AMERICAN GOVERNMENT
A Brief Introduction

Second Edition

AMERICAN GOVERNMENT
A Brief Introduction

Second Edition

Max J. Skidmore
Marshall Carter Wanke

St. Martin's Press   New York

Library of Congress Catalog Card Number: 76-41545
Copyright © 1977 by St. Martin's Press, Inc.
All Rights Reserved.
Manufactured in the United States of America.
098
fedc
For information, write: St. Martin's Press, Inc.,
175 Fifth Avenue, New York, N.Y. 10010

cover design by Mies Hora

cloth ISBN: 0-312-02450-9
paper ISBN: 0-312-02485-1

CONTENTS

AMERICAN GOVERNMENT
A Brief Introduction

Second Edition

1 INTRODUCTION

Citizenship and Public Policy

Different men often see the same subjects in different lights.

Patrick Henry

Governments are the mechanisms that human groups employ to protect themselves from internal and external threats and to establish the policies that will provide the most favorable conditions for pursuing their lives. Because they are among the most nearly universal of human institutions, it is natural that they should be taken for granted and therefore poorly understood. When something is so common that its existence is hardly ever questioned, its influence may not be fully recognized. Many persons may be concerned about forms of government, or about the details of specific policies or actions, but rarely do they consider the nature of government itself.

Politics in Everyday Life: The Individual and the Community

Government touches virtually all of us each day in one form or another. We see government function in the person of the postman delivering the mail, the police officer on the corner, the clerk at the district office of the Social Security Administration, the drill sergeant, and the agent conducting an investigation into the beliefs and behavior of some citizen or group. Sometimes its effects are beneficial, sometimes detrimental, but they are always important. Where government is popularly elected, the people have some control, potentially, over the broad outlines of the policies that affect them so greatly, but they will fail to exercise their influence effectively if they are not adequately informed about basic issues and about the ways in which government operates. The study of government and politics is therefore an essential part of every citizen's education.

To begin to understand politics, you must become familiar with the basic structures and processes of American national, state, and local governments. This, however, is merely the beginning of knowledge. Beyond the basics are formal and informal relationships within and between the various levels of government, differing approaches to the study of government and politics, and the frequent divergence of reality from appearances. Above all, to understand politics, you must develop the ability to analyze critically and to determine when it is appropriate to accept political statements, when to reject them, and when to remain skeptical until better information is available. If this is difficult, it can also be exciting.

Politics is everywhere. Much of what may seem at first to have little to do with politics is in truth intensely political. Politics is related directly to our view of life, our relations with others, our judgments of right and wrong, and our perceptions of the world. *Politics*, in brief, is the means by which human beings collectively organize their affairs. It centers on the ways in which the person adjusts to the group and, conversely, the manner in which the group accommodates persons who differ vastly from one another. Aristotle described politics as the "architechtonic science," the one that is fundamental to all others. It is through politics that societies determine what can be done, what should be done, and what is done. Participation in political life can help each person realize his or her own potential by helping to shape the larger community.

Politics in America is both collective and individual, concerned with the group and with each person. It deals with the rights of the individuals as fully as with the duties. Similarly, it deals with the obligations of the community as fully as with the rights. The task of the democracy has always been, and remains, to establish a society in which the rights of the individual and those of the community are recognized and protected, and the duties of both are observed and fulfilled. Because of the constant tension between individual and social needs, no political system has ever fully succeeded in performing the task. However, the goal is not to achieve perfection but to seek it, to do the best that is possible.

In a popular government political participation is not only a right of the people but also their responsibility. Unfortunately, in the United States the latter too often is ignored. Two thousand years ago the ancient Greeks recognized that human beings are fundamentally social animals. Political life is the foundation of the social order; by failing to participate, a person loses a major dimension of his human potential. The fundamental civil right of the American citizen is the right to vote, yet voter participation in this nation is shockingly low. Voter participation is only one small factor in whether the political system works or not, but it is one of the more obvious indications. The 1972 presidential election provides a case in point. Presidential elections routinely bring about a higher vote than other elections, but in the 1972 contest, which returned Richard Nixon to office, only about 55 percent of the potential voters cast their ballots. Nixon's approximately 61 percent of the vote constituted a landslide, one of the greatest in American history, but because of the low turnout only about one-third of the eligible voters chose the winner. In the 1976 election, the voter turnout was even lower; only about 54 percent of the electorate cast their ballots. These statistics are worrisome because they indicate an unwillingness on the part of many Americans to make their political system work—an unwillingness that could result eventually in the end of constitutional government.

In the past decade, our political system has been beset by a series of urgent crises as well as by more subtle but no less dangerous difficulties, such as encroachments on individual privacy, the tendency among many to reject legitimate political processes, and an increased willingness to accept authoritarian measures. These problems highlight the delicate balance between personal rights and public needs that is the essence of politics. The overriding political realities of these years were Watergate and the involvement of the United States in a war in Indochina.

The Vietnam War not only brought about innumerable difficulties, and intensified countless others, but itself became an immeasurably complex phenomenon. It led to a discussion of America's role in the world; of the nature of communism; of the uses, limits, and dangers of power under modern conditions; of the role of war and the conduct of warfare; and even of the purposes of domestic policies. It led to troubled thoughts about the nature of the state and government and reopened the historical American questions of selective conscientious objection or civil disobedience, on the one hand, and revolution, on the other. Certainly there has been no "radicalization" of mainstream American views and beliefs, but it is significant that the questions receive any attention at all, and the mainstream may well have altered direction somewhat.

None of the questions raised by Vietnam has brought a clear answer, but each has required thought and judgment. Historically, military conscription—the draft—has been thoroughly unpopular in the United States, even in time of all-out war. In peacetime it was unthinkable. In the early 1950s, however, it burst upon the American scene as a full-blown part of the "American Way of Life." The questions surrounding

"Oh, I like reforms O.K., but not <u>sweeping</u> reforms."

the Vietnam War directly stimulated a reexamination of its desirability. It was also true that the conscription of middle-class young men was one reason why the war was questioned. Without it, assuming that the war could still have been conducted, the deaths of young and old Vietnamese might have gone unexamined. Related to the war, but less directly, were such questions as urban blight, poverty admidst affluence, racism, and individual liberties that long have troubled the American political system but took on new urgency in the 1960s. Technology, wealth, and good will alone were unable to provide the answers, even when they were applied. Vietnam dramatized the need for choice in the use of resources—financial and human—and it jeopardized liberties as government and the war's opponents brought the war home.

Watergate, the name for that complex of events having to do with the abuses of governmental authority by the Nixon administration, brought with it a concern for morality in politics and perhaps some renewal of an awareness of the importance of limitations upon power. There have been scandals in government before, but none of the magnitude of Watergate. It reflected an attempt to expand executive dominance beyond constitutional limitations, to overwhelm not only other branches of government but the rights of citizens as well. This overt assault upon the Constitution was beaten back, with the assistance of some fortunate accidents. We cannot always count on good fortune. If we are to have better government, we must learn from the hectic events of the recent past and guard against repetition. The struggle to get and keep good government begins with individual understanding of the foundations and forms of American politics and its main concerns, as they were and as they are now; it can proceed only if maintained by an alert and concerned citizenry.

The Political and Cultural Background of American Democracy

The roots of American political ideas and the American governmental system reach far back, even beyond the beginnings of the thirteen colonies. The notion that men are created equal can be traced to ancient classical thinkers as well as to the beginnings of Christianity. The writings of both Plato and Aristotle generate the idea that an ethical government must operate according to law. This principle has developed through the years into the modern doctrine that the government should be one of laws, and not of men. The ideas of limited government and constitutionalism long were prevalent in the English tradition, dating most dramatically from the Magna Carta in 1215, when King John was forced to accept limitations on his power. These ideas were transplanted into the new American environment.

The earliest voluntary settlers came to America's shores largely for economic or religious reasons. Of those coming because of religion, the Pilgrims arrived on the Mayflower to found the Plymouth Colony in 1620, and the Puritans settled in Massachusetts Bay a decade later. Both groups sought religious freedom for themselves, but they did not in turn extend freedom of worship to others. The Puritans drove Roger Williams from the Massachusetts Bay Colony, for example, because he challenged the prevailing orthodoxy to denying that the state should have the power to control religion, by advocating freedom for other religious beliefs, and by denying the right of white persons to seize Indian lands. When he established the colony of Rhode Island, he attempted to put his beliefs into practice, and Rhode Island led the way toward democracy for the rest of the colonies. Even the Puritans, however unwillingly, made their contribution to the development of democracy, because their beliefs regarding church government led to congregational control and freedom from an ecclesiastical hierarchy. This had political implications far beyond the confines of the churches.

Others came because they could not advance themselves in the old society. Such persons as fourth sons, adventurers, convicts, and debtors flocked to the New World, where many flourished. Ambition also carried merchants, tradesmen, and farmers across the Atlantic, to settle mainly in the middle and northern colonies, and planters established large plantations for commercial agriculture in the South, and rapidly developed a labor system based upon human slavery. Subsequently, many German and Scotch-Irish farmers moved into the western backcountry, reflecting a westward movement that, almost from the beginnings of European settlement here, seemed to encourage independence and individualism.

From earliest times Americans sought to defy authority and promote individual gain. Because of their memories of European despotisms, they designed their new governments carefully to limit the exercise of political power. The basic principle dominating the discussions that led, ultimately, to revolution and the breaking of ties with England was that all persons have a right to self-government, that no government has the right to rule without the consent of those who are governed. Thomas Jefferson, author of the Declaration of Independence, captured the intellectual impetus for the revolution in words that sound radical even today. In that document he asserted that all are equal, that government legitimately can receive power only from the people, and that the only justification of government is to secure the right of the people to life, liberty, and the pursuit of happiness. These sentiments were an extension of centuries of English tradition and had been embodied most fully in the writings of the English theorist John Locke. As shaped by decades of American experience, supplemented by the theories of separation of powers from Montesquieu in France, and expounded by Jefferson, they became the keystone of American political thought. The primary principle, then and now, is that the government is the servant of the people, not their master.

There were, of course, striking contradictions in practice to the principles that Americans professed to follow. The most apparent was the forcible exclusion of some groups from the framework of rights, notably black slaves and Indians. Moreover, although Americans designed the system to restrict the exercise of governmental power, they were unconcerned with restricting the exercise of private power. The Founding Fathers could hardly have foreseen the huge concentrations of private power that would soon accompany the development of the corporation and the industrial state.

With the coming of the twentieth century, the most prominent features in American society were cities, social and geographic mobility, and industrial enterprise. No other people in history have rushed so quickly into cities, and away from the countryside, as have Americans. Many basic American attitudes, however, developed when the United States was a white, Protestant, rural, Anglo-Saxon nation and have persisted with little change. Many Americans still approach politics with orientations suited for simpler times. For example, many still tend to agree with Jefferson that cities are places of evil and corruption and that virtue attaches to rural living and the agrarian life, at the same time that they enjoy and are dependent upon the advantages of urban living. This was shown dramatically in the national contempt for, or indifference to, the threatened financial collapse of debt-ridden New York City in 1975-1976. The tendency to condemn the urban life is paradoxical considering that well over two-thirds of us live in central cities or the suburbs that surround them. The great metropolitan areas of the nation are like magnets, attracting and repelling. This ambiguous affection may account partially for some of our urban problems today. Other paradoxes abound in contemporary America. We venerate the settled life although we no longer live it, and there is a continuing, and fashionable, effort to "return to the land," though we are essentially an urban people. Similarly, we are individualistic and nationalistic; we are humane and belligerent; we prefer small government and adopt big government; we are contemptuous of authority and elect officials on platforms of "law and order." In short, contradiction seems to be the hallmark of American civilization today.

Constitutional Democracy

The basic principles of the American system of government are equality, government only by consent of the governed, and protection for minority rights. It is a simple matter to identify instances in American history that are in sharp contrast to the tenets of American political thought. Approval of slavery and systematic injustices toward the Indians are only two instances. In addition, there have been blatant violations of human rights and dignity in the practice of racial segregation and in the relocation of Japanese-Americans during World War II.

White Americans have suffered violations of the protections listed in the Bill of Rights as well. Beginning with the Alien and Sedition Acts of 1798, the United States government and the states have all too easily passed laws that have severely restricted the exercise of free speech whenever dissent threatened established modes of order. There have been numerous violations of rights and basic courtesies committed by Congress itself, notably in the activities of the House Committee on Un-American Activities (later titled the House Committee on Internal Security, then finally abolished) and by the late Senator Joseph McCarthy. Examples must also include the murders by governmental forces of both black and white students on college campuses, and the brutalization and harassment of peaceful protestors by government agents in many parts of the nation. As the sordid revelations of the last few years (culminating in the Nixon administration's "enemies list") have indicated, *government* lawlessness constitutes one of the major "law and order" problems in the United States.

Nevertheless, a political system cannot be evaluated fairly by examining only its failures. The task facing students of politics is to determine the suitability of America's political goals and the degree to which the American government is achieving its goals in general, and to propose and work for improvements whenever they appear to be needed.

Much of the world today lives under various forms of *authoritarianism*, in which such rights as exist are granted to the people by the government, rather than being inherent in the people. In the American system the power ultimately is lodged in the people, and they grant power to the government, which exercises it within strict limitations, at least in theory. This notion of a republican government—one that is free, representative, and limited in power—rests upon two fundamentals: democracy and constitutionalism. There may be conflict at times even between these fundamentals. *Democracy* implies consent by the governed and popular control of the government expressed through majority rule;

constitutionalism implies limitations on power, even democratic power. In other words, the majority should rule—but not to the extent that it oppresses the minority. A democracy without limitations could be chaotic and destructive of the minority; a constitutional state without democracy could become irresponsible or corrupt. A constitution comprises principles that allocate power to various agencies and set limits on its use. Thus, in a democracy majority rule is the most basic principle, but a constitution is necessary to curb potential abuses of the majority. Where popular government under the rule of law exists, we have a *republican* form of politics, or a *constitutional democracy*.

Analyzing the Workings of the American System

Political scientists in recent years have attempted to develop measures to evaluate the effectiveness and the impact of public policies, at best a formidable and complex task. At a more basic level, there are various "models," or frameworks, that political scientists use to analyze and interpret a governmental system. Many have been applied to American politics. The most simplistic is a model of democracy based on *mass participation*, wherein the people retain power and direct the policies of their government. This is the model that tends to be presented to public-school pupils and probably is responsible for much of the disillusionment that develops when young adults confront complex reality. At the other extreme, the *power-elite* model sees the American system as dominated by a fairly small group, controlling industry, the military and civilian wings of government, the professions, and trade and labor organizations. Members of the power elite may move from one segment to another, but collectively they form a group, unresponsive to the people, that sets policy and determines even the most detailed aspects of American life.

The model that most political scientists tend to accept as the best description of the workings of American constitutional democracy is the pluralist model. "Pluralism" here does not mean a society that is free for diversity. Rather, it refers to a group theory of politics. According to the *pluralist* model, American society is dominated by powerful organized groups, and the government serves essentially as a broker, or referee, among them and also frequently participates as an interest group itself. Each group works for its own interests, and the government serves to coordinate and facilitate compromise, so that the most powerful groups will obtain most of what they desire while they will be antagonized as little as possible. The people may have access to power through these groups, causing some observers to emphasize their popular nature, though critics view them as channels for elite domination. It is, of course, an oversimplification to speak of the "government" as a monolithic force because goverment agencies are powerful interest groups that often lack coordination with other agencies and sometimes even work at cross-purposes. The Public Health Service, for example, works to discourage smoking, while the Department of Agriculture works for subsidies to tobacco farmers and spends money to encourage smoking abroad.

Many of the writers on pluralism argue that it is not only an accurate description but also a desirable one. They see politics in a pluralist system as "realistic," that is, based upon self-interest rather than moral or idealistic considerations. The proponents of pluralism believe that attempts to base politics upon principle would result in a multiplicity of warring factions that would tear the social fabric asunder, and they contend that the compromises of self-interest are the best guide for society just as the "invisible hand" was to have ordered society's economic progress in Adam Smith's view of capitalism. Pluralism reflects the contentment of the great majority with the status quo that emphasizes material possessions, conformity, and political apathy. Pluralists imply that apathy is actually a good thing, that it sustains the system, because the masses, if they were to participate fully and make use of their political potential, would tend to be hostile to diversity and civil liberties. (The indications from research, however, are not clear on this issue.) Although the critics scorn the middle-class life style that is the essence of pluralist politics for its mediocrity, conformity, and materialism, the pluralist writers finds its virtues of stability and prosperity for millions more important. Many, in fact, believe that this is all that a political system is capable of providing.

It is difficult to quarrel with those who maintain that American politics tends to operate as the pluralist model describes it. But the system does upon occasion rise above the operation of pluralist politics. Possible examples may be the Test Ban Treaty and the civil rights and voting rights acts of the 1960s. In general, however, the pluralist model seems to describe accurately the day-to-day workings of American government.

Those who reject the pluralist perspective generally do not deny that it presents a reasonably accurate view, but they challenge its desirability. They argue, for one thing, that it places extreme emphasis upon organization. The only group powerful enough to participate in pluralist politics is the organized group. It leaves the unorganized out of account, except insofar as they share interests with the organized. Of course, it may be argued that the unorganized should therefore organize, but the critics contend that circumstances often make organization difficult, if not impossible. Another inadequacy charged against a pluralist system is that the process ignores individual citizens, who theoretically are the primary units of a democratic society. They are unlikely to be heard, even if correct, unless they succeed in uniting. This means that pluralist politics has produced a radical, and in some ways substantially unexamined, change in democracy. It has shifted our political focus from the individual to the group. Admittedly a society of more than 200 million persons has little chance of placing primary emphasis upon unorganized individuals, but this should itself increase concern about population size. Moreover, pluralism provides only a rudimentary conception of the public good. It defines the public good only as that which flows from accommodation and compromise among competing powers. The general public, like the individual, is left out of account.

The critics of pluralism further charge that its value judgments are openly elitist and that they center on power alone and ignore ethical considerations. It is cynical indeed, they say, to conclude that the people are too foolish to have an effective hand in governing, or that the only ethics that is "realistic" results from selfish competition among the powerful. Unintentionally or not, this amounts to open repudiation of the principles of the Declaration of Independence. The justification for government under pluralism shifts from the protection of life, liberty, and the pursuit of happiness to the protection of the right of powerful interests to compete or cooperate with other powerful interests. Political equality is dismissed in favor of open acceptance of political inequality. Government by consent of the governed becomes government by the power of the governor. Opponents of pluralism thus see the model as a smug subversion of the American Revolution.

The controversy over pluralism is largely confined to academic circles, but the implications are broader and touch upon the very meaning of American democracy. This topic ought to be a matter for greater public debate.

Suggested Readings

Carl Bernstein and Bob Woodward. *All the President's Men.* New York: Simon & Schuster, 1974. The classic treatment of the Watergate investigations by the two reporters whose diligence led to much of the disclosure.

Jimmy Breslin. *How the Good Guys Finally Won: Notes from an Impeachment Summer.* New York: Ballantine, 1976.* An unusual and insightful view of the Nixon administration.

Richard Harris. "Watergate Prosecutions." *New Yorker*, June 10, 1974. A valuable work by one of the most careful observers of American politics.

J. Anthony Lukas. *Nightmare: The Underside of the Nixon Years.* New York: Viking, 1976.*

Jarol B. Manheim. *Déjà Vu, American Political Problems in Historical Perspective.*

New York: St. Martin's Press, 1976.* An interesting treatment of some contemporary political themes and their backgrounds.

Dan Rather and Gary Paul Gates. *The Palace Guard.* New York: Warner, 1975.* One of the best popular treatments of the background of Watergate.

Jonathan Schell. *The Time of Illusion.* New York: Vintage, 1976.* One of the best pictures of the atmosphere of the Nixon White House.

Theodore C. Sorenson. *Watchmen in the Night: Presidential Accountability After Watergate.* Cambridge, Mass. M.I.T. Press, 1975.*

Bob Woodward and Carl Bernstein. *The Final Days.* New York: Simon & Schuster, 1976.

*Available in paperback.

THE CONSTITUTION

Enlightened statesmen will not always be at the helm.

James Madison

Origins

The situation in the new American states after they had gained their independence from England seemed to call for some form of political association. Because there was as yet no American nation and each state was independent and jealous of its prerogatives, unanimous approval of the thirteen was required if they were to be bound together in any semblance of a federation. It is not surprising, therefore, that the states remained the primary centers of power under their first experiment with union, the *Articles of Confederation.*

In September 1774, prior to the outbreak of the Revolution, delegates from twelve of the colonies had assembled to form the First Continental Congress, but resolutions from that body did not effectively change British policy. Its successor, the Second Continental Congress, which had convened in May 1775 after the war began, had coordinated and directed the military efforts of the colonies. This Congress, in which each colony had one vote, adopted the Declaration of Independence on July 4, 1776, and laid the foundation for the Articles of Confederation, submitted to the states for ratification in November of 1777. By 1779, all of the states had ratified the document except for Maryland, which delayed its approval until March of 1781, after other states had ceded certain western lands to the nation. With Maryland's approval, the Articles became effective.

The Articles established a central government consisting solely of a unicameral, or one-house, Congress in which each state delegation had one vote. Important actions required the approval of nine states, and amendment of the Articles required the assent of all thirteen. There was no separate executive or judiciary, although Congress was given limited judicial functions regarding marine matters and interstate disputes. Initially Congress created committees as needed for executive actions but soon found it necessary to appont permanent departments under its control. The "president" was not the chief executive but rather the presiding officer of the Congress. The Articles declared that "each state retains its sovereignty, freedom, and independence" and that the states had entered into a "league of friendship with each other" (Articles II and III).

Clearly, the government that the Articles established was more a consultative council serving to reflect the views of the states than it was the government of a nation. The arrangement was a league of largely independent units, not a nation state in the modern sense. The greatest difficulty appears to have been finance. The Congress could place levies on states for funds to operate, but there was no way it could enforce payment. All attempts to enact a tariff to provide a source of national revenue failed. Such an action required unanimous approval of the states, and at least one state always would oppose the tariff. Moreover, Congress had no authority over citizens, who were subject only to the governments of their respective states.

Considering the circumstances, a good deal was accomplished under the Articles. Such agenices as the Departments of Foreign Affairs, War, and Finances, all of which Congress created in 1781, could well have evolved into a cabinet government. This parliamentary form might have been more efficient in many ways than the present government. With the cession of western lands to the nation, moreover, the United States came to be something more than a mere league of sovereign and independent states; there now were national lands, held in common. The most significant governmental action of this period was the adoption of the Northwest Ordinance of 1787. This act prohibited slavery in the Northwest Territory (the national lands north of the Ohio River) and established an orderly procedure for the admission to the confederation of any state, created from the region. Ultimately, the territory became the states of Ohio, Indiana, Illinois, Michigan, and Wisconsin. This innovative approach to the handling of territorial areas set a precedent not only for the future development of states carved from other national lands but also for the evolution of colonial units into self-governing nations elsewhere in the world. Additionally, the ordinance provided a bill of rights guaranteeing contracts, jury trials, freedom of religion, and the right of habeas corpus for inhabitants of the territory. When the new government took charge of the nation after the adoption of the Constitution, it readopted the provisions of this great ordinance. The prohibition of slavery in the Northwest Territory was one of the most important actions of the Congress under the Articles of Confederation. It set the tone for much of the future development of western lands, and if Congress had gone further and had adopted Jefferson's suggestion that slavery be prohibited in all western lands, north and south, it might have averted much of the severe sectional strife that later developed. Unfortunately it did not.

Despite the accomplishments, definite inadequacies were apparent in the Articles' political arrangements. Because it had been granted so little power, the central authority would have had difficulty functioning as a true government under the best of circumstances, and the circumstances were not the best. Moreover, one flaw in the Articles of Confederation was fatal. Congress had no way to enforce sanctions upon either citizens or states and thus could not exercise effectively even those limited powers it was supposed to have. Many leaders, especially those who favored strong central power and a greater national identity, concluded that the government was far too weak to continue unchanged.

Delegates from all of the states except Rhode Island met in Philadelphia in 1787 to discuss the Articles of Confederation and to suggest changes that would remedy the weaknesses and encourage a viable national government. Despite the limited purpose of the convention, the delegates quickly concluded that the nation's difficulties could be eliminated more effectively by a new governmental structure than by one that attempted to preserve the arrangements of the confederacy. Just as the new nation had come into being by means of a violent reaction against authority that led to a revolution, so the first stable and enduring government gew from disobedience to authority. The delegates ignored the orders that they had received and produced one of the most remarkable documents in the political history of the world, the United States Constitution.

The Constitution was the result of a series of hard-fought compromises as well as basic agreements. Ultimately, all thirteen states approved the new document, but only after considerable debate with fierce, often bitter, controversy over ratification in several, and only after those who were skeptical of the new proposals exacted a promise that the First Congress under the new government would propose a "bill of rights" for ratification by the states. The Bill of Rights, in the form of the first ten amendments, thus became a part of the new Constitution. The entire period was characterized, not only by dissension, emotion, and factional interest but also by political speculation and theorizing of an extraordinarily high order by a group of remarkable men. It was a period of ferment that produced many profound political writings and codified many enduring principles of political wisdom and morality. In addition, it was a time of remarkably high participation in politics with people everywhere hotly debating the proposed charter. By this process, they brought the Preamble to life.

In recent decades historians have persistently questioned the accomplishments of the Founding Fathers and their motives. In 1913 Charles A. Beard published his famous study, *An Economic Interpretation of the Constitution of the United States*, in which he contended that the prime purpose of those who designed the new government was to limit democratic tendencies and ensure financial security and gain for themselves and the wealthier classes. Certainly it appears at first glance that the Constitution may be a conservative repudiation of the radicalism of the Declaration of Independence, but further consideration suggests that Beard's argument overstates the case. Unquestionably, the Declaration is more "radical" and more democratic in spirit than the Constitution. The Constitution is full of checks upon the power of the people. Its rigid provisions for amendment, for example, require more than a majority and do not permit popular participation in the process. It establishes a powerful Supreme Court that is composed of appointive justices with essentially life tenure. It requires affirmative action on all legislation by a Senate that originally was not subject to popular election and that still, as part of the federal design, represents areas rather than population. The Electoral College and many other features incorporated into the Constitution are far from the radical individualist spirit of the Declaration.

Nevertheless, some of the antidemocratic provisions of the Constitution can hardly be classed as reactionary. Appointive judges with lifetime tenure, for instance, enable the courts to defend liberty in situations when a democratic body might restrain it. The Constitution reflects a profound fear of concentrations of power. Its general function is to limit the power of the government and the nation state, even power based upon popular consent—a function that is, in the historical sense, profoundly liberal. The authors of the Constitution undoubtedly were influenced by personal considerations and by economic factors. Beard performed a service in calling attention to the role of economics, which should no longer be ignored, but he exaggerated the importance of this role in charging that economic issues were the sole criterion by which the authors of the Constitution shaped the new government. Similarly, although it is true that the Constitution is more conservative than the Declaration, it can hardly be classed as a "sell-out" of the principles of the Revolution, as some have alleged. By the standards prevailing throughout the world, the Constitution was uniquely liberal. Despite its restrictions on majority rule it provided for a government that was based on the power of the people and that was more democratic than any other.

The men who created the Constitution and worked for its adoption had faith in institutions. They believed that their goals of a just and free society could be achieved if the proper institutions could be established. Power was necessary, but it was also dangerous. Only the right balance of institutions could permit the necessary exercise of power and simultaneously prevent abuse by its wielder. The system that they designed incorporated their conceptions of what American society should be. On the fundamental qeustions, they were in agreement. There should be a national government, and it should have sufficient power to govern adequately. But that government should also be limited. The ultimate power must rest with the people, who would exercise it through directly and indirectly elected representatives and through appointed officials. The system must also be federal in some manner, permitting the existence of both national and state governments.

Such agreements on fundamental matters reflected a shared background and the wide acceptance of the basic tenets of American political thought. There were, nonetheless, extreme divergences of opinion on matters of specifics. Tensions existed between the wealthy and the workers, between large states and small, between coastal and backcountry areas, between small agriculture and large, between manufacturing and agriculture, between debtors and creditors, between slaveholding interests and the rest of the nation, between nationalists and those whose allegiance remained solely with their states, between advocates of various religions or none; in short, the variety of sources for conflict was astonishing. The founders recognized this and worked to accommodate it. The Constitution to a considerable degree reflects both the myriad tensions and antagonisms that were prevalent and the process of compromise that gave it life. Some of the tensions have dwindled, but others have arisen in their place. Despite the national uniformity of freeways, hamburger chains, and television entertainment, the United States remains a very diverse nation, as illustrated by the "discovery" of the American South in the 1976 campaign. On balance, the potential for conflict probably is greater today than before. It is a testimony to the practical wisdom of the founders that their creation, splendid but not perfect, has survived to this day.

Principles

LIMITED GOVERNMENT

The foremost principle of constitutionalism is that power shall be limited. Any constitution, as noted in chapter 1, is a set of restrictions on the exercise of governmental power, and any nation that observes such a set of restrictions is a constitutional state. It is the performance that counts, not the form. The Soviet Union, for example, has a written constitution, but because the Soviet rulers ignore its requirements when they deem it to be in their best interests to do so, the U.S.S.R. cannot be considered a constitutional state. On the other hand, Great Britain has no single written document that could be identified as a constitution, yet it has a definite set of principles, developed in centuries of struggle, that strictly govern practice; Great Britain is, therefore, a constitutional state. Every provision of the U.S. Constitution makes explicit the notion of limitations on governmental power in general and on the power of governmental agencies in particular. Our Constitution; in fact; has become a model for nations throughout the world to imitate.

All constitutions are worthless unless the people and the officials of the government think that they should be observed and work to protect and preserve them. Although there have been numerous instances in which constitutional principles have failed to guide action in the United States, the general record is good. The pattern has been to uphold the Constitution and to observe limitations on governmental action. Limited government thus remains, as it must, the key principle of our constitutional system. The government, therefore, must respond to the values of the people and protect individual rights, not create or interpret values for the people. Anything else would be a severe blow to the principle of limited government, and hence to the Constitution itself.

POPULAR SOVEREIGNTY

Another key principle of the American constitutional system is *popular sovereignty*. According to the principle the people have the ultimate power, if they should choose to exercise it. They create the power and delegate it through the Constitution to the government, although they do not control the workings of the government directly, even through elections. In addition, there are those checks already noted that prevent the people from controlling decisions. Nevertheless, under the Constitution the government does not create power and grant rights to the people. It is the people who permit the government to act and who are the theoretical holders of power. The basic theory that is consistently threaded throughout American political thought, and upon which the Constitution and the government are based, is that the government governs only with the consent of the people. If the people were to withdraw support from the government, it could no longer rule legitimately. This problem has not yet confronted the nation. From the beginnings of government under the present Constitution, the people have consistently supported the system. Although the Civil War may seem to be an exception, both sides even then sought to preserve what they considered to be the system that the Founding Fathers intended. They may turn against a particular party or administration, but they have never turned against the system of government.

SEPARATION OF POWERS

One of the most basic principles of the Constitution is one that gave rise to the "presidential" form of government, namely, the *separation of powers*. The Constitution provides for an elected executive, the President, who heads the executive branch with its administrative agencies and who is chosen independently of the legislative branch, the Congress, and is not responsible to it. These two branches are supplemented by a third, the judiciary, headed by the Supreme Court. Many persons consider the three branches to be equal, but the Constitution clearly gives the Con-

"It's Called Separation Of Powers — We
Separate You From Your Powers"

from *Herblock Special Report* (W. W. Norton & Co., Inc., 1974)

gress the central power if it chooses to exercise it. Nevertheless, in recent decades the President has overshadowed Congress, and the courts are a distant third as holders of power. Each branch has powers of its own and checks over the other two branches. There is some formal overlap, such as the role of the Vice President, who sits as president of the Senate even though he is a member of the executive; another is the quasi-judicial function that Congress exercises when impeaching officials and trying those who have been impeached. There is considerably more informal overlap, such as the quasi-legislative and quasi-judicial functions assumed by many executive agencies in issuing regulations and hearing disputes, and the holding of military reserve commissions by many members of Congress (a practice now under attack in the federal courts). Nevertheless, the three branches retain considerable independence. The classic description of the operation of the separate branches is that they provide *checks and balances.*

The founders designed the government so that all legislation must originate in Congress. Even here there are checks, because the Congress is *bicameral*—that is, divided into two houses, the Senate and the House of Representatives—and both houses must approve all laws in identical form. The President is responsible for administering the laws, and the courts adjudicate disputes and settle questions regarding matters of law. This is in contrast to the *parliamentary form* of democracy, in which the executive is selected by the legislature and serves at its pleasure and in which, additionally, there may be a considerable mixing of roles in some institutions as in Great Britain's House of Lords and Privy Council. (Each of these bodies retains certain judicial functions, although the former is a house of the legislature and the latter is essentially executive in nature.)

Many political scientists dislike the principle of separation of powers because checks and balances lead to considerable inefficiency. For example, one political party may control the presidency at the same time that the other controls the Congress. It is even possible for the Congress to be divided, with the House of one party and the Senate of another. In the parliamentary system, if the executive cannot work with the parliament, there immediately are new elections. In the presidential system, the situation contines until the next regularly scheduled election, which means that an impasse may continue for as long as four years. Even so, the system was designed deliberately to limit power, and if it raises the likelihood of inefficiency, the founders considered this to be a small price to pay. Their purpose was, as James Madison put it in *The Federalist*, No. 51, to insure that "ambition must be made to counteract ambition." Too many have lost sight of the wisdom and of this principle and have allowed ambition to feed upon and to support ambition.

In recent years, the power of the President has increased tremendously. It may be that too much power, rather than an inability to exercise power, is the greatest defect of the presidential form of government. In foreign affairs, despite the allocation of collateral powers and checks to the Senate, the American President is probably the most powerful, and least accountable, official on Earth. Even some of the political scientists who a few years ago criticized the possibility of governmental inefficiency resulting from checks and balances now complain that there are far too few checks. Historically, the President has had to share domestic powers more broadly, but in this century—particularly in the decades after World War II—Congress has found many of its traditional checks no longer effective, or practically impossible to invoke. Even impeachment is so cumbersome and so serious as to appear virtually impossible to use successfully unless the situation becomes critical. No doubt Richard Nixon would have been impeached, and probably removed from office, had he not resigned. Nevertheless, even with the Watergate scandals and the accompanying revelations of political espionage and sabotage directed by the White House, the constitutional mechanisms for redressing abuse of office were extremely sluggish. Impeachment or the threat of impeachment can obviously be effective, but neither could succeed under conditions requiring even moderate speed. It is fortunate for the nation that events did not outrun the complicated and awkward procedures established to handle them; if similar conditions were to recur, the result might not be so favorable.

JUDICIAL REVIEW

Although nowhere mentioned in the Constitution, the power of judicial review must be considered one of the foremost principles of the American constitutional system. *Judicial review* is the power of the courts to declare acts contrary to the Constitution to be void. Chief Justice John Marshall's decision in *Marbury* v. *Madison* (1803) first asserted the power to declare an act of Congress unconstitutional, and this decision became a firm principle of American constitutional law. There is considerable evidence to indicate that the Founding Fathers assumed that the courts would have this power by virtue of the fact that all actions must be consistent with the Constitution to be valid. If a law were inconsistent with the Constitution, the courts simply would refuse to uphold it. This is the argument that Alexander Hamilton advanced in *The Federalist*, No. 78, and it is discernible in the records of the Constitutional Convention.

Judicial review is an American development that followed logically from the existence of a written constitution. Other nations have copied the practice until today, in one form or another, it is fairly widespread, in the sense that in most new nations with a written constitution based upon American or British governmental principles, the courts will be asked to exercise judicial review. Few nations, however, give a general grant of judicial review even to their highest courts, and very few high courts have shown much willingness to exercise even limited judicial review. This is especially the case where doing so would require overruling the government. Of course, it should be pointed out that in the United States as well, despite its long experience with judicial review, the Supreme Court has relatively rarely declared an act of Congress or of the federal executive to be unconstitutional and usually will go to great lengths to avoid doing so. This is because the Court must rely upon persuasion and leadership because its power falls far short of that of the President or of the Congress. Not only does the Supreme Court lack the power to enforce its own decisions, but the Constitution gives Congress control over the Court's most significant power—the ability to hear cases appealed from lower courts. The Court is much less reluctant to strike down state laws or executive actions.

FEDERALISM

The Founding Fathers demonstrated their originality when they devised the framework of American *federalism*. They saw as their urgent task the strengthening of the national government and the development of a nation state, but they did not intend to obliterate or even to weaken severely the existing states. Their solution was to provide a geographic distribution of power between a strong central government and strong constituent units, the states, with each level exercising power directly over the individual citizen within its prescribed sphere of action. The resulting federal system has served, in varying degrees, as a model for other nations throughout the world. Although the term "federal" was not a new one, the innovations of the Founding Fathers gave it new meaning. Previously, it denoted what we would today call a confederacy (see chapter 3).

Constitutional Change

INFORMAL DEVELOPMENT

Students of government frequently divide constitutions into two classes, rigid and flexible, depending upon the ease with which they can be amended. The Constitution of the United States is difficult to classify in these terms. Although it clearly is rigid in form—that is, it is most difficult to amend—it has been relatively easily adapted to changing conditions merely by differences in interpretation made possible by judicial review. This is partly a result of the tradition of constitutional interpretation as it developed, but it is also a function of the language of the

Constitution itself. The Constitution is extraordinarily brief; it deals with broad statements of principle rather than with the details of governmental operation. The framers showed their inspiration most clearly in limiting this basic law to fundamentals. Probably no document that required constant amendment could have commanded the lasting respect that the U.S. Constitution has enjoyed, nor have become so familiar to the general public. Constitutions that specify every aspect of governmental operations (e.g., those of India or Texas) require amendment for the most minor change in detail; the Constitution of Texas has been altered over 200 times in the last hundred years. The U.S. Constitution, by contrast, has allowed substantial evolution in practice without radical or rapid change in the original document's basic principles.

In addition to judicial review, presidential practice, congressional action, and custom have contributed to the process of development. For example, the Constitution clearly grants to the President the power of veto over legislation passed by the Congress. Until the presidency of Andrew Jackson, however, presidential vetoes were rare, and many were of the opinion that the veto would be exercised only in narrow and clearly defined cases. But President Jackson infused new importance into the veto by using it whenever he desired. This changed constitutional practice without changing the Constitution as a document. Both loose and strict interpretations of the veto power were consistent with the requirements of the Constitution, yet Jackson's precedent had a major effect upon the subsequent operation of the government.

Similarly, in the last few decades Congress has adopted many pieces of legislation giving quasi-legislative powers to certain executive agencies. No formal constitutional amendment was involved, but there has been radical revision of the structure of the government and the traditional conceptions of the powers and duties of the executive and the legislative branches. The force of custom has also contributed to change, as can be seen in the position of political parties in modern America. They are so fundamental to the operation of American government that they may almost be thought of as basic to the constitutional system, yet the Constitution itself contains not one word about political parties.

So potent have some of the unwritten traditions of the presidency been that formal amendments have been passed to ensure their continuance. The original Constitution, for example, specified that the powers and duties of the office of the President "shall devolve on the Vice President" in case the President dies, resigns, or is unable to "discharge the powers and duties of the said office." President William Henry Harrison died in 1841, shortly after having taken office, and for the first time this provision of Article II of the Constitution had to be applied. There was immediate question whether the Vice President, John Tyler, actually became President or was merely to be "Acting President." Tyler settled the issue by insisting that he was President, and subsequent Vice Presidents who succeeded to the office were not even faced with the question. The Twenty-fifth Amendment, ratified in 1967, made this long-established tradition part of the written Constitution. Section 1 reads, "In the case of the removal of the President from office or his death or resignation, the Vice President shall become President." When Gerald Ford succeeded Richard Nixon, there was no question of his status as President, despite his having been appointed Vice President under the provisions of Section 2 of the Twenty-fifth Amendment, rather than having been elected.

In the case of presidential terms a longstanding tradition was violated and was rapidly restored by a formal amendment. After having served two terms as President, George Washington declined a third term, thereby establishing a precedent that continued until the time of Franklin D. Roosevelt, who not only broke the tradition by running for a third term but won and continued on to win a fourth. After his death Congress proposed the Twenty-second Amendment, placing into the language of the Constitution the two-term limitation that had existed, by custom, until 1940. The amendment was ratified in 1951 and so restricts any President after Truman.

CONSTITUTIONAL AMENDMENT

The process of formal amendment is long and difficult. In order to be adopted, an amendment to the Constitution must first be proposed by a national body and then ratified by the states. The Constitution specifies two methods of proposing amendments, but the only one that has ever been used is proposal by Congress, requiring a two-thirds vote of both the House and the Senate. The other method is by a national convention, called by Congress when two-thirds of the state legislatures request it.

Ratification must be by three-fourths of the states, and here also there are two methods. Congress specifies which is to be used. With one exception, all amendments have been submitted to the state legislatures for approval. If Congress directs, however, the states call conventions to consider an amendment and approval by conventions in three-fourths of the states is necessary for ratification. This latter method has been used only once, in the case of the Twenty-first Amendment, which repealed the Eighteenth (Prohibition) Amendment. The rural, fundamentalist forces that had supported Prohibition in the first place still were dominant in many state legislatures, and ratification by the legislatures thus was unlikely. Congress, as a result, specified consideration by conventions rather than legislatures, recognizing that conventions would be more reflective of the overwhelming public desire to eliminate Prohibition.

The Bill of Rights and Civil Liberties for Americans. The first ten amendments to the Constitution form the *Bill of Rights*, one of the most important features of the American system of government, yet probably one of the most misunderstood. Contrary to popular opinion, the courts have consistently held that the Bill of Rights was designed to protect a citizen against actions by the national government only, not against actions of a state. The Supreme Court first ruled upon the applicability of the Bill of Rights to the states in the case of *Barron v. Baltimore* in 1833. In that decision Chief Justice John Marshall declared for the Court that the first ten amendments had never been intended to limit state governments.

Throughout their history Americans have tended to fear the power of the national government and to be less concerned with the power of the states. Apparently they feel more comfortable with state governments because they believe, rightly or wrongly, that the states are easier to control since they are closer or are less dangerous because they are not as powerful. This feeling certainly is reflected in the history of the Bill of Rights, which was adopted because of fears that the new national government would encroach upon the lives of citizens and the functioning of states. Not all Americans shared these fears, of course; the Constitutional Convention avoided including a bill of rights at all, and many believed, Hamilton among them, that it would be superfluous to include one. Those of Hamilton's persuasion felt that since the purpose of the Constitution was to limit governmental power, the Constitution was, itself, a bill of rights. So pervasive were people's fears of Big Government, however, that those who opposed a bill of rights had to agree to include one in order to persuade some of the states to ratify the Constitution. Chief Justice Marshall's opinion was probably consistent with the intentions of those who devised the first ten amendments (James Madison attempted to secure passage of protection for citizens against state action, but failed), and the Court has never overruled *Barron v. Baltimore.*

The result was that for years there was a great discrepancy between those rights that were national and those that were recognized by the states. Fortunately, the situation has changed even though the first ten amendments in themselves still do not limit state action. The breakthrough came with the ratification of the Fourteenth Amendment in 1868, shortly after the Civil War. This amendment prohibits a state from making or enforcing any law "which shall abridge the privileges or immunities of citizens of the United States"; from depriving "any citizen of life, liberty, or property without due process of law"; or from denying "to any person within its jurisdiction the equal protection of the laws." It defines citizens as "all persons born or naturalized in the United States." For more than half a century the Court interpreted the Fourteenth

Amendment so narrowly that there was no significant change in practice. In the period of reaction during and following the First World War, however, when many states placed severe limitations upon freedom of speech and the press, the situation became potentially so oppressive that the Court finally was induced to act. In 1925, in *Gitlow* v. *New York*, the Court held that the freedoms of speech and the press, which the First Amendment protects from abridgment by Congress, are so fundamental to American life that they are "protected by the due process clause of the Fourteenth Amendment from impairment by the states." So far as the U.S. Constitution is concerned, therefore, it is the Fourteenth Amendment that protects a citizen from state action, not the Bill of Rights.

Most of the protections of the Bill of Rights have now been extended by action of the Fourteenth Amendment to limit state governments. The late Justice Hugo Black believed that the Fourteenth Amendment extends the entire Bill of Rights to protect a citizen against state action; the nearest the Supreme Court came to agreeing with him was in the case of *Adamson* v. *California* (1947), in which a minority of four justices so ruled. Of course, the state constitutions themselves contain bills of rights, most of which are similar to, and some even more extensive than, the national Bill of Rights. However, the people of a state can usually amend their constitution relatively easily, so that a state bill of rights is inadequate protection against inflamed public opinion. On the other hand, it is noteworthy that states on many occasions have been in advance of the federal government on a variety of issues. The Virginia Declaration of Rights, for example, was a model for the federal Bill of Rights. The present situation is that state practices with regard to freedom of speech, religion, assembly, association, search and seizure, and self-incrimination must meet the national standards set by the Supreme Court, and that the right to counsel (if necessary, to be furnished by the government) is guaranteed in both state and national criminal proceedings. The practices of the states vary from state to state and also differ from federal practice in such matters as jury trials, grand juries, and standards of procedural fairness.

It is difficult to predict what the future of the Bill of Rights and Fourteenth Amendment protections will be. Many citizens seem unconcerned or even hostile to them. In addition, several members of the current Supreme Court shaped by the Nixon administration have expressed disagreement with the theory that has extended the limitations to state governments. They will certainly not support additional extensions and might perhaps vote to rescind some of the extensions that now do limit the states.

The Bill of Rights sets down those limits upon the central government and guarantees of individual liberty from governmental encroachment that the citizens of the early republic believed to be necessary to the maintenance of a free society. Indeed it was for those limits and guarantees that Americans fought a revolution. They then forced them upon the proponents of the Constitution by their determined agitation during the ratifying conventions.

The First Amendment protects the core freedoms: freedom of worship, speech, press, and peaceable assembly. It also provides for the separation of church and state and for the citizen's right to petition the government. The Second Amendment secures the right to a citizen's militia, which illustrates that there was a widespread fear of a standing military force as a threat to a free society. Constitutional authorities deny that it guarantees individual citizens a right to purchase, own, or bear firearms. Despite this there is often more outcry over the "sacred" guarantees of the Second Amendment than over infringements of other rights listed that truly are basic to a free society.

The Third and Fourth Amendments deal with the right of privacy. The Third protects against requiring citizens to provide food and shelter for soldiers in peacetime and limits such requirements in time of war. The Fourth secures the rights of the people to protection against unreasonable searches and regulates judicial procedures.

The Fifth, Sixth, Seventh, and Eighth Amendments set forth the rights of persons accused of crimes and require strict procedures to protect both persons and property from arbitrary actions. These amendments establish the basic rules of fairness in judicial proceedings, specifying that no person shall be required to testify against himself, that trials must be speedy, that the accused must be permitted to confront his accusers, and that he must be able to compel witnesses to testify in his behalf, as the state can do for prosecution witnesses. It protects against *double jeopardy*, which means that a person acquitted by a federal court cannot be brought to trial in another federal court on the same charge. This prevents an unscrupulous or overzealous government from continually retrying those persons whom it wishes to condemn until it finds some court that is willing to convict. As interpreted by the courts, these amendments limit officials from obtaining confessions by trickery or coercion, they require jury trials in all criminal prosecutions and most civil cases and fairness in the selection of jury members, and they establish the right to consult with a lawyer at any stage of the proceeding. These amendments have been subject to detailed interpretation because they set forth some of the basic procedural protections designed to maintain rights when they are most endangered, that is, when the citizen is in conflict with the government. Consider the implications, for example, of being tried, after having been accused of a criminal act, without the right to confront accusers or to compel witnesses for the defense to testify, while the prosecution has full powers of subpoena. Such situations have occurred in the past in state courts and were frequent in colonial days.

The Ninth Amendment provides that the mere fact that a liberty is not mentioned in the Bill of Rights does not indicate that it is not a right of the people. It has been cited, for example, as a device to protect the people from governmental damage to the environment. The Tenth was added to protect the states from the accretion of too much power on the part of the central government.

The Other Amendments. Although the Constitution is nearly 200 years old, and political and economic conditions are unbelievably different from those existing at the time of its writing, by early 1977 there had been only twenty-six amendments. The first ten amendments came so soon after the Constitution itself that they may almost be considered a part of the original document. The remaining sixteen produced considerable changes, some major and some minor.

The Eleventh Amendment, ratified in 1798, was the first adopted after the Bill of Rights and is designed to prevent a person from bringing suit against a state in a federal court without the consent of the state involved. This was a reaction to the Supreme Court's ruling in *Chisholm* v. *Georgia* (1793) that federal courts could accept a suit brought against a state by a citizen of another state, which the states feared would give the federal judiciary too much power over their affairs. The Twelfth Amendment was adopted in 1804 to prevent a repetition of the confusion that occurred in the presidential election of 1800. In that year there was a tie vote between Thomas Jefferson and Aaron Burr, who were candidates for President and Vice President of the same party. This occurred because the original constitutional provision required the Electoral College to vote for President and Vice President simultaneously without distinguishing their votes. The election was thrown into the House of Representatives where there was considerable unpleasantness before Jefferson finally emerged as the winner. The Twelfth Amendment established a new arrangement that provided for separate votes for President and Vice President, thus preventing the inevitable tie votes and adapting the Constitution to the rise of a party system with each party offering candidates for both offices.

There were no more amendments until the Union victory in the Civil War brought about three more. The Thirteenth, ratified in 1865, abolished slavery. The Fourteenth came three years later and is one of the most important parts of the Constitution. Among other things, as discussed earlier, it established a national basis for citizenship and provided protections for civil rights and liberties against state encroachment. Its original purpose was to insure the freedoms of the newly emancipated blacks and to extend citizenship to them. The year 1870 saw the last of the Civil War amendments, the Fifteenth, which prohibited restrictions on the right to vote based upon race or color. As history indicates, it takes more than a constitutional amendment to guarantee a right; black citizens were routinely denied the right to vote throughout much of the South until at least the mid-1960s.

The next two amendments, both ratified in 1913, were the result of the ferment of the late nineteenth and early twentieth centuries that had brought forth strong third parties, such as the Populists, and led to the Progressive Movement. The Sixteenth Amendment secured the right of the national government to adopt an income tax and overturned the 1895 Supreme Court decision, *Pollock* v. *Farmers' Loan and Trust Co.*, that had denied the government this power. The Seventeenth took the power to elect senators from state legislatures and gave it directly to the people.

The Eighteenth Amendment of 1919 was the disastrous Prohibition amendment, which led to the beginnings of truly organized crime in this country and greatly increased the national disregard for law and order.

The ratification of the Nineteenth Amendment in 1920 guaranteed to women that they would be admitted to the vote on the same basis as men. It was the largest single extension of the democratic principle in the history of the Constitution.

The Twentieth and Twenty-first Amendments were both ratified in 1933. The Twentieth revised the beginning dates of presidential terms and congressional sessions. It shortened the period after an election before new officeholders assumed power in order to eliminate the long "lame duck" situation, and it clarified certain points pertaining to presidential succession. The Twenty-first repealed the Eighteenth Amendment and thereby eliminated national Prohibition, but (probably as the price of adoption) it guaranteed any state that wished it the right to prohibit the importation, transportation, or use of liquor.

The Twenty-second Amendment, restricting a President to two terms in office, did not come until 1951. The next amendment, the Twenty-third, was ratified a decade later, in 1961, and granted the right to vote for President and Vice President to residents of the District of Columbia by providing the District for the first time with electors in the Electoral College. This extension of democracy was followed in 1964 by the Twenty-fourth Amendment, which denied the states the right to restrict voting in federal elections through the use of a poll tax.

The Twenty-fifth Amendment, adopted in 1967, empowers the President to fill the office of Vice President, if it becomes vacant, contingent upon the approval of his choice by both houses of Congress. It also provides procedures—rigidly restricted, of course—by which the Vice President may exercise the powers of the President under certain conditions in which the President may be physically or mentally incapable of exercising them himself.

The latest amendment, the Twenty-sixth, was ratified in 1971. In yet another great extension of the democratic principle, it lowered the voting age to eighteen. In early 1977 the proposed Twenty-seventh Amendment—prohibiting legal, economic, or political discrimination on the basis of sex (the "Equal Rights Amendment")—was under consideration by the state legislatures.

The Constitution Today: Shield Against Arbitrary Government?

As the press of population and the call for increased security, both domestic and external, become greater, the likelihood of arbitrary government increases considerably. The judiciary generally is the thin black line between the citizen and improper actions by the government. This is not to imply that the government is filled with persons eager to stifle liberty. Most officials of the government—elected, appointed, or career—are decent persons who only want to do their jobs. The more subtle and more frequent difficulty stems from insensitivity to the demands of constitutional procedures on the part of both government and governed. The measures that lead to arbitrary government may be as much the result of popular demand as of a desire by ambitious officials for more power.

The task of a free society is always to insure the rights of the community without violating the rights of individual citizens. In the wake of increasing concern over airline hijacking, for example, every person who flies on a commercial airline is now subject to personal search. The average citizen probably favors this practice, believing that the increase in his or her personal security outweighs the invasion of personal privacy. However, there have been some, such as former Senator Vance Hartke of Indiana and columnist William F. Buckley, Jr., who consider the searches to be a violation of constitutional rights.

This is the kind of judgment that continually faces free societies. How much protection is necessary, and how much may liberty and privacy be restricted to achieve it? Many interest groups are actively involved in this struggle over security and rights.

The airline example is a small instance and one over which there is not very much controversy. But the important question is: How much care do people and government have for constitutional protections when their personal interests are not immediately affected? Unless there is general concern, and unless the issues are recognized for what they are, the protections of the Constitution may be eroded quietly and slowly. Such erosion may result from the people's fears as much as from the govern-

Shadowed

ment's desires. These incremental changes are rarely obviously wrong or totally unjustified, but small actions create a pattern that could lead to an invasion of the most fundamental of the liberties that the Founding Fathers designed the Constitution to protect.

As mentioned earlier, no constitution can protect the rights of individual citizens unless the citizens offer it support. In a time such as this, when there are threats to constitutional protections from both the populace and government officials, it becomes all the more necessary to stress the fragile nature of constitutions. The people must be alert to every invasion, deliberate or inadvertent, of personal and group liberties. The preservation of the Constitution must be the first principle of constitutional democracy.

Suggested Readings

Hannah Arendt. *Crises of the Republic.* New York: Harcourt, Brace Jovanovich, 1972.*

Bernard Bailyn. *The Ideological Origins of the American Revolution.* Cambridge, Mass.: Harvard University Press, Belknap Press, 1967.*

Charles A. Beard. *An Economic Interpretation of the Constitution of the United States.* New York: Macmillan, 1956; first published in 1913.

Max Beloff. *The American Federal Government.* New York: Oxford University Press, 1959.

James Fenimore Cooper. *The American Democrat.* New York: Vintage, 1956.*

Roy P. Fairfield, ed. *The Federalist Papers.* Garden City, N.Y.: Doubleday, 1961. Classics of American political writing.

Carl J. Friedrich and Robert G. McCloskey. *From the Declaration of Independence to the Constitution.* New York: Bobbs-Merrill, 1954.*

Richard Harris. "Annals of Law." *New Yorker,* April 5, 12, and 19, 1976. An examination of the current status of the Fifth Amendment and the abuse of the grand jury system.

Forrest McDonald. *We the People.* Chicago: University of Chicago Press, 1965. An attack upon the Beard position.

C. Herman Prichett. *The American Constitution.* 2nd ed. New York: McGraw-Hill, 1968. One of the most thorough treatments of American constitutional development.

Clinton Rossiter. *The Political Thought of the American Revolution.* New York: Harvest Books, 1963.*

E. E. Schattschneider. *Two Hundred Million Americans in Search of a Government.* New York: Holt, Rinehart and Winston, 1969.*

David Wise. *The Politics of Lying: Government Deception, Secrecy, and Power.* New York: Vintage, 1973.*

Benjamin F. Wright. *Consensus and Continuity.* Boston: Boston University Press, 1958.

*Available in paperback.

3

FEDERALISM AND NATIONALISM

The Development of the American Nation

It is not by the consolidation, or concentration of powers, but by their distribution, that good government is effected.

Thomas Jefferson

The Federal Union

When the authors of the U.S. Constitution established the outline of the American federal system, they devised a scheme that has shaped the whole of American political development and has been widely copied in other nations. In all probability, they had no clear idea of the direction that the new system would take, and they had no precedents to guide them; they were forced to innovate. How could they create a nation that would truly be a nation without arousing the fears and jealousies of thirteen separate states, each virtually a nation in itself? Federalism was their answer.

It was obvious that there would have to be some form of geographic distribution of power. The states were political and historical entities dating back to the colonial charters granted by the English crown. Neither the historical setting nor the preferences of the citizens would have permitted any move toward a unitary government. Under a *unitary form of government*, which Britain and France were developing, one central government has authority to govern a nation without intervening political subdivisions (variously called states, provinces, cantons, *Länder*, or republics). There may actually be subdivisions of a sort, but they are essentially agents of the central government. On the other hand, the experience under the only other form then existing, a confederacy, had been unsatisfactory. A *confederacy* is more a league of nearly independent units than a nation state as we think of one today. The true power lies with the subdivisions. The central authority, if any, is very weak and has no direct jurisdiction over the citizens of the subdivisions.

Because the only existing alternatives appeared to be impractical, the Founding Fathers were forced to create a new form that would, they hoped, combine the energetic central government of a unitary system with the strong subdivisions of a confederacy. The new form took the name of "federalism," which gave new meaning to an old word, previously synonymous with "confederacy." The implementation of *federalism* meant that the citizen henceforth would be subject not merely to a state, as under the Articles of Confederation, and not merely to a central government, as were the English, but to two governments, state and national, each "sovereign" within a specific jurisdiction. The American federal system retained strong states with powers that the national government could not abolish and added a strong national government with powers that were safe from action by the states. Each level of government had direct authority over the individual citizen and could levy taxes and enforce penalties. Figure 1 compares the federal form of government with the unitary and confederate forms.

The U.S. Constitution is the source of authority for all governments in the United States. The powers of the national and state governments are apportioned by the Constitution, as Figure 2 shows. The Constitution specifically delegates certain powers to the national government, among them, the power to perform such national functions as coining money, declaring war, regulating interstate and foreign commerce, and conducting foreign policy. Other powers that it delegates to the national government, such as the power to tax, confer concurrent jurisdiction— that is, they are powers that both national and state governments may exercise. The Constitution forbids certain powers to the national government, others to the states, and yet others to both. Nowhere does it list the powers of the states. These are considered to be "reserved," and, under the Tenth Amendment, every power not delegated to the national government or prohibited to the states is reserved to the states or the people. Each state has its own constitution, which confers powers upon the government of the state, within the framework of the U.S. Constitution, and structures the exercise of those powers. Every state law must be consistent with that state's constitution, and all state constitutions must be consistent with the U.S. Constitution.

FIGURE 1. Territorial Structure of Governments

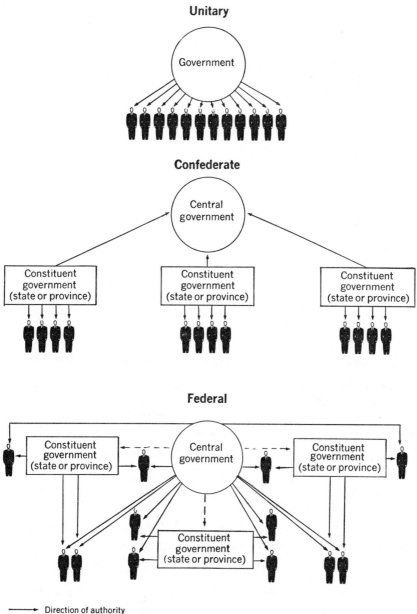

Unitary

Confederate

Federal

———▶ Direction of authority

— — ▶ Direction of authority when exercised within limited jurisdiction

FIGURE 2. Governmental Powers in the United States

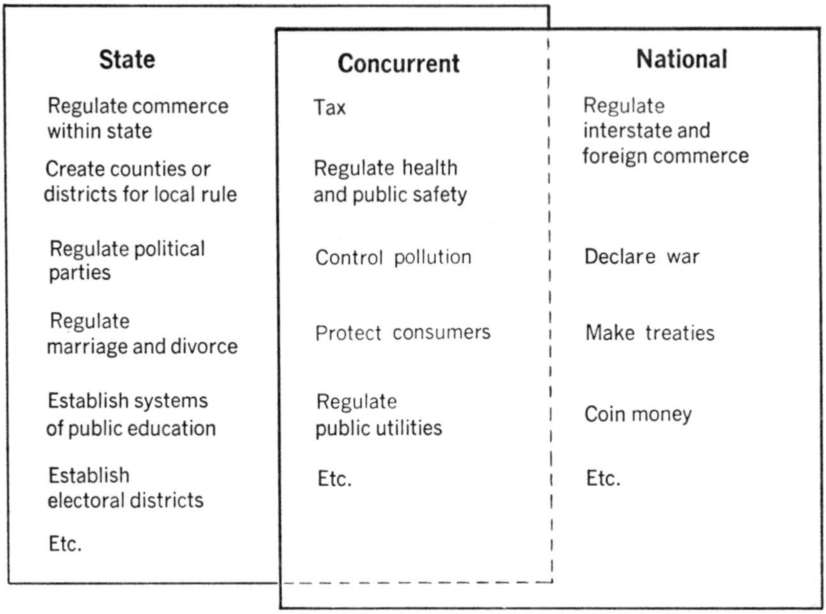

State	Concurrent	National
Regulate commerce within state	Tax	Regulate interstate and foreign commerce
Create counties or districts for local rule	Regulate health and public safety	
Regulate political parties	Control pollution	Declare war
Regulate marriage and divorce	Protect consumers	Make treaties
Establish systems of public education	Regulate public utilities	Coin money
Establish electoral districts	Etc.	Etc.
Etc.		

THE DISPERSAL OF POWER: STATES AND THEIR DIVISIONS

Under federalism each of the states has a complete government, exercising legislative, executive, and judicial powers. Below the state-government level there is a host of other governments, variously estimated at between 80,000 and 100,000 separate units nationwide. These are the municipalities, counties, and school and special districts that disperse the power of decision throughout the system.

The major division in most states is the county, which may range in size from 150 inhabitants (in Loving County, Texas) to 2 million or more (in Harris County, Texas; Cook County, Illinois; or Los Angeles County, California). In some states, counties trace their origins to colonial days and have a strong sense of identity; in others, they may be new creations. In all states they are completely the creature of the state government, which can alter their boundaries or charters as it wishes, and which uses counties as administrative arms. They often do not follow the separation-of-powers principle, being governed by a board of commissioners (sometimes called a "county court," although not a judicial body) that is both executive and legislative in nature. County judicial bodies, or courts, may or may not exist. Reformation of county government is an unexciting and rather specialized concern, but it is becoming increasingly important as counties become responsible for controlling land use and providing basic services such as police protection, transportation, and hospitals for their residents, many of whom may not live in municipalities offering such services. The county relies heavily for its revenues upon the property tax, which has become a major issue in the politics of tax reform.

In all states there are municipalities, ranging from the incorporated giants with their own charters, such as Detroit, to the smaller cities incorporated under general law, and even smaller towns and villages that enjoy no special powers and are often dependent upon counties and special districts for services. Cities with charters granted by the state, which specify powers and responsibilities, are normally governed by elected councils and mayors (although a city manager may replace or supplement the mayor). These units of government usually have basic responsibilities in the provision of services such as education, health care, police and fire protection, and amenities such as parks, museums, and recreation facilities. They raise funds by taxing incomes or sales, by borrowing, and by receiving state and federal aid. Many of the older and larger cities in the United States are collapsing under the weight of increasing social responsibilities and shrinking sources of taxation as the population shifts to suburban areas but wishes to have continued urban advantages as well. The near bankruptcy of New York City in 1976 is only one case. Washington, D.C., is sliding quietly into bankruptcy as well, and a number of other cities may follow it over the edge if some basic restructuring of political power and responsibility does not occur in urban politics.

In addition to these units of government there is a network of school and special districts. School districts, with elected boards, have been in existence for a long time. They derive much of their funds from property taxes and bond issues (which are actually loans that local voters must approve). Such services as water provision, sewage disposal, conservation, and transportation are increasingly being entrusted to special districts as well. These districts may tax, spend, and borrow money. Because they are easily created or restructured by the state as the need arises, they offer quick solutions to sudden problems. They may be governed by either elected or appointed boards. On occasion special districts amass enormous powers, which handicap other political units. The most remarkable example is the Port Authority of New York, actually an interstate agency. At one time it was under the leadership of Robert Moses and held virtually total control over the city's transportation. In fact, through a carefully constructed system of interlocking boards and authorities, often controlled by Moses himself, the basic shape of New York City and much of the state—in parks, roads, and housing—was dominated by a single, nonelected official for nearly fifty years. The accountability of special districts is thus another critical, if somewhat narrow, concern. There is also a need to coordinate the activities of their ever-increasing number and variety.

All of these divisions are subordinate to the state in some way, which makes their relationship to the state quite different from the relationship of state and federal governments (although occasionally, as Moses discovered, they can be placed in an impregnable position by tying them to a constitutionally protected power such as that of issuing bonds). In fact, the states are essentially unitary systems, and could function well, unchanged, if the federal union suddenly disappeared. Many of them, indeed, are larger than most independent nations. The responsibilities of governing states such as California, Pennsylvania, Illinois, Texas, and New York—aside from foreign affairs—are easily as great as governing the Netherlands, Denmark, or Belgium. Nevertheless, under the federal system another authority—the national government—also governs the same territory as the state, and under the Constitituion neither is permitted to infringe upon the powers of the other. In general this relationship has been respected, although there is considerable pushing and shoving as well as grumbling about aggressive bureaucrats from Washington or obstreperous locals interfering with the conduct of the other's affairs.

Such a highly complicated system requires some mechanism for settling disputes, not only between a state and the national government, but between neighboring states. This mechanism is the federal court system, usually the U.S. Supreme Court. So long as it stays within the limits of its powers under the Constitution, the national government is supreme. Under the terms of Article VI, federal laws and treaties are the "supreme law of the land," although they may not conflict with the Constitution as interpreted by the Supreme Court. Thus any state law, even if otherwise within the state's power to enact, that conflicts with federal law or treaty is invalid.

THE CHANGING BALANCE OF FEDERALISM

There is little today that remains exclusively under the jurisdiction of the states because the interpretations of the Constitution by the Supreme Court, beginning soon after the nation's founding, have tended toward the expansion of national powers. States today set their own tax policies, exercise police powers, and establish their own educational, health, and welfare systems. Even in these traditionally state activities, there is considerable federal participation through grants-in-aid, the single largest source of revenue for every state, which require that state functions meet federal standards. The exclusively state functions must also meet constitutional requirements, which gives the federal courts jurisdiction over them in certain situations.

This does not mean that federalism is dying or that the states are not vigorous, thriving political entities. State governments are growing at a rapid rate and, like local and national governments, constantly perform more functions.

The states today have dual identities: they are governmental entities with powers and responsibilities of their own, and they voluntarily act as administrative arms for many federal-state cooperative programs. Any person who believes that the national government ignores the states, or that it seeks to reduce their powers wherever possible, should spend some time in a federal agency in Washington. Generally, the slightest hint that an action may incur broad displeasure among state agencies sends federal bureaucrats scurrying for cover.

There are very few purely federal domestic programs; most require state involvement and active state cooperation. Although generalizations are dangerous, it probably is safe to say that federal agencies, as a rule, are *too* sensitive to state desires, rather than not sensitive enough, a situation that often permits the continuation of such things as racial segregation in the public schools and discriminatory welfare practices based upon state or regional prejudice. Lack of action on the part of Congress has often allowed these and similar violations of constitutional requirements to continue until the federal courts have been forced to act. Even when Congress and the courts have acted, the timidity of the bureaucracy, a lack of interest, or even a covert hostility on the part of the administration can delay considerably the righting of wrongs.

The federal principle is rooted firmly in American governmental institutions. The Senate, where every state is equally represented, expresses the purest form of federalism, but other institutions of government (excepting only the Supreme Court) reflect the federal principle in varying degrees. The U.S. House of Representatives, for example, was designed to represent the people, not the states, and representatives are allotted to the states on the basis of their population. Nevertheless, the fact that each state, no matter how small, is entitled to one representative means that even the "people's branch," the House, must reflect the existence of states to some extent. The Electoral College also is based within the states, reflecting both population size and the states as units, since each state is entitled to the same number of electors as it has members of Congress. In the event that the Electoral College fails to select a President, the selection falls to the House of Representatives, where, however, each state delegation, regardless of its size, may cast only one vote. The political parties themselves are state-based and are considerably stronger at the state and local levels than at the national level. Therefore, although the balance of powers has shifted considerably toward the national government, there is little likelihood that federalism is on its way out.

But is this federal vitality a good thing? Has federalism outlived its usefulness? Some scholars believe that it has, and others vigorously dispute them. It is true that federalism has certain disadvantages. There may, for example, be a great divergence between the laws of one state and those of another. The drivers of interstate trucks are well aware of this because they must be certain to meet the varying requirements of weight, height, length, and width of every state through which they will be driving, and they will be stopped in each one to be sure that they do meet them. Variations in divorce laws have also caused disputes in the past, with instances in which persons are considered to be divorced in one state but not in another. In general, however, the "full faith and credit" clause of Article IV of the Constitution insures that such inconveniences will be held to a minimum, and under normal circumstances each state must recognize the actions of other states.

The critics of federalism, though, appear to have strong arguments when they point out that the existence of states has permitted the perpetuation of injustices such as racial segregation and the infringement of various civil rights and liberties because the Bill of Rights did not limit state action. On the other hand, segregation began because the national government either was unconcerned or was sympathetic to bigotry. Under such circumstances, it could well have existed on a regional basis in a unitary state. For example, the Supreme Court decision that permitted the South and border areas to become thoroughly segregated, *Plessy* v. *Ferguson* (1896), occurred long after the adoption of the Fourteenth Amendment, which was designed, among other things to guard against state infringement of the rights of racial minorities. Moreover, it was not until the presidency of Woodrow Wilson, well into the twentieth century, that the District of Columbia instituted formal racial segregation. The same inferences apply to state violations of other civil rights and liberties. If they, like segregation, are permitted by the Supreme Court, by the Congress, and by the President, and are approved or tolerated by the people, it would appear that the cause is not the federal structure but public attitudes.

Some dissatisfaction with federalism has come from those who saw the national government of the 1960s as the leading force for justice, civil rights, and civil liberties in the American political system. This perception of the role of the national government during that period is correct, as is the recognition of the reactionary nature of many state governments throughout much of American history, especially in the 1950s and 1960s. Less known and little recognized, however, is the role played by many of the state governments themselves in leading the national government in the fields of justice, civil rights, civil liberties, and in the implementation of wide-ranging social programs.

One example can be found in the courts of this land. The supreme courts of many states are now considered in advance of the U.S. Supreme Court on numerous issues. This was not always the case. Under the leadership of Chief Justice Earl Warren, whom President Eisenhower appointed in 1953, the Supreme Court was highly innovative. Warren retired in 1969, however, and the Nixon appointees so changed the Court's character that in many cases it rapidly rejected the libertarian emphasis that had been so prominent. Because of this shift, the courts of many states—including Alaska, Hawaii, Maine, Michigan, and South Dakota—have demonstrated innovation on certain subjects far exceeding that of the current U.S. Supreme Court. The Supreme Court of the State of California, in fact, has long been considered by many judicial scholars to be considerably beyond the national Court. It has preceded the latter in many decisions, such as those outlawing capital punishment, and both it and the Supreme Court of New Jersey have held that, under their state constitutions, property taxes are an inequitable means of funding public schools, although the U.S. Court continues to reject such claims founded upon the national Constitution.

Similarly, many states have been in advance of the national government in other respects as well. States such as Minnesota and Colorado passed legislation establishing civil rights for racial minorities far earlier than the first truly significant federal civil rights legislation of 1964. The state of Wyoming allowed women to vote almost thirty years before the Nineteenth Amendment. There are controversies today between the national government and state governments that wish to set certain health, safety, and quality standards higher than those required by Washington. For example, the federal government has sought to prevent states from requiring safety provisions for nuclear power plants more rigorous than those required by the Nuclear Regulatory Commission (formerly the Atomic Energy Commission), whose standards some states and prominent scientists have criticized as dangerously lax. Federal agencies have also moved to prevent some states from enforcing noise restrictions at airports that exceed federal standards, or from insisting that bacon and hot dogs be of higher quality than that required by the federal government (which permits them to consist overwhelmingly of fat and water). It is easy to identify instances of recalcitrant states being forced by federal action to humanize their policies and to abide by the U.S. Constitution. It is equally easy to overlook other instances when states have been in advance of the federal government, which at times has even retarded the development of progressive policies within the states.

Federalism has been accused of being cumbersome and inefficient. It is, but this is not necessarily a disadvantage. A government that is too efficient may be dangerous, and, if too much inefficiency can create tremendous social and political problems, so can too much efficiency. Federalism is another way of separating governmental powers so that they are not all in one place. It is probable, as the proponents of federalism believe, that the confusions of federalism would make it somewhat more difficult for a political leader who is willing to violate constitutional restrictions upon his power to gain dictatorial control. It it also true, as critics point out, that federalism tends to delay many needed social programs because of disputes about who should do what.

Some adherents of federalism assert that it helps bring the administration of programs closer to the people because most federal programs are administered by the states. This is consistent with the views of the early democratic theorists, who believed that the people would be more concerned with local and state governments and would be better able to follow their activities. For some reason, however, this has not proved to be the case. The high level of corruption in many local and state governments attests to the general lack of concern with them, as does the fact that elections with national issues at stake, especially presidential elections, routinely bring out a much higher voter participation than do other elections. It is questionable whether the average citizen is any better informed about a state or local program than about one administered directly from Washington.

Some of the solid advantages of federalism are that it can provide political experience at the state and local level for future national leaders and that it can permit states to experiment with and assess programs before they are adopted by other states or by the entire nation. When the national government adopted the Social Security Act in 1935, for instance, it included a provision for Old Age Assistance to help states pay pensions to the elderly who were in need. Wisconsin had begun such payments decades before and had been followed by several other states, thus giving experience upon which the federal planners could rely.

The most obvious advantage of federalism is that it can help to adjust governmental requirements to local or regional conditions. This is especially true in countries that have varied ethnic, linguistic, or religious groupings concentrated by region. Generally speaking, the United States has no regionally distributed groupings of this kind, but there are substantial cultural differences between regions originally based on ethnic and other distinctions. Texas, for example, is very different from Vermont. Federalism also appears to offer some advantages because of the sheer size of the nation, which makes some sort of administrative subdivisions almost a necessity.

It should be evident that American federalism has evolved to such an extent that it would hardly be recognized by the founders. The process has been long, with only one dramatic and sudden development—the Civil War. It is to be expected that a system that was designed as an innovation, and was more or less the result of a pragmatic compromise, would change considerably, not only as the nation gained experience with it, but as the conditions of life changed through time. The framers of the Constitution seemed to expect this by wording that document's provisions for federalsim in very general terms, which allowed and encouraged change. Although it has expanded and matured, the system nevertheless remains truly federal. There are strong state governments that the national government cannot eliminate, and the states retain powers that are safe from interference by the national government; conversely, the national government cannot be eliminated by the states, nor can they infringe upon its powers. Some states originally asserted the right to "nullify" the operations of federal laws within their territory, or to "interpose" state power to shield citizens from the federal government. Such doctrines were never accepted legally and were laid to rest by the Civil War. To be sure, some southern states exhumed them after the Supreme Court outlawed school segregation, but this was mere chest beating on the part of a few state officials.

Not every nation that appears on paper to be federal meets the criteria outlined above. There are many truly federal states in the world in addition to the United States, such as Canada, Australia, Switzerland, and the German Federal Republic (West Germany), although the United States stands out even among these in the breadth of its federalism and, in particular, in the possession of a truly federal judicial system. There are other nations that are federal in structure but not truly federal in practice. Brazil, for example, has varied, depending upon the government in power, between a federal state and one in which the national government removes most, if not all, power from the states. Nevertheless, its formal structure appears similar to that of the United States. The Soviet Union is another interesting case. Each constituent republic is guaranteed autonomy by the Soviet constitution, but the constitution permits the central government to retain such tight control that it even approves the budgets of the constituent units. Therefore, although the structure is designed to be truly federal, and many of the formal constitutional and legal provisions ostensibly preserve the federal structure, the Soviet system in many respects functions almost as if it were unitary.

The Growth of National Power

In the early years of the nation a great controversy arose between the *strict constructionists*—those who believed that the national government's powers were limited to those clearly specified in the Constitution—and the *loose constructionists*—those who argued that the Constitution itself "implied" certain powers that could be inferred from those that were listed. The strict constructionists, led by Jefferson, insisted that it would be dangerous to accept the inferred interpretations that the loose constructionists, led by Hamilton, continually advanced.

The argument burst forth in full bloom when Hamilton, as Secretary of the Treasury, proposed that the national government charter a national bank. In 1791 President Washington requested Jefferson, his Secretary of State, to prepare an opinion as to the proposed bank's constitutionality. Jefferson argued that nowhere in the Constitution was there authority permitting the national government to issue a charter, and that to do so would expand its powers more than the Constitution intended. The government was limited, he insisted, to those powers specifically *noted* in the Constitution. In rebuttal Hamilton prepared a closely reasoned document justifying the doctrine of *implied powers*, saying that any power that the Constitution enumerated was directed toward an end, and that any means to that end, unless specifically forbidden by the Constitution, were therefore also permitted. Washington accepted Hamilton's argument and, when Congress passed the act establishing the bank, signed it into law.

Although the national government created a bank, the controversy over strict versus loose construction of the Constitution continued, despite the fact that Jefferson, as President, used the doctrine of implied powers to justify such things as the annexation of the Louisiana Territory in 1803 and the embargo of foreign trade in 1807. If there ever had been doubt as to the eventual outcome, the Supreme Court tipped the balance. Several decisions handed down under the influence of the great Chief Justice John Marshall strengthened the national government and encouraged the nationalizing tendencies. The classic expression of the Court's preferences for the Hamiltonian view came in 1819 in the case of *McCulloch* v. *Maryland*. The Chief Justice wrote that although the government is one of strictly limited powers, if the goal is constitutional, then any means to that goal, if they are consistent with the goal and are not forbidden by the Constitution, are also constitutional. This decision, which denied the state of Maryland the power to tax a branch of the Bank of the United States, has become a firm fixture in American constitutional law.

It was the Civil War that finally laid to rest most of the questions regarding national supremacy. The Constitution plainly declares, in Article VI, that treaties and federal laws, so long as they are consistent with the Constitution, are to be the "supreme law of the land" and that they also bind state judges. Before the Civil War, some had argued for the right of secession as the final recourse of a state that opposed national policy, but the Civil War settled the issue in practice and the Supreme Court subsequently settled it in law. The Fourteenth Amendment, which followed the war, provided the basis for national citizenship and strengthened the federal judiciary's power to review state actions to force compliance with national policy. For years the courts restricted their interpretations of the Fourteenth Amendment, limiting its impact on the states, but in the last few decades it has become the vehicle for national insistence upon a system of civil rights and liberties for Americans regardless of state policy.

At the end of the nineteenth century reformers looked to the central government as their ally in controlling socially destructive interests such as the great manufacturing and transportation trusts, and they endowed it with new regulatory powers. The Great Depression of the 1930s intensified national power by presenting the nation with such tremendous difficulties that only the national government could possibly be strong enough to deal with them. Following quickly upon the depression was World War II, which required even more national power. In the years following this war the wartime state continued because of cold war tensions, the demands of world leadership, and the fears of many that America is ever in danger of becoming weak. No nation in modern times can fight a major war without devoting considerable time and energy to it on a national basis. The demands of war and of defense in a world that fears war are by far the greatest forces that strengthen nationalizing tendencies. Those who favor less federal government and more military forces are asking the impossible; the military is a major part of the government. The centralization brought about by the Great Depression was considerable, but that caused by the Second World War and the military policies of the postwar years, including Korea and Vietnam, make the centralizing tendencies of the depression pale into insignificance by contrast.

Political forces, of course, are not the only ones that have encouraged tendencies toward centralization in this country. Technological forces, largely beyond democratic control, have also played their part.

The automobile (with its interstate highway system) and the computer, to name only two, have revolutionized our lives and the character of the nation with no planning or forethought whatsoever. Developments in communications—the telephone, movies, radio, and television— similarly have strengthened centralizing tendencies by reducing regional differences and substituting an invisible web of common and simultaneous experience.

Recently there have been calls to return some power and responsibility to the states, to curb the nation's centralizing tendencies. Until the last few years, most such concerns were thinly disguised excuses for racism or were attempts to justify attitudes based upon selfish interests. Now, however, many who earlier advocated strengthening the powers of the national government have concluded that a government sufficiently strong to accomplish their goals may also be sufficiently strong to work against them and to become repressive. This theme was a major part of campaign oratory in 1976. Whether the fears of big government are justified and whether a change in direction is possible, only time will tell. All too frequently, as W. H. Auden remarked, "time will say nothing but 'I told you so.' "

The Growth of Nationalism

Originally, white Americans were nothing but transplanted Europeans. They brought with them European ideals, outlooks, and practices, which they modified to make more or less consistent with the new and primitive environment. By the time of the Revolution, a change had occurred. No longer were Americans local representatives of other societies and cultures; they had instead developed a strong national consciousness and a thriving new culture of their own. It is not possible to determine at what point in history Americans became conscious of themselves as American, but many factors clearly contributed to the development of a specifically American character.

At the close of the Revolution, Crèvecoeur, a French immigrant to America, asked in his *Letters from an American Farmer* the question, "What, then, is this American, this new man?" He answered that everything here regenerated those who had been European into something new, a new man with a new psychology different from that of the European. With a vastly greater potential for movement, both socially and geographically, Americans were less rooted to the soil than were their European counterparts, but they nonetheless had a greater stake in society. In a land permeated by democratic theory, they conceived of the nation and the government as their own.

Paradoxically, the very mobility and rootlessness of Americans—a people who, to some extent cut off from their ties with the past, had carved out a new world in the Western Hemisphere—have encouraged the development of a particular kind of nationalism. In 1893 the historian Frederick Jackson Turner read a paper entitled "The Significance of the Frontier in American History" at a meeting of historians in Chicago. Turner's "frontier thesis" sought to explain the development of the American character by attributing it to the existence of a frontier that continually called Americans forth from the cities to the American West. He concluded that it was the westward movement with its wilderness experience that developed the American qualities of self-reliance and democracy.

Turner's thesis is inadequate in many respects, and it ignores how Americans were, and are, connected to the rest of the world, but it is noteworthy that it immediately struck a responsive chord in the hearts of Americans, and for a time that it seemed to be a complete explanation. It told Americans that historians had concluded what they had known instinctively all along—that they were unique, that they were totally separate from the old and corrupt institutions of Europe, that they could make their own way in the world. And make their own way they did. They swept across a continent, virtually exterminating the Indians as they went. They seized, purchased, or negotiated for a vast expanse of land that had been owned by others, from Florida, through the huge interior region of the Louisiana Purchase, on to the Pacific coast, taking Texas and the arid lands of the Southwest in passing. Not even the ocean stopped them, as they pressed onward to accumulate the distant lands of Alaska and Hawaii. Wherever Americans went, they carried their traditions and institutions with them, ultimately carving new states from all these territories.

This movement to acquire new land and to incorporate it into a new American empire came to be called *Manifest Destiny*. Americans, from the highest government leaders to the everyday citizen, believed that it was America's destiny to engulf the continent, to bring enlightenment to "inferior" peoples, to spread the benefits of American civilization, and to expand the Union. Before the end of the nineteenth century the United States had spread from the Atlantic to the Pacific and was looking west and south for new worlds to conquer.

Manifest Destiny in its classic form ended on the shores of the Pacific, but the thirst for expansion was not dead. The impulses that had fed it in the middle of the 1800s resurged in the 1890s to continue into the twentieth century as open imperialism. Because of its intense nationalism and its tremendous wealth and resources, the United States succeeded in annexing Hawaii, seizing the Philippines, wresting Cuba from Spain and reducing it for a time to a virtual American possession, interfering (along with other countries) with the sovereignty and internal affairs of China, and asserting the right to police the manners and morals of the Latin American nations.

Nationalism has become one of the major forces in world affairs, often overshadowing everything else including social class, race, and economic or political considerations. It seems characteristic of the modern world that all peoples and their governments are intensely nationalistic, especially the newer states. Marxists long assumed that the interests of the working classes would lead workers of various nations to unite against capitalists. In reality, the forces of nationalism have become so strong that there is relatively little trans-national social and political current, with the exception of the great multinational corporations. Even the so called wars of national liberation tend to be self-consciously nationalistic movements.

Intense nationalism developed early in the United States, partly, it seems, as a reaction to the European institutions from which many of the early American settlers had fled. Throughout our history, it has taken varied forms. It has led to some of the most impressive acts of international generosity in world history, such as the Marshall Plan, which helped to rebuild a Europe that had been ravaged by war, just as it has upon occasion led to irrationalities, such as the excesses of the McCarthy period in the 1950s, the removal of Americans of Japanese ancestry to concentration camps during the Second World War, and the Palmer raids of the post-World War I era. At its best and at its worst, American nationalism has reflected the strengths and the weaknesses of the nation. More than that, it has reflected the energy of America in a powerful manner.

Americans have much to be proud of. American political thought has been an enlightening force throughout the world for 200 years. American economic accomplishments are probably the most impressive that the world has ever known. But American pride can lead to contradictions, such as that pointed out by Mark Twain and other critics of American imperialism in the Philippines early in the twentieth century. How can a democratic nation maintain democratic ideals at home and subvert them elsewhere? Can democracy stop (as politics is supposed to, but rarely does) at the water's edge?

Pride has led the nation into military excesses, such as the War in Southeast Asia, the longest war in American history despite the fact that it was never declared. It is generally true that war is simply incompatible with constitutional democracy. Democracy stresses open discussion; war

demands secrecy. Democracy thrives upon dissent and disagreement; war represses all opinion not consistent with the waging of the conflict. Democracy is based on the solution of problems by reason; war is based on solutions by force and violence—the greatest possible breakdown of law and order. Democracy places value on the individual; war subjects the individual to a rigid authoritarian rule. Unfortunately, the same nationalism that is built on democratic theory and the American past can, if unrestrained, lead into the very situations that are most destructive of the institutions that brought forth the nationalistic pride.

Two of the most prominent characteristics of the American character have been a sense of mission and a belief that nothing was beyond the power of the American nation to accomplish. World War I struck a blow at both of these. Americans had gone into the war with highly idealistic aims; they had intended to "make the world safe for democracy." Instead, there was repression at home, with a Sedition Act making it a crime to criticize the government and resulting in the jailing of almost 2,000 persons, and there was disillusionment with the postwar settlements abroad as the victors fought for national advantage at the expense of democratic principles. Both the high idealism and the subsequent disillusionment resulted in part from Americans' naive tendency to accept views so oversimplified that they failed to understand the significance of world happenings.

America then turned inward, symbolized by the Senate's refusing to grant President Wilson's plea to join the League of Nations. The government even incorporated into law the racist doctrines that earlier had encouraged imperialism, adopting restrictive immigration legislation that effectively excluded those of certain races and severely restricted the immigration of others. Internally, the government made no move to eliminate or reduce segregation and other racist policies and, in fact, as often as not appeared to encourage them.

World War II partially restored American confidence and enabled Americans to point with pride to impressive industrial and technological feats, but the subsequent development of the cold war and America's insistence that only the United States and the Soviet Union were "world leaders" brought further disillusionment. The oversimplified viewpoint that assumed that other nations must accept the leadership of one of the two "superpowers" reflected the general lack of awareness of the strength of nationalism in countries other than the United States. It impeded awareness of the wish of other nations, especially in the so called developing areas, to direct their own political futures independently of the major power centers. Such failures of understanding contributed greatly to the tragic developments in Southeast Asia, which, to some extent, resulted from an exaggerated nationalism that caused many American leaders to misinterpret situations elsewhere in the world.

Suggested Readings

Herbert Agar. *The Price of Power: America Since 1945.* Chicago: University of Chicago Press, 1957.*

Stephen E. Ambrose. *Rise to Globalism: American Foreign Policy 1938–1976.* Baltimore: Penguin, 1976.*

Yehoshua Arieli. *Individualism and Nationalism in American Ideology.* Baltimore: Penguin, 1966.*

Jack Bass and Walter De Vries. *The Transformation of Southern Politics.* New York: Basic Books, 1976.

Walter H. Bennett. *American Theories of Federalism.* University, Ala.: University of Alabama Press, 1964.

Valerie Earle, ed. *Federalism: Infinite Variety in Theory and Practice.* Itasca, Ill.: Peacock, 1968.*

Daniel J. Elazar. *American Federalism: A View from the States.* 2nd ed. New York: Crowell, 1972.*

Roy P. Fairfield, ed. *The Federalist Papers.* Garden City, N.Y.: Doubleday, 1961.

Herbert Jacob and Kenneth N. Vines. *Politics in the American States.* Boston: Little, Brown, 1976.*

Max Lerner. *America as a Civilization.* New York: Simon & Schuster, 1957.

Jarol B. Manheim. *Déjà Vu: American Political Problems in Historical Perspective.* New York: St. Martin's Press, 1976.*

Michael McGiffert, ed. *The Character of Americans.* Homewood, Ill.: Dorsey, 1964.*

Frederick Merk. *Manifest Destiny and Mission in American History.* New York: Vintage, 1963.*

Michael D. Reagan. *The New Federalism.* New York: Oxford University Press, 1972.

Alexis de Tocqueville. *Democracy in America.* 2 vols. New York: Vintage, 1957.* A classic view of American democracy in the nineteenth century.

M.J.C. Vile. *The Structure of American Federalism.* New York: Oxford University Press, 1961.

*Available in paperback.

4 THE EXECUTIVE PROCESS

An Imperial Principle?

> Nothing can well be imagined more directly contrary to common sense than to suppose that millions of people should be subjected to the arbitrary, precarious pleasure of a single man.
>
> Jonathan Mayhew

The executive as an institution, a position, and a function has been dominant throughout history and across cultures. Many political systems have been governed by one person or group of persons combining all the powers of government, ranging from the simple head of the family to the dictator, sun king, divine ruler, or emperor. Although a separate legislative body or judiciary might have existed, it was subject to the will of the executive. By contrast, there are few terms or forms for legislatures; if the number of words for an institution is indicative of importance in culture and history, legislatures and judiciaries rank far behind executives. Systems in which the legislature has the predominant power, the parliamentary systems, are in a minority. Even where parliamentary systems exist, the power has shifted in the twentieth century to the executive. The American Constitution, although based on the ideas of separation of powers and the checking of each branch's powers by other branches, does give preeminence to the legislature. As we approach the third century of the Constitution, however, the executive has stepped to the center of the stage, rising partly on the discarded or delegated powers of the Congress.

Varieties of the Executive in America

In one original draft of the Constitution the American executive was to have been elected by the Congress. In another the President was to be elected by the people. Eventually both of these plans were rejected and a compromise devised. The President would not be merely a tool for realizing the will of the legislature, nor would he be a direct instrument of the people. The state legislatures would choose as many presidential electors as they were assigned members in Congress. This Electoral College would then pick the best two men from among the citizens to be the President and Vice President. With the development of the party system it became the custom over the years, although not required by the Constitution or federal law, that the electors simply cast all of their votes for the candidate of the party winning the majority of popular votes in the state. Thus the American presidency has moved closer to the popularly elected office proposed at the convention by Gouverneur Morris as a bulwark against legislative tyranny.

The Constitutional Convention established the basis of modern executive power. The presidency was to be a single office, the Vice President having essentially no powers of his own. The executive was to be independent of the Congress and have a national constituency, whose voice would be heard through the state-based Electoral College. Powers were allocated to the President in military and foreign affairs and, somewhat more vaguely, were implied in domestic affairs. Together these specifications created a new kind of executive role.

The commentary that follows concentrates upon the national executive, but much of it applies to the states as well. The office of governor strongly resembles that of the presidency in the domestic sphere, and the state bureaucracies share the strengths and weaknesses of Washington administrative agencies. However, there are some general distinctions to note, and some other exceptions will be mentioned in the detailed discussion.

Governors are typically hemmed in by greater constitutional restrictions than are Presidents, and in some states they are clearly subordinated to the legislature. Their power is shared in most cases with other elected executive officials—lieutenant governors, attorney generals, treasurers, auditors, secretaries of state—and the governors have little if any control over them. Often the voters will even select a cabinet drawn from both parties. In addition, the major functions of state government may be under the control of independent boards and commissions—subject only to limited gubernatorial control by appointment of some part of their membership during a single term. All of this must be set against the context of state constitutions, many of which take a very narrow view of the permissible limits of state power. Having said this, it must be noted that executive power is growing in the states, reflecting the general shift of power in American political history. Most of the governors possess one resource that is denied to the President, the *item veto*, which enables them to veto portions of a bill as well as the whole bill. On balance, then, the executive offices at state and national levels are more similar than distinctive, despite differences in practice.

This generalization collapses at the local level. Here there may be strong executives, charged with the full range of local powers and responsibilities, but in other cases the legislature is virtually supreme. County government often is entrusted entirely to a council of some kind, and many cities have a dominant legislature with a weak mayor or city manager. The special districts fit this pattern too. The greatest variety in politics is expressed at the local level, which is accordingly difficult to discuss except in contrast to the relatively uniform ideas that prevail in state and national structures.

The Growth of Executive Power

There have been powerful men in the presidency from the beginning. Thomas Jefferson, for instance, used the presidency as an active part of government, and he dominated the federal government of the time. The office itself, however, has grown in strength since Jefferson's day. After Jefferson's terms, in fact, the Congress came into its own. For most of the nineteenth century attention focused on the men and activities of Congress. Only the strong Presidents stand out in this period: Andrew Jackson and Abraham Lincoln. Lincoln in particular assumed powers usually held by Congress, sometimes ignoring the Constitution in his struggle to hold the Union together. In the eyes of many historians and political scientists, Lincoln achieved the most powerful presidency in American history, lacking only modern technology. After Lincoln came another series of men less powerful and less well known than many members of Congress. As the twentieth century opened, the balance slowly began to shift. In the first three decades of the new century the presidencies of Theodore Roosevelt and Woodrow Wilson were matched by the passive years of William Howard Taft, Warren G. Harding, Calvin Coolidge, and Herbert Hoover, but with the coming of the New Deal the presidency passed to an almost unbroken line of men who believed that the office could be, and should be, expanded. At the same time the circumstances of history were producing demands from the public and from other parts of the political system that virtually forced the presidency to expand, even under a man such as Dwight D. Eisenhower, who had not wanted greater powers. Richard Nixon, though supporting the idea of restricted federal powers and the restoration of state powers, still assumed an executive role as great as that of any of his predecessors—

perhaps the most extensive in history—to implement his views of a good society. His successor, Gerald Ford, and the 1976 challenger, Jimmy Carter, both spoke in terms of limited powers while advocating programs that would require continued executive preeminence. Franklin Roosevelt, Harry Truman, John Kennedy, and Lyndon Johnson, on the other hand, clearly expressed and acted upon their preference for a powerful presidency in a powerful national government as the best way of solving the crises of twentieth-century life.

It is significant that Lincoln, the most powerful President of the nineteenth century, was chief executive during the cruelest and most exhausting war ever fought by the United States. Other nineteenth-century Presidents who made their mark also tended to do so in military or in foreign affairs: the war against Mexico, the Indian wars, the purchase of Louisiana. Only Jackson in the years after Jefferson can be said to have expanded the powers of the presidency by dealing with largely domestic issues as he extended influence to the frontier elite. The tendencies that brought forth the most powerful Presidents in the nineteenth century have accelerated in the twentieth and have been supplemented by others. The reasons for the growth of presidential power are fourfold.

First, there has been the increasing involvement of the United

States during the twentieth century in world politics and in the wars endemic to those politics.

Second, the increase in the power of the presidency has been related to the growth in size and power of the entire executive branch. The Constitution itself barely mentioned the executive departments and made no statement on their role. The executive bureaucracy of the federal government has grown into an enormous elite, served by a great mass of clerks. Today it employs nearly 3 million workers and spends a quarter of the gross national product. The President's position as head of this bureaucracy gives him power that far exceeds that of Congress, which has only a few thousand employees and a relatively small legislative budget—unfairly singled out for criticism in the 1976 campaign as evidence of congressional self-seeking and wastefulness. In particular the control of the executive budget—in effect the national budget—vested in the President by Congress itself in 1921 has allowed the President and his staff to shape national policy, in so far as it can be shaped by money (see pp. 60–61 for further discussion of this issue).

Third, executive power has been augmented by developments in technology and changes in society in the twentieth century that have made the President the most visible political figure. The public identifies him as the head of the political system and of the country; few can identify all, or even some, of their state's congressmen, state and local representatives, and judges. Nearly everyone can name the President. The President is able to command television appearances and set their conditions. His activities are usually accorded a prominence in the news that no single congressman, and perhaps not the Congress itself, can match.

Finally, the type of political campaigning and the political history of the United States since 1932 have weeded out passively oriented presidential candidates. Most of the men who have competed for the office in the past forty years have been strong personalities, clearly oriented toward an expanding presidency regardless of their personal political philosophies on the role of the federal government or the role of the government in general.

The President and His Policy Makers

The federal executive may be divided into two parts: first are the elected leader and his policy subordinates, some two thousand appointive offices, under the direct control of the President, which constitute the policy head of the executive branch; second are the bureaucracies, controlled today by civil service hiring on the basis of merit rather than on the basis of patronage or class considerations.

The President is the official with which the Constitution primarily concerns itself. It is his powers and responsibilities that are defined in Article II, following the blunt statement that "the executive power shall be vested in a President of the United States of America." The Vice President is basically only a safeguard against vacancies in the office of President. The office of Vice President has only one power of itself, that of presiding over the Senate and casting a vote in the event of a tie. Even that power is not described under the article dealing with the executive. The first Vice President called it the "most insignificant office ever conceived," and John Nance Garner, one of Franklin Roosevelt's Vice Presidents, said that the job was "not worth a pitcher of warm spit."

The vice-presidency is important as a stepping stone to higher office. Thirteen Vice Presidents have succeeded to the presidency. Four filled out the term of a dead President but had none of their own. Four were subsequently elected after filling a term, and four others were elected on their own after completing terms as Vice President. The thirteenth, Gerald Ford, completed the term of President Nixon after his resignation but did not win election on his own. Only in recent decades, however, has the office become an important newsmaker. Nixon and Johnson, as well as Hubert Humphrey and Spiro Agnew, were all personally energetic and ambitious men, and they created interest in themselves, with the help of the President. Attention naturally centered on Ford and Nelson Rockefeller as the first nonelected Vice Presidents, and on Ford as the almost certain successor to Nixon during the deepening Watergate crisis. The President, however, still controls the circumstances of the Vice President. He can give his subordinate a great deal of responsibility and visibility, grooming him as a successor, or he can keep him in the White House closet. The disappearance of Rockefeller from the public eye followed quickly upon the obvious intention of President Ford to seek his own term and to choose a different vice presidential candidate. President Carter's choice of Vice President Mondale to serve as his top adviser and the coordinator of his staff is without precedent. Mondale appears to be in a position to become the most powerful Vice President in history. This, of course, will depend upon his retaining Carter's confidence.

Most eyes focus on the President; his hands alone hold the reins. His powers are a combination of constitutional grants, statutory additions by Congress, additions grafted on by custom and accident, and his personal attributes and abilities. A good deal will always depend upon the President's personal ability to persuade others, to keep on top of the situation, to make the best of his political status and authority without pushing his powers beyond the limits of others' endurance and causing a confrontation. He is faced with demands from many different constituencies. A careful use of these demands can increase his political stature, whereas mistakes may compound each other and drag him down under the burden. The President has to deal with the enormous bureaucracy and keep it from subverting his policies. He must keep his major advisers and executive heads from becoming too independent, too important in their own right, perhaps with an eye to higher office themselves. He must deal with Congress as an institution and meet the additional demands of his party's members in Congress. Members of his party outside Congress will expect his support and help as the unofficial leader of the party, and his personal supporters may have conflicting needs. The nation as a whole is the President's constituency as head of state; the world outside also will make demands on him in this role. He and his office will be the target of pressures from most of the interest groups in the nation. A major mistake in any one of these areas can tarnish a shining performance in the rest.

The President is assisted by the chief executive officers of the various departments, by his Executive Office, and by his own personal staff. The Cabinet, which is generally composed of the Vice President (if the President so chooses), the department heads, and certain important White House officials such as the National Security adviser—the exact composition varying with each administration—is not comparable to the cabinet of a parliamentary government. Although each department or agency head has certain "constituencies" (business, labor, foreign governments) to which he or she must respond, these officials are ultimately responsible only to the President. He is the only person who can fire them, barring impeachment—a long-established principle that has been confirmed by the Supreme Court. No amount of public pressure can admit a department head to this policy-making council once he or she has fallen from favor, nor even save his or her job, as Nixon's first Secretary of the Interior, Walter Hickel, discovered.

DOMESTIC AFFAIRS

The President has wide authority in domestic matters. Table 1 summarizes his powers in this area.

In this century the nominations of executive officers and federal judges offered by the President have rarely failed to be confirmed by the Senate. During the nineteenth century the Senate refused to grant consent far more frequently, rejecting a quarter of the judicial appointments alone. Today the confirmation hearings may be used to publicize congressional disagreement with policy in the office under consideration. In the end, however, following the tradition that the President is entitled to have the appointees he wants, the Senate usually confirms. This also extends to the personal advisers of the President, discussed below, whom

TABLE 1 The President's Role in Domestic Affairs

Domestic Power/Role	Source	Check
Appointment and removal of major policy makers	Constitution, Article II, Section 2, for appointment; removal by tradition	Confirmation by Senate if the Congress so determines. Article II, Section 2
Head of the executive; chief administrator	Constitution, implied in Article II, Sections 2 and 3	Subject to congressional approval of the number and structure of departments, etc. Article I, Section 8
Executor of the laws	Constitution, Article II, Section 3	Congress alone may make law. Article I, Section 1
Budget preparation	Budget and Accounting Act of 1921	Congress alone may appropriate funds. Article I, Section 9
Impoundment/transfer of funds	Tradition; possibly statute	Budget Act of 1974
Initiator of legislation	Constitution, implied in Article II, Section 3	Congress alone may make law. Article I, Section 1
Veto	Constitution, Article II, Section 7	Excepting ten days or less before adjournment, Congress may repass. Article II, Section 7
Convene special sessions and adjourn Congress if the houses disagree on the time	Constitution, Article II, Section 3	Congress determines all other procedural matters. Article I, Section 5
Executive order	Tradition	????
Executive privilege	Tradition; Supreme Court case *(U.S.* v. *Nixon)*	Supreme Court ruling in *U.S.* v. *Nixon*
Head of state and symbolic leader of the nation	Constitution, implied in Article II; tradition	????

the Senate does not require to be ratified. These appointments are to some extent a source of patronage for the President, who generally chooses nominees from his own party.

As head of the executive branch the President is also the leader of the entire federal bureaucracy. He and his executive heads may issue orders changing the regulations and practices of various agencies. He may reorganize the Executive Office, which includes his advisory agencies and his personal White House staff, as he sees fit unless Congress objects within sixty days. Reorganization of the executive departments or creation of new ones requires action by Congress. A President may attempt to avoid this by reorganizing his own staff along the lines he prefers and then requiring the executive departments to go through this staff in order to consult with him, although this has usually aroused criticism and been quietly halted.

As executor of the laws the President is effectively free to determine how much attention will be devoted to various areas. If he is confident of public support, he may even openly refuse to implement a policy approved by Congress. Even though the Constitution requires the President to "faithfully execute" the laws, Presidents have argued that this does not bind them to execute laws that they believe are intrusions into executive powers. Congress cannot force the President to take action except by using its monetary powers to deny him funds for some other project. Executive discretion has become a necessity as the amount of federal legislation mushrooms, yet at the same time it gives the President great power in shaping policy. The Constitution has no remedy. There was one attempt by Congress to utilize impeachment proceedings as a means of attacking a President whose policy it found offensive, against Andrew Johnson, but it failed by one vote. Other efforts to impeach were directed at John Tyler and Herbert Hoover but failed completely. The nearly certain impeachment of Nixon in 1974 ended with his resignation from office under this threat. In general, the only effective remedy remains in the hands of the people, through denial of reelection or the creation of sufficient pressure for resignation. Beyond this the only remedy is the President's personal moral code and sense of history.

Congress created the budgetary powers of the President in 1921 and extended them in 1939 by putting the budget agency in the Executive Office, where the President could easily control it. Prior to that the executive departments submitted their requests to Congress separately, and it was up to Congress to determine the priorities. In the present arrangement the President, assisted by the budget agency, now called the Office of Management and Budget (OMB), presides over the determination of priorities. Departments submit requests to the OMB, which can reshape them as it wishes. No requests are submitted directly to Congress, although some powerful agencies with close ties to a congressional committee may in fact do so informally. All but four governors have similar powers.

There have been some brief efforts in Congress to establish a "legislative budget," as a means of enabling Congress to check executive power by setting its own priorities, but these efforts failed, ending in a 1974 compromise which elevated Congress to the position of a more careful check writer. Congress is to blame for much of the escalation of executive power that produced the excesses of the Nixon administration. It had permitted the practices of impoundment and transfer of funds to develop. *Impoundment* is the presidential practice of refusing to spend funds appropriated by Congress, and *transfer* refers to the spending of funds for purposes Congress did not approve, particularly for military objectives. The legality of both of these practices was uncertain. Congress had, prior to the Nixon years, authorized the President to effect savings in administering programs, but this had never included the right to refuse to spend funds for administering a program at all. Still, after the Second World War Congress had given at least implied consent to this by allowing impounding to increase, frequently not even protesting. The Nixon administration simply expanded an established practice, even though the total rose to many billions of dollars, as it made increasing use of impoundment to kill programs that the law required but which the President and his men opposed.

The 1974 reforms did not take full effect until 1976, and the effects are too recent to assess fully. The President must now submit his budget proposals to Congress within fifteen days after it convenes each year. To coordinate their responses, the Budget Committee of each house must recommend overall spending amounts, including recommendations by category, to the appropriations committees by April 15. By May 15 there must be agreement between the houses on spending levels, and appropriations must be completed by September 25th. In addition, the President is required to submit all proposals for new spending at least a year in advance, so that Congress may have sufficient time for thorough consideration, aided by the professional staff of the new Congressional Budget Office.

The use of impoundment has been severely restricted, following numerous federal district court decisions that declared its implementation by Nixon to be illegal. The Supreme Court backed the decisions in February 1975 by unanimously ordering Ford to release funds for water pollution control that were originally impounded under Nixon. Either house may now block an impoundment by passing a resolution that is not subject to veto. No program may be abolished through impoundment without the explicit consent of both houses. President Ford was careful to obtain congressional approval when he wished to defer or reduce spending on a program (perhaps as a result of his long career in Congress as well as the new requirements). Any future violations of the reform provisions can readily be tested in court so long as Congress remains interested in its powers and responsibilities.

The power of the President over budgeting matters is part of his role in legislative matters. A second major legislative role of the President is based upon his power to suggest legislation to the Congress. Through the State of the Union message, in which he yearly lays down the outline of his administration's programs, and the periodic suggestion of legislation that he thinks "necessary and expedient," in the Constitution's phrase, the President and the executive branch have become the source of most national legislation. Since the Second World War this power of the presidency has become increasingly important to the legislative process. Perhaps two-thirds of all legislation originates in the executive branch today. If the minor bills are excepted, executive inspiration has accounted for nearly four-fifths of the major proposals passed by Congress in the years since the war. The White House is now expected to draw up legislation and present it to Congress as part of an overall administration program. The congressional leadership, whether of the President's party or not, has failed to respond with a program of its own; instead, it merely reacts to White House proposals. Various congressmen, particularly senators, may introduce legislation, and some few will draw up major bills, often with the help of interested organizations. A major proposal on the health-care system, for instance, may have the backing and assistance of the American Hospital Association or the Committee of 100, a union-backed coalition. The resources of the executive branch, however, and the political purpose and will of its single head, are far greater than those of Congress, which are divided among its elected leaders and its committee heads and additionally split by party lines. The executive has assumed a great deal of the legislative power, through both presidential initiative and congressional default.

If the White House proposals are mutilated by Congress, or if that body passes other legislation not acceptable to the President, he may use the veto, having ten days to do so. Congress may then repass the bill over the veto, unless it has adjourned within the ten-day period. Repassage of a vetoed bill requires a two-thirds vote of each house. The possibility that Congress may repass a bill makes the veto much less useful to a President than a final veto. Additionally, the veto is a general veto rather than the item veto possessed by some of the state executives; thus, the President may not veto only part of a bill but must accept it or reject it in its entirety. If an unrelated item is added in a "rider," he must reject the entire bill in order to reject the rider. Some legislation that the President does not like may be forced upon him by attaching it to material he is intent upon having. (In some states governors are saved from this dilemma by requirements that legislative acts deal with only one subject.)

The final legislative power of the President, that of convening special sessions of Congress, is essentially an emergency power. If a crisis of some kind occurs when Congress is not in session, the President may summon it to meet. Of course, there is no assurance that Congress, once convened, will act favorably on the President's request. Special sessions have become rare in the twentieth century, because the regular sessions of Congress now consume most of the year.

Through executive privilege and the executive order, the President's actions may escape scrutiny by the Congress. These two powers have evolved from historical necessity and exist only by implication, if at all, in the Constitution. *Executive privilege* originally meant that the President himself could not be called upon to testify before Congress, a privilege held to be necessary under the separation of powers. By extension, his few personal assistants were also free from testifying. This right of refusal underlines the difference between the President and a prime minister in parliamentary government. The prime minister, during "question time," may be ruthlessly interrogated by any and all members of the legislature, a probing that cannot be escaped by refusal to appear.

The contrast has grown sharper in the post–World War II years as Presidents have gradually extended the privilege to more and more of their ever more important advisers. For example, persons holding such positions as Assistant for National Security and Assistant for Domestic Affairs, not subject to Senate confirmation, have also not been subject to congressional questioning. In 1973 the Nixon administration expanded the interpretation of the privilege, ruling that no members of the executive office would appear before Congress even after they left office, although it subsequently retreated from this position and did permit them to testify. Critics in and out of Congress have noted that the effect of executive privilege has been to diminish sharply the congressional ability to share in policy making. If Congress cannot question those who are the effective determiners of policy in the executive branch, its ability to analyze those policies and suggest changes or alternatives is substantially reduced. Although the Nixon administration backed down on executive privilege to a large extent in the Watergate hearings—partly under direction from the federal courts—the practice itself remains substantially uncurbed.

An *executive order* is a directive issued under the authority of the President, either by him personally or by one of the executive departments. Congress could not conceivably consider and pass as law every minute change that needs to be made in the bureaucracy as circumstances change, and so it has allowed the executive this quasi-legislative activity. Executive orders usually involve a change in the regulations of an agency or an action that must be taken to implement legislation or enforce a provision of a treaty or of the Constitution as the courts interpret it. Most of these are not controversial, but some post–World War II executive orders have generated disputes, and a number of recent orders have actually involved major policy changes. In the Kennedy administration, for instance, military bases were desegregated by executive action. Also, the Nixon administration made major changes in matters such as tax structure and day-care eligibility by changing regulations. Thus an executive order may involve a change in policy no less significant than many of the changes submitted to Congress for approval. There have been challenges to some of these orders; a suit was brought against the changes in the Treasury Department regulations, for example, but with no success. Critics of the expansion of executive orders have pointed out that they mark another intrusion of the President into legislative territory, adding to the imbalance between President and Congress in the twentieth century.

Devising a means to control the executive order without crippling governmental efficiency is difficult. Perhaps, after the publication of the order, Congress could be given a period of time in which to examine the order which would then take effect unless Congress disapproved it. The burden of examining the mass of executive orders would be substantial, but the members of Congress have the power to provide themselves with the staff necessary to do this, just as they have the power to give the executive the authority and staff necessary to issue executive orders. The difficulty lies where it often does, in the slow awakening of Congress to its loss of power and the even slower devising of ways to restore it.

FOREIGN AFFAIRS

The foreign policy powers given to the President in the Constitution are summarized in Table 2. The major ones are his powers as Commander in Chief of the armed services, with the implied right to initiate hostilities, and his treaty-making power. In the early days of the republic, when the armed services numbered only 1,000–2,000 and the United States shunned the entanglements of the old world as Washington advised, these powers seemed insignificant. As the armed strength of the

TABLE 2 The President's Role in Foreign Affairs

Foreign Power/Role	Source	Check
Treaty making	Constitution, Article II, Section 2	Ratification by two-thirds of voting senators. Same
Appointment of ambassadors and other officers	Constitution, Article II, Section 2	Confirmation by Senate. Same
Recognition of other nations and receiving ambassadors	Constitution, Article II, Section 3; recognition implied	????
Commander in chief and initiator of war	Constitution, Article II, Section 2, and implied	Declaration of war and military funds only by Congress. Article I, Section 8; War Powers Act of 1973
Executive agreement	Tradition	????; possibly statute requiring agreements to be submitted to Congress for its information

United States rose in the nineteenth century, the power of the President increased. When the United States assumed a major, and for a time the dominant, role in world affairs, the President accordingly became a world leader. The weapons technology of the twentieth century, spurred by the cold war and culminating in the nuclear age, gave the President enormous powers, which were inevitably reflected in increases in domestic might. The exercise of foreign policy powers parallels that of much of the domestic powers: the President takes the initiative, and Congress reacts. The active role belongs to the President.

The Constitution provided checks both to the President's treaty-making powers and to his powers as Commander in Chief. Only the Congress can declare war, and presumably it need not wait to be asked to do so by the President. Congress alone can raise and equip an army, and the Constitution limits appropriations for that purpose to two-year periods, unlike any other appropriations. Treaties must be submitted to the Senate and ratified by approval of two-thirds of those voting before they are legally binding on the United States. (This process has been puzzling to some nations, which have regarded the signature of the American representative as constituting a commitment that is not erased by Senate rejection of the agreement.)

In the two centuries since the framing of the Constitution the checks have gradually lost most of their effectiveness. Congress has declared war on only five occasions, but dozens of military actions have been undertaken and continued by the executive without benefit of a formal declaration. Many of these initiatives did not result in any major fighting (e.g., the landing of American troops in Lebanon in 1958, ordered by Eisenhower to protect a pro-Western government there). Other "undeclared wars" have assumed outsized dimensions. The Mexican War in the nineteenth century and the Vietnam War in this century were the subject of bitter criticism by part of the public and by some congressmen, leading to suggestions that the war-making powers of the President be curtailed. After a long series of proposals by some members, including many conservatives, that would require the President to obtain congressional approval for his military actions within a set period of time, the Congress in late 1973 enacted such a proposal. As expected, the President promptly vetoed it, but the Congress at last had been aroused, and the required two-thirds majority in each house voted to overturn the veto. The new law requires the President to notify Congress within forty-eight hours if he sends troops into another nation, and to withdraw them after sixty days unless Congress approves the action. The law provides further that Congress may force troop withdrawal during the sixty-day period by a majority vote that is not subject to veto. There are practical difficulties with this law, including the possibility that Presidents could be tempted to direct short but exceedingly destructive actions in order to accomplish their purpose before the end of sixty days. Despite the inherent difficulties, however, Congress felt that some such action was necessary; otherwise its power to declare war would remain a dead letter, and the war-making powers would remain almost completely in the President's hands.

Similarly, the check exercised by the Senate over relations with other countries in treaties has declined in significance in the twentieth century with the decline in the use of treaties. Instead, the executive has turned to the executive agreement. In its original form, the *executive agreement* was simply a compact with another national head or delegate, not requiring Senate concurrence; the subject matter might be the details consequent to a treaty or administrative problems generally not serious enough to require a treaty. As the years passed, however, executive agreements have been used increasingly to deal with major problems without submitting the action to the Senate. In fact, executive agreements outnumber treaties in the twentieth century. The President thus has further increased his control over foreign affairs. In addition, many of these agreements were concluded with no notice to the Senate of their existence, let alone to the public. Although executive agreements are not binding on successive administrations unless those administrations consent, they do commit the United States in the eyes of the other nation in many cases, and dozens of agreements are still in force from past administrations by consent. The discovery by the Senate Foreign Relations Committee of a number of secret agreements involving military support of nations such as Ethiopia, Laos, and Spain led to consideration and passage of legislation requiring all agreements to be submitted to Congress at least for its own information, although no right of congressional veto was established. The executive agreement, and its control by Congress, poses problems paralleling those in controlling the executive order. Executive agreements developed as a necessary means of conducting the minor details of American interaction with nearly 150 nations; to forbid them or to require that all agreements be treated as formal treaties would cripple conduct of our foreign relations. Yet if Congress does not find some way to bring the substantive executive agreement under control, its treaty powers will continue to wither, and its present minor role in foreign policy to dwindle.

Through his appointment of ambassadors to other nations, subject to Senate confirmation, and his power to receive ambassadors, not subject to Senate approval though carrying with it the power to recognize those nations, the President acts as the head of state. He is the determiner of which nations we will have relations with and on what basis. There is no way that Congress can force the President to recognize or to refuse recognition to any nation, although it may attempt to do so by not allocating the funds necessary to establish relations. There have been some occasions when confirmation of an ambassadorial nominee was held up while the Senate expressed its disapproval of the policy in regard to the nation that was to receive the ambassador, but this has never been much more than a symbolic gesture. Since the beginning of the republic, it has been generally regarded as the rightful role of the President to take the lead in foreign affairs. Even when this means slighting or ignoring congressional directives, there has rarely been protest. For instance, Congress passed a law in the 1940s requiring congressional action to revalue the dollar. In recent years the President has unilaterally directed reevaluation of the currency and Congress has lodged no complaint, on the grounds that foreign speculators would benefit from the advance knowledge of a devaluation, to the economic disadvantage of the United States, if the President sought consent.

THE LIMITS OF PRESIDENTIAL POWER: WATERGATE

The first limit on any President's power is his own personality and capabilities. Each man has his own strengths and weaknesses, which help to shape the results of his action. Presidents can choose White House and executive office staffs to help compensate for this. Those who are not good administrators of personnel can partly overcome this lack by choosing an assistant who is and giving him or her the job of supervising the choice of executive appointments. Similarly, Presidents can supplement their strengths, choosing other advisers whose strong points reflect their own. Skillful selection of staff can reduce the limits imposed by inherent capabilities but never eliminate them. The decisions must ultimately be made by the one man, the President, and his intellect, judgment, and personality are critical.

The President is subject to many other limitations, some traditional, some laid down in the Constitution, some determined by circumstances. Although he can try to stretch his powers through reinterpreting the Constitution, the survival of constitutional democracy obliges him to abide by it and by decisions of the courts. When Truman interpreted his powers as Commander in Chief to allow him in the Korean War to seize the steel mills during a strike, his opponents quickly obtained a Supreme Court ruling to the contrary, and he was forced to back down. Moreover, even when there is no constitutional or legal bar, action is limited by the degree to which other powerful persons accept it. Congressional leaders, the President's own advisers and executive heads, the bureaucracy itself, leaders of other nations, pressure group interests, and, in some cases, the general public may all be able to thwart presidential plans. A President's resources are great, but they are limited; even allocated carefully and thriftily, they will probably not cover all of his goals. The past restrains him; commitments in foreign policy, for instance, are not easily reversed. The costs of attempting to reverse them may hamper him in some other policy. Domestic programs build up powerful constituencies that will resist change. Finally, the acceleration of problems in the mid–twentieth century makes many of the President's routine chores today equal to emergency conditions in the White House of the past. This imposes limits of time and information. There are deadlines that must be met, vast amounts of information that the President must sift through, and the greater problem of getting enough information. There must be decisions on a vast array of domestic and foreign issues, some of which are new in this century and impose staggering burdens, such as nuclear weapons, biological warfare, control of international corporations, and the military uses of space. And, in the end, it may all be undone by some chance event somewhere—by mobs in Birmingham, a grounded U-2 plane in Russia, a forgotten tape recorder, or a bullet in Dallas.

The problem of limits to executive power was at the root of the Watergate crisis that engulfed the second Nixon administration. The true origin of Watergate was not the burglary of the national Democratic offices in the Watergate buildings along the Potomac in Washington. It began with the expansion of executive power in the years following the depression and in the consequent damage done to the delicate constitutional balance of powers. The system was already far out of balance when the first Nixon term began in January 1969. Presidents had come to see themselves as rightfully dominant over the rest of the political system. At the same time the problems of war and economic dislocation had led to ever more visible and strident dissent. The enormous powers of the presidency made it all too easy to attempt to eliminate opposition—an attempt that nearly succeeded—and the belief in the near perfection of the presidency made it all too easy to see opposition as intolerable.

In July 1970 the Federal Bureau of Investigation (FBI), the Central Intelligence Agency (CIA), the National Security Agency (NSA), and the Defense Intelligence Agency (DIA) were notified by the White House of a plan for collecting information about and starting action against dissidents—including breaking and entering, opening mail, wiretapping, bugging, and infiltrating dissident groups and constantly harassing them through criminal prosecutions. One of the originators of the plan had already advised the President that most of these tactics were illegal, and the formidable head of the FBI, J. Edgar Hoover, objected on the same grounds. It is uncertain what then became of the plan, officially. In retrospect it appears that much of it was carried out informally, through the new Special Investigation Unit (SIU) in the White House.

The SIU was created in 1971, after the publication of the *Pentagon Papers* on the American role in Vietnam had drawn the fury of the Nixon administration. Known informally as the "Plumbers" (stopping leaks of information), the SIU was directed by White House officials. The SIU was directly connected with what former Attorney General John Mitchell described as "White House horrors," including the Watergate burglary itself. It conducted an earlier burglary of the offices of a psychiatrist who had treated Dr. Daniel Ellsberg, the principal defendant in the *Pentagon Papers* case, in the hope of discrediting him. The Plumbers also investigated a potential rival in the 1972 presidential race, Senator Edward Kennedy; tapped telephones of those suspected of giving or receiving information about the administration's present acts and future plans; and placed fabricated cables in State Department files in an abortive attempt to place the blame for the 1963 assassination of the Vietnamese leader Ngo Dinh Diem on the late President Kennedy (and so further damage Senator Kennedy). The burglary at the Watergate was part of a comprehensive plan that originated with the Plumbers and the Committee to Re-Elect the President with the approval of some of the top officials in the administration.

In September 1972 the trial of the accused burglars began under Judge John Sirica of Federal District Court in Washington. The proceedings were immediately recessed until after the elections in November, which returned the President to office by a resounding margin over the Democratic nominee, George McGovern. Watergate played only a bit part in the concluding months of the campaign, but as the second Nixon administration was triumphantly inaugurated, events were converging upon its collapse through Watergate. The opening event was the conviction of the seven accused. Judge Sirica, in a controversial move, postponed sentencing to give them time to reconsider their refusal to cooperate with the continuing investigation of Watergate. Frantic discussions of clemency in exchange for silence ensued in the White House. Eventually one of the seven, James McCord, exposed the story in a long and detailed letter to Judge Sirica. The necessity for some congressional action, long resisted, now became painfully obvious.

In May 1973 Senator Samuel Ervin's committee to investigate campaign abuses began its televised hearings, which instantly became a public sensation. For the first time the people heard administration and campaign officials discussing criminal actions and began to recognize the serious misconduct of those in office. Talk of impeachment for the first time moved from fantasy to possibility. The hearings continued throughout the summer. An audience of many millions heard the quiet statement by a White House official that he had directed the installation of an elaborate tape recording system in the White House upon Nixon's initiative. Incredibly, it seemed, there would be taped evidence of the entire Watergate period in the White House.

The Special Prosecutor, former Solicitor General Archibald Cox, and the congressional investigators moved immediately to subpoena the tapes. The White House resisted; upon being pressed, the President gave orders to fire the Special Prosecutor. Stunned by the furious outpouring of disapproval that followed, the President agreed to a new Special Prosecutor. The war over the tapes ended with a unanimous Supreme Court decision against the President, a key development that, by requiring the President to release the tapes, probably turned the tide in the direction of his removal or resignation. A second front then opened when it was discovered that a tape was missing and another tape was interrupted by an 18½-minute erasure at a vital point. The question of impeachment loomed ever larger.

In the closing months of 1973, the Judiciary Committee of the House was charged with the duty of determining what, if any, charges should be recommended to the whole House. This committee, consisting of twenty Democrats and sixteen Republicans, all lawyers, conducted protracted and painstaking studies of evidence from all sides. In July 1974 the Judiciary Committee concluded its preliminary work and went before the public with televised hearings on specific charges.

These debates themselves were yet another education for the public. Rarely is Congress, or any part of it, seen at work; there was general agreement that the Judiciary Committee conducted itself splendidly. And when the questions were put to a vote, an overwhelming bipartisan majority voted to recommend impeachment on two grounds: a misuse of government powers and obstruction of justice. A similar majority recommended a charge of interference with the constitutional process of impeachment itself by refusing to provide information to the committee. Finally, any question of partisan bias was shown to be baseless when many of the Democratic members joined with most of the Republicans to reject two other proposed articles of impeachment.

Preparations for the House vote on the recommended articles, and the probable Senate trial, were underway when the President released the missing tape at last on August 5. The "smoking gun" was finally in court; the words of the President himself recorded his complicity in the effort to cover up the illegal acts that his aides had committed. Senior Republicans redoubled their efforts to persuade him to resign in the face of the virtual certainty of impeachment and conviction. Three days later the President replied with an address to the nation announcing his resignation at noon the following day.

Earlier Nixon had appointed Representative Gerald Ford Vice President when Spiro Agnew resigned the office. This was the first exercise of the Twentieth-fifth Amendment; previously there had been no provisions for filling a vacant vice presidency between elections. When Nixon resigned, Ford succeeded to the presidency, bringing a wave of relief to the nation. A mixture of indignation and puzzlement followed shortly when the new President pardoned Nixon, thus short-circuiting the judicial process.

There is still serious unfinished business that goes beyond personalities. Watergate represents the near destruction of constitutional government in the United States, an almost inevitable result of the aggrandizement of the powers of the presidency in the past decades of depression, war, and domestic upheaval. The process of restoring constitutional government that began with the impeachment proceedings was not completed by a resignation. Some of the basic issues of Watergate have been aired in the Congress and in the country, but others have not yet been confronted.

The central issue in terms of executive power is the need for checks against the abuses made possible by the development of the "imperial presidency." First President Ford and then, to an even greater extent in his early days in the presidency, Jimmy Carter have made efforts to humanize the office. Nevertheless, the expansion of executive power gives the President and his subordinates a staggering range of responsibilities and a very free hand in running the bureaucracy to meet them. Moreover, the mechanisms for investigation and prosecution of official abuse of such powers lie within the same agencies that may have abused power. Proposed reforms would establish defenses against government lawlessness. One proposal would create a new division within the Justice Department with responsibility for government corruption of all kinds, other than that perpetrated by very high officials who might well override this division. The American Bar Association has suggested that these extraordinary cases be assumed by the office of a special prosecutor. Along with these two mechanisms, a congressional agency—an Office of Congressional Legal Counsel—might be formed to assist the legislature in suits against the executive branch when they are needed (and to defend it against the executive as well). These new proposals could help to protect against the subversion of free and honorable government by those sworn to uphold it.

THE FUTURE

The imperial presidency itself and the argument of national security which has supported it still very much dominate American politics. The executives of the twentieth century, and some of their predecessors, have acted aggressively to make the presidency into a powerful central office. They acted from a combination of personal enjoyment of power and a desire to see their own vision of the social good become reality. A good deal of the executive expansion involved seizing powers from Congress, which sometimes meant nothing more than taking what was offered on a silver platter. Congress has delegated many of its powers to the President over the years, although no President in the twentieth century has delegated any power to Congress, as a few did in the congressional heyday of the nineteenth century.

The central role played by the President in the political system is not likely to change, even if the legislature should reassert some of its authority. In the nuclear age the central position of the President in war making is unlikely to be displaced, and the general control of the executive over foreign affairs is authorized by the Constitution itself. At best, although Congress can hope for a greater share of the responsibility of setting the limits of American action, it will make little policy. In domestic affairs Congress originally had the major role, and the need to restore its rightful share of power is more pressing. The shift to executive dominance is already a *fait accompli* in many areas, however, and the role of executive leadership in the progress of American society is accepted and celebrated by much of the public and by many intellectuals, although some recently have come to have second thoughts. Recapturing powers lost or given away is always much more difficult than their forfeiture. For those powers specified in the Constitution, a check is also specified, and Congress must find some way to reassert that check. Those powers that have been developed by the executive "from scratch," such as executive privilege, are much more difficult to control; new checks must be devised. Outside groups that are affected may become part of the control process by challenging executive action in the courts. The public itself can assist by indicating to the President and the Congress public reaction to executive action. In turn the press bears a large responsibility for making knowledge of executive actions and their implications available to the public. In the end the President will still have the great power to act first, to seize the initiative. This, too, is one of the lessons of Watergate. Despite the clear and present dangers of the imperial presidency revealed by Watergate, and the pressing need to deflate the office's bloated power, very little concrete reform has in fact been realized. In part this is because public and politicians allowed themselves to believe that the resignation was a solution to, rather than a symptom of, the problem. In part, however, it is because the structure of American politics, shaped by twentieth-century circumstances, is unlikely to permit very much reduction in executive power. The best that we can hope for is that it be carefully watched.

The Bureaucracy: A Capital Offense?

ROLES OF THE BUREAUCRACIES

The federal bureaucracies, and their state and local counterparts, bear a closer resemblance to the bureaucracies of other nations than do other parts of our political system to their foreign counterparts. Bureaucracies tend to have the same characteristics whether they are located in Washington, Paris, or Moscow. As they grow in size and responsibilities, bureaucracies have assumed leading roles in various governmental functions and may even eventually dominate some of them. The American bureaucracy is no exception. In their day-to-day administrative actions, the federal (and other) bureaucracies carry out quasi-legislative and quasi-judicial functions as well as executive ones. Since the beginning of the New Deal, when their size and cost escalated, the bureaucracies have become some of the nation's most powerful interest groups; in turn, many of the major private interest groups have found a home in the recesses of the bureaucracy. The bureaucracies themselves have become major policy makers.

The bureaucracies are also important for their symbolic and practical impact on the public. Although the President and his Cabinet may be the most visible part of the executive, bureaucratic agencies are the only part of the system that most people will encounter personally. This applies with even more force at the state level. Internal revenue agents, post office clerks, motor vehicle inspectors, social security and welfare workers, pollution control officers, and the highway patrol—all are part of the executive, charged with administering the laws and implementing the policy of top officials. The daily workings of the bureaucracy bring legislative acts and executive wishes to life, often in a form somewhat different from that which their originators intended. For many, contact with administrators will be all they know of government and its purposes.

The federal bureaucracy is not discussed in the Constitution—in contrast to most state charters—except as an aid to the President. It is accountable only through the accountability of the President, who appoints the major heads. However, most of the employees are not subject to direct control by the President or the Cabinet but are, rather, part of the Civil Service, under an independent commission that controls their hiring and conditions of service. This reform was instituted in the 1880s after growing discontent with patronage was brought to a head by the assassination of President James Garfield at the hands of a presumably disappointed office seeker. Most states and cities, with the notable exception of Chicago, have also adopted a civil service system. Its advantages are obvious. The institution of Civil Service, however, does tend to reduce the control of the chief executive over the army of functionaries who administer the law and who may not administer it as he wishes.

THE GROWTH OF BUREAUCRATIC POWER

In 1789 at the outset of the Republic, only the departments of State, Treasury, and War existed, plus the positions of Attorney General and Postmaster General. The federal establishment numbered less than 1,000. Today there are eleven departments (see Table 3), and their heads

TABLE 3 Major Federal Executive Agencies*

The Cabinet†	The White House	Selected Independent Offices
State (original)	White House Office	Nuclear Regulatory Commission
Defense (original [as War Dept.])	Office of Management and Budget	Federal Reserve System
Treasury (original)	Council of Economic Advisers	General Services Administration
Justice (1870)‡		
Interior (1849)	National Security Council	National Aeronautics and Space Administration
Agriculture (1862)	Domestic Council	
Commerce (1903)	Council on Environmental Quality	Civil Service Commission
Labor (1913)		
Health, Education, and Welfare (1953)	Energy Resources Council	Veterans Administration
Housing and Urban Development (1965)	Presidential Clemency Board	Civil Aeronautics Board
Transportation (1967)	Federal Property Council	Federal Communications Commission
	Office of the Special Representative for Trade Negotiations	Federal Power Commission
	Council on International Economic Policy	Federal Trade Commission
	Special Action Office for Drug Abuse Prevention	Interstate Commerce Commission
	Office of Telecommunications Policy	National Labor Relations Board
	Council on Wage and Price Stability	Securities and Exchange Commission

*As of December 1976.
†Dates are those of establishment.
‡NOTE: The Attorney General was a member of the original Cabinet, but the Justice Department was not created until later.

constitute the main part of the Cabinet, with the Postal Service and Postmaster General now eliminated. In addition to the thousands of divisions in these departments, there are some 3,000 other advisory committees, boards, commissions, councils, conferences, panels, task forces, and the like; not even the government itself knows how many there are. Whatever the exact figure, it is many times the number of employees in 1789.

State governments, and to some extent municipal governments, have seen a similar growth and dispersion of power. Many state constitutions have established detailed administrative structures with specific functional divisions, such as public health, highways, welfare, higher education, energy regulation, banking, insurance, liquor control, and public safety. Some cities have their own boards, such as the New York City Parks Commission, which, as mentioned in chapter 3, helped Robert Moses in his rise to power. These agencies are sometimes allowed to establish their own hiring practices, and they may be nearly independent of the chief executive. Such autonomy may result in the same failure to regulate or otherwise carry out intended functions that plagues much of the federal bureaucracies. Reform is even more difficult where constitutional change or permission of the state legislature is needed.

THE INDEPENDENT AGENCIES

Outside the normal framework of the executive bureaucracy at the national level are the independent offices and agencies. Such agencies may be classified as administrative (e.g., the Federal Reserve System Board of Governors), regulatory (e.g., the Federal Trade Commission), and corporate (e.g., the Tennessee Valley Authority). Other independent offices are listed in Table 3. These bodies, created by Congress beginning in 1887, are run by executive heads appointed by the President. Their responsibilities lie primarily in the economy, particularly in regulating some aspect of the economy such as the production and distribution of energy resources. A great deal of federal power is concentrated in such agencies, which together form what is essentially a fourth branch of government. The boards of commissioners and the like that govern them are formally independent of the President because they serve staggered, fixed terms of office that limit his power to control through appointments. In the 1976 Democratic presidential campaign this autonomy was subjected to much criticism, particularly directed against the Federal Reserve Board and its control over credit and monetary policy.

Despite these complaints, the independent agencies have become increasingly subject to presidential management in the last few decades. The appointment power, however limited, does give the President some access to these agencies, and he also maintains budgetary control. Many critics of the independent agencies have suggested that they have become supporters of the industries that they are supposed to regulate and no longer fulfill their purpose; in addition their increasing subservience to the President in some instances increases the President's power in the economy. Other critics of the "fourth branch" have called for even greater presidential control to prevent administrative programs from being undercut by contradictory agency policies. Still others have suggested that the agencies should simply be abolished on the grounds that they have failed to regulate the economy for the benefit of anyone but the interests they are supposed to regulate. Whatever the solution may be, it is certainly clear that this complex area of administration is one of those most in need of reform.

THE SPECIAL PROBLEM OF THE PENTAGON

Much of the growth of the bureaucracy in this century is the direct result of the expansion of the Defense Department. It employs approximately half of all civilian federal workers, in addition to the several million men and women in the armed forces. The second largest department, now an independent agency, is the Postal Service. Far behind these two is the Department of Health, Education, and Welfare, with less than a tenth of the Defense Department roster.

The distribution of the budget also determines to a large extent the influence of the various departments in the government policy-making process. Again the Department of Defense leads, with the largest single departmental allocation, roughly one-third of the budget. Additional military-related expenditures, such as veterans affairs, military aspects of foreign aid and the Food for Peace program, the space program, military work of the Nuclear Regulatory Commission, interest on the national debt resulting from past wars, and the like increase the defense share. The highest estimate is that defense spending accounts for two-thirds of the budget. Regardless of which estimate one accepts, defense spending represents an enormous factor in the economy. Some 20 to 25 percent of the economy is dependent in some way on military expenditures. Few congressional districts are without a military installation or contractor. The interrelationship between the upper levels of the Pentagon staff and the upper levels of military industries is close. Hundreds of retired military leaders and heads of civilian agencies have found work in defense industries, and a smaller contingent of men leave the industries and join the Pentagon or the White House staff. This economic strength combined with enormous staff size make the Defense Department more equal than its peers, the other departments. Any change in federal spending priorities must of necessity involve the Pentagon.

REFORM

The impact of the Pentagon on the shape of government policy is still a major problem, despite the defusing of the draft issue and the reduction in military size represented by the volunteer army. Military spending is on the increase, illustrated by President Ford's request for some $104 billion in direct defense costs in fiscal year 1978. Indirect costs will also increase as pensions and other benefits escalate as a result of the improved conditions of service of the volunteer army. There has been little reform in the formulation and supervision of the defense budget nor in the vast apparatus that it supports.

The growth of the bureaucracy at all levels in both numbers and divisions is another troublesome area. Elimination of unnecessary or unsatisfactory agencies almost never occurs. In the last fifteen years, for example, 236 new federal departments, agencies, or bureaus have been created, and only 21 have been disbanded. Several Presidents in the past three decades have proposed radical reshapings of the executive branch, but they have succeeded only in creating three major new departments. Powerful interests and employee organizations strenuously resist the idea that "their" agency should be terminated or merged with others. The result is an incredible division of authority, with literally dozens of agencies having conflicting roles in such areas as services to the poor, drug control, and intelligence gathering. Control of such a vast apparatus is difficult, if not impossible. The need for reform is evident, yet political difficulties will make it exceedingly hard for President Carter to carry out his campaign pledge to carry out such reform. There are encouraging signs, however. In April 1976 Colorado passed a *sunset law*, which requires periodic review of all government programs and agencies and the abolition or reorganization of the ineffective ones. As a result, government structure is no longer perpetual power. Other states are in the process of enacting similar reform, and a subcommittee of the Senate has begun consideration of a federal sunset law. Once again, federalism may prove to be the source of creative change in the United States.

Freedom of information is yet another item of continuing difficulty, and here too the states have provided valuable examples. Extracting information, or knowing what information should be available from government agencies, is done only with great patience—partly a consequence of the sheer complexity of the government and partly a consequence of the bureaucratic passion for anonymity and secrecy as a professional prerogative. Despite the Freedom of Information Act of 1967, the flow of information has not measurably quickened. Most agencies have deftly fitted the information they wished to withhold into one of the nine categories of permitted reasons for secrecy. Tighter standards for disclosure *and* for protection of privacy have been established in some of the states. Congress needs to look again.

Finally, there is need for reform of the kind and amount of information government agencies can collect and what they can do with the information collected. The revelations of 1975 and 1976 on the spying activities directed against citizens by agencies such as the CIA, FBI, and DIA brought attention to part of the problem. Reforms by individual agencies, such as the FBI's decision to limit surveillance to about 3 percent of those previously under scrutiny, are welcome. However, the basic issue of control over intelligence activities remains essentially unresolved. The superficial reforms made are in effect worse than no reforms because they obscure the issue rather than eliminate it.

The data that have been and are being collected in every area of life represent an uncontrolled explosion of an ever present bureaucratic impulse. As the computer has come into wide use (there are some·60,000 in the federal executive branch), the problem of invasion of privacy grows. Every smidgen of information ever collected can be easily stored, collated, and retrieved. The problem is compounded by illegitimate collection of information, but even the massing of legitimate information poses a threat. Relatively few persons came under the illegitimate political scrutiny of the army intelligence service, but almost every adult in America is the subject of one or more government dossiers. (Adding private forms such as credit data, the average adult is documented in some ten records.) The list of the different kinds of forms on which the federal government collects information is itself nearly 400 pages long!

In a profound sense, government by bureaucracy is incompatible with democracy. Bureaucracy by definition is a form of organization based upon routine and efficiency, and individual considerations and exceptions are inconsistent with the regulations. A government concerned with individual problems may occasionally be inconsistent and inefficient; a democracy can hardly escape individual problems. The ability of the bureaucracy to escape executive supervision also means that it is not subject to popular control, a major criterion of democracy. But bureaucracy seems inevitable, so ways must be found to limit its worst tendencies. The answer lies in developing more effective political leadership of the bureaucracies. This does not necessarily mean greater control by the President, although substantial presidential supervision is needed if the executive is going to be able to implement his policies. Congress can also play a major role. It already has an effective investigatory arm in the General Accounting Office. If this body were given increased staff and authority, and the support of the Congress when it trod upon tender toes, the Congress would be able to play a greater policy-making role. And the development of two sources of control, both accountable to the public, would bring the bureaucracy into at least indirect accountability to the public and give the public more security against arbitrary action, a necessity for democracy.

Suggested Readings†

James D. Barber. "Passive-Positive to Active-Negative: The Style and Character of Presidents." *Washington Monthly*, October 1969.

Carl Bernstein and Bob Woodward. *All the President's Men.* New York: Simon & Schuster, 1974. One of the major Watergate books, subsequently a film.

Edward F. Cox, et al. *Nader's Raiders Report on the Federal Trade Commission.* New York: Grove, 1969.*

Thomas E. Cronin. *The State of the Presidency.* Boston: Little, Brown, 1975.

Norman Dorsen. *None of your Business: Government Secrecy in America.* Baltimore: Penguin, 1975.*

Roy P. Fairfield, ed. *The Federalist Papers.* Garden City, N.Y.: Doubleday, 1961.

Robert Fellmeth. *The Interstate Commerce Omission: The Public Interest and the ICC.* New York: Grossman, 1970.*

John J. Fialka. "Battle of the Barons." *Washington Monthly*, May 1976. The problem of bureaucratic reform.

Louis Fisher. *Presidential Spending Power.* Princeton, N.J.: Princeton University Press, 1976.* Major study of presidential financial control.

Morton H. Halperin, et al. *The Lawless State: The Crimes of the U.S. Intelligence Agencies.* Baltimore: Penguin, 1976.*

Louis Koenig. *The Chief Executive.* New York: Harcourt Brace Jovanovich, 1968*

Louis M. Kohlmeier, Jr. "The Regulatory Agencies: What Should Be Done?" *Washington Monthly*, August 1969. A critical view of the politics of the "fourth branch."

Arthur Millar. *The Invasion of Privacy.* Ann Arbor: University of Michigan, 1971.

Richard Neustadt. *Presidential Power.* New York: Signet, 1964.* A classic study of presidential powers, said to have greatly influenced JFK.

Charles Peters. "The Fireman First Principle." *Washington Monthly*, March 1976. More on bureaucratic reform.

Dan Rather and Gary Paul Gates. *The Palace Guard.* New York: Warner, 1975.*

George Reedy. *The Twilight of the Presidency.* New York: Harcourt Brace Jovanovich, 1970.*

Ben Roberts. "Tying the Imperial Purse Strings." *Washington Monthly*, September 1975.

Arthur Schlesinger, Jr. *The Imperial Presidency.* Boston: Houghton Mifflin, 1973.

Walter Shapiro. "The Intractables." *Washington Monthly*, May 1976.

Theodore C. Sorenson. *Watchmen in the Night: Presidential Accountability After Watergate.* Cambridge, Mass.: M.I.T. Press, 1975.*

Peter Woll. *American Bureaucracy.* New York: Norton, 1963.*

Bob Woodward and Carl Bernstein. *The Final Days.* New York: Simon & Schuster, 1976.

*Available in paperback.
†See chapter 1 for additional readings on Watergate.

5

THE LEGISLATIVE PROCESS

Congress, The People's Branch?

Laws should have no other end ultimately but the good of
the people.

Thomas Paine

In every society there must be some way to formulate basic rules
governing relationships among the members and between each person
and the group. In modern political systems this is the legislative process,
which culminates in the formal passage of laws by bodies designated to
act as rule makers for the whole. This process not only produces those
rules necessary to preserve a cohesive community but introduces some
measure of collective action in deciding upon policy. In democratic nations it provides, at least in theory, a voice for the people in governing the
state.

Although nearly all contemporary political systems incorporate
some form of collective decision making and some "primitive" societies
have virtually total participation in governing, leaders throughout human
history have frequently exercised the full powers of government with little
if any institutional check. The development of legislatures in the Western
world is largely the result of a deliberate effort to prevent one-person rule.
In some societies a group or council of some sort has functioned as the
interpreter of tradition and the formulator of new rules of procedure to
meet changing conditions, but these rules seem to have contributed less
to the growth of legislatures than did efforts by nobles to restrict the
arbitrary power of kings and to have their own interests represented in

decisions of state. The legislative process as we know it evolved gradually, serving to regulate political life and theoretically to represent the people collectively.

Types of Democratic Legislatures

In the Western democratic nations legislatures have taken two predominant forms. The majority are *parliamentary:* the legislature chooses the executive, and there is no separation of powers. If there is a serious disagreement between the executive and the parliament, the issue is presented to the people in new elections to determine whether the former leadership retains power or surrenders it to another party. Typically, there is considerable party discipline or responsibility in such systems— that is, the party has a large measure of control over the votes of its members in parliament. The system is designed both to allow people to participate in deciding the major direction of governmental policies and to give them some assurance that the government will follow the broad outlines that the winning party advocated during the elections.

Parliamentary governments are an outgrowth of the principles that evolved in England over a period of centuries. As a rule, they split the executive into two parts, the head of state and the head of government, but there are some exceptions (such as the arrangements in certain African states) in which the two are combined. In Great Britain the monarch is head of state; in nonmonarchical parliamentary nations the head of state usually is designated a president. The *head of state* exercises primarily ceremonial functions, such as conferring the honors specified by the government, receiving ambassadors and visiting dignitaries, and otherwise performing symbolic acts. Some heads of state do have powers in a crisis situation, such as the disputed elections in Nigeria in 1964 or the 1975 parliamentary troubles in Australia. Many have the duty of officially appointing the prime minister or acting as commander in chief of the armed forces. The real power in parliamentary governments, however, lies with the *head of government*, who usually is called the prime minister. This official, along with other ministers or department heads whom the parliament selects from among its own ranks, truly exercises the power of the executive.

The other major type of democratic legislature is found in the United States and in those countries having a *presidential form of government.* The primary principle distinguishing the two forms is *separation of powers.* The legislature is elected for a specific term, and the president is elected separately, also for a definite period of time. Major elections cannot occur irregularly, as they may in a parliamentary system, but must take place only at prescribed times in a regular cycle. The independence of the legislature and the executive means that the two may significantly disagree for a considerable period. If this happens, the system provides no way to consult the people through new elections. Many political scientists dislike separation of powers for this reason. They believe that it can lead to deadlock in government and that the parliamentary system is more efficient. Others, however, prefer the presidential arrangement because it institutionalizes stability. There cannot be a rapid succession of governments as has sometimes happened in some parliamentary systems, such as in France under the Third and Fourth Republics and in Italy. In Italy, for example, there have been some three dozen changes in leadership since the Second World War.

A rather new form of government combines the parliamentary and presidential principles, providing a strong and independent executive superimposed upon a more or less traditional parliamentary system. Variations of this hybrid form can be seen in France under the present Fifth Republic and, until recently, in the Republic of Korea. Many of the Third World nations, such as Tanzania and Zambia, have experimented with such arrangements. In these forms of government the president occupies a position similar to the most powerful of presidents in presidential systems. Outwardly the functioning of the legislatures approximates that of legislatures in parliamentary systems, but their importance tends to be considerably diminished because of the independently powerful executive. In fact, most of these experiments have ended in military coups or in the total emasculation of the legislature.

Legislators: Delegates or Free Agents?

Because the legislature is the body that adopts rules binding upon the whole of society, it plays a vital role in all liberal democracies. Nevertheless, there is no firm agreement regarding the proper function of legislators, even though political theorists frequently have concentrated upon them and their role as representatives of the people. At the one extreme are those who believe that members of a democratically elected legislature should simply reflect the wishes of those who put them in office, that they should function as delegates from the people to the representative body. At the other extreme is the point of view set forth so well by the conservative theorist Edmund Burke after his election to the British House of Commons in 1774. Burke indicated that the voters elected him to Parliament to represent the best interests of the nation and that he would exercise his best judgment, regardless of the wishes of the people.

To some extent the question is one of constituency. Do legislators represent their districts or the entire nation? Do they represent the desires of the people or the people's "best interest" when the two seem to diverge? Is it proper for legislators to follow their judgment of what is best if they know it to be against the people's desires? Is it honest of them not to do so? The answer inevitably depends upon the definition of democracy and may be influenced by the kind of government under study. For example, one could argue that the "delegate" interpretation is less appropriate in a parliamentary system than in a presidential system because the people at least in theory have more frequent opportunities to check their representatives and remove those from office with whom they often disagree. In a presidential system, in which people are given little opportunity to express their displeasures effectively except during regularly scheduled elections, the advocates of the "delegate" system might have stronger arguments. In the United States there is little popular discussion of these issues, and many studies indicate that legislators express considerable disagreement among themselves as to what their proper function should be.

The notion that representatives should serve purely as delegates may seem simply too unrealistic to be taken seriously in a large modern state. Many writers have demonstrated that the people know very little about the actual effect of their representatives within a legislature, and that even those who have some familiarity with their legislator's voting record are unlikely to know whether it truly reflects his or her positions. The legislator may have worked to weaken a bill for which he or she voted, may have succeeded in killing a bill before it ever reached a vote, or may have voted against a bill that in principle he or she would support hoping thereby to work for a stronger one. The possibilities are endless. The "will of the people" is probably even more difficult to ascertain. The science of polling can provide considerable information, but it is far from perfect. The legislator's mail may be a strong indication of the way the people think, but it may not reflect their thoughts adequately. In all probability, on most complex issues the people are insufficiently informed to give a meaningful opinion. If there is strong opinion, will it remain, or will it shift? Although "public opinion," in the popular sense, may exist, it is doubtful whether legislators could follow it completely if they were to try.

On the other hand, if legislators are able to determine existing public opinion, should they completely disregard it? If they were to do so could democracy survive? Many persons believe that legislators should vote their consciences and that they should work to educate the public if in their view its opinion is wrong. Nevertheless, few legislators could blatantly disregard public opinion very often because of the necessity of facing reelection.

As with many questions in politics, this one can never be answered completely. The American political system is one of adjustment and compromise and is often simply a search for anything that works. Members of most contemporary legislatures operate under many guises: they do attempt to represent their constituents' interests, they do act according

"When my distinguished colleague refers to the will of the 'people,' does he mean his 'people' or my 'people'?"

to their consciences, and they do respond to special interests. Sometimes they behave in one way and sometimes in another. Many legislators, in fact, appear frequently to serve as delegates simply because their own beliefs reflect those of their constituencies. Clearly, the voters can affect their legislators to some extent; clearly the legislators can exercise some independence; and clearly the system is imperfect. Some issues probably are better resolved by one approach, others by another. The arrangement works—often poorly—but it does work.

The Functions of American Legislatures

The framers of the Constitution obviously intended the Congress to be the center of the political system in the United States and to be the preeminent branch of government. As noted in the previous chapter, during the twentieth century Congress has lost or surrendered much of its power and influence to the President. This is not unique to the United States or to the national government. Similar tendencies are apparent in other democratic nations, and they are at work in state governments as well, although to a somewhat lesser degree because of the tight restrictions that state constitutions tend to place on the powers of governors and because of the governors' lack of power in foreign affairs.

For better or worse, it is generally accepted that the prime motivating forces in American governments are generated from executive branches and that legislatures are unlikely to become significant initiators of policy. Although there may be exceptions in some state governments and even more at the local levels, where, as noted before, the pattern of government often differs from the traditional American bicameral legislature and separated powers, the national government gives every indication that it will continue to be dominated by the executive branch, despite the reforms that have resulted and may yet result from Watergate.

This is not to say that the Congress will be, or has been, a rubber stamp. Like most other legislatures in democratic nations the Congress considers policies proposed by the executive, and it may reject or revise as well as adopt them. It is also perfectly free to propose its own. In fact, as a result of congressional criticism of some practices of the Nixon administration, there have been efforts to inject more energy into the Congress in its dealings with the executive branch that would increase congressional initiative in formulating policy. This is particularly true with regard to budgetary and fiscal matters. After years of criticizing Nixon's conduct of the war in Indochina, Congress in 1973 finally acted by including in an appropriations act that Nixon had requested a prohibition against spending any money from any source on military activities in Indochina. The

President vetoed the measure, and the House majority that voted to overturn the veto fell short of the required two-thirds. Congressional leaders threatened to attach the same prohibition to another appropriations act, this time one that was essential to the continued operation of some governmental offices, serving notice that the President must accept some restrictions upon his power or bring the government close to a halt. Eventually Congress and the President compromised on a law setting a date beyond which the bombing and other military activities had to cease. It is worth noting that such a vote of no confidence in executive policies in a parliamentary system would have caused the government to fall, bringing about new general elections.

In 1974 Congress adopted a reform program (mentioned in the previous chapter) that was designed to provide procedures permitting a more effective role for the legislative branch in budgetary policy. It established a new Congressional Budget Office to be headed by a congressional appointee and supplied with a professional staff, and it created within each house a new Budget Committee. (Four of the states also have strong legislative budget agencies.) The program was fully effective by 1976; it set forth a timetable for budget decisions and required that all matters affecting the budget—including taxes, spending, appropriations, deficits, and surpluses—be coordinated through the new committees.

The impoundment crisis precipitated by the Nixon administration, also mentioned in the previous chapter, served to reassert congressional control over the budget. Now, the President must inform Congress of his intention either to defer spending appropriated funds or to impound them. Either the House or the Senate can reject a deferral simply by passing a resolution so stating. In the case of a proposed impoundment, both the House and the Senate must pass a resolution approving it within five days after being informed of the President's intention, or else it is rejected.

In each chamber the Budget Committee has jurisdiction over matters of presidential impoundment or deferral of funds. In the Senate, however, because the chairman of the Appropriations Committee, John McClellan, insisted upon full jurisdiction for his committee, there was a compromise. The leadership was determined that the reforms would be substantive, so the Budget Committee did receive jurisdiction, but in order to avoid offending Senator McClellan, one of the Senate's "old guard," his committee was given concurrent jurisdiction, as was any other committee that previously had authority over any subject that would be affected by the proposed actions. Because the reforms did not become fully operational until 1976, it is still too early to be certain of their full impact.

In general, Congress is asserting itself somewhat more than in the recent past, but it still hesitates to push for maximum advantage in its relations with the executive. The explanation may be timidity, reverence for the presidential office or fear of its power, simple inertia, poor organization, lack of will or leadership, or any combination of these. For many reasons the presidency is likely to remain the primary source of policy initiation. The executive is more cohesive and less cumbersome than the Congress, and the President can put forth some claim to a national constituency that Congress, although it is a national legislature, cannot. The Congress also speaks for the people, but by its very nature it speaks with many voices, and it is unlikely to match the President in his appeals to the people as their chosen head. In addition, the importance of foreign affairs in contemporary national life gives maximum disadvantage to the Congress and maximum advantage to the President.

LAWMAKING

The American legislature as a representative assembly has many functions, but the most central is the passage of laws. The range of legislation is almost unlimited because nearly any subject can become the basis for legislative action. In addition, needs change as do desires and even tastes, and so legislation is continually revised and reconstituted to avoid stagnation and injustice. Because the legislature must adopt laws binding on all, there will inevitably be some injustice even when the laws are well designed and well administered. It is the responsibility of the legislature to keep such injustice at a minimum by insuring, among other things, that the coercive force of the laws it passes is no more than is absolutely necessary and that the rules for conduct that it prescribes are those that truly are needed, and no more.

Ideas for legislation come from constituents, parties, interest groups, the legislators themselves, and an endless variety of other sources. The primary stimulus is the executive branch, but it too responds to the ideas of others, including those of members of the legislature.

Many of the acts that Congress adopts have been introduced in previous sessions but for one reason or another did not succeed. Even some proposals passed with administration support have gained that support only recently, and have originated in earlier sessions of Congress. It is thus difficult if not impossible to determine the original sources of most legislation, and it may be that there is a tendency to exaggerate executive influence and underplay the role of Congress itself. Whatever the origins of legislation, it is the Congress that sifts the competing demands and arrives at the compromises that become the laws of the land. Regardless of the degree to which it initiates policies, the Congress indelibly stamps its imprint upon them.

In addition to the passage of statutes, lawmaking involves other functions. Under the Constitution, the Congress participates in the adoption of *treaties*, which constitute a special kind of law binding two or more nations to certain conduct and regularizing relations between them. This function is limited to the Senate, which must approve any treaty by a two-thirds vote. The initiative in treaty making is formally reserved to the President, who negotiates and then presents them to the Senate. Another form of lawmaking deals with the fundamental law, the Constitution. The Congress has the power to propose constitutional amendments by a two-thirds vote of both houses.

OVERSEEING THE ADMINISTRATION

Following closely behind the making of law in importance is the function termed, with unconscious irony, *legislative oversight*. In order to assure itself that the executive branch is administering the laws in the way Congress intended, various congressional committees scrutinize the operations of the hundreds of governmental programs. Congress has many weapons at its disposal in dealing with the President and his administration, if it should choose to exercise them. It can pass new legislation, even over a presidential veto. More often, it will attempt to influence program administration by the "power of the purse."

One powerful tool is the General Accounting Office, headed by the Comptroller General. GAO reports to Congress, not to the President, and has full authority to conduct investigations into any use of funds or into the administration of any program. Special interests both in and out of the government sometimes succeed in suppressing or weakening GAO reports, but the agency's potential is limited only by the willingness of Congress to use it.

Congress must appropriate all money that the government spends. If it is unhappy with a specific program, Congress may reduce or eliminate the appropriation for that program. Rarely is anything more vital to any administrator of a government agency than the agency's relations with the House and Senate appropriations subcommittees. Some members of Congress, because of their key committee appointments, exert extraordinary control over certain executive officials and their agencies. Often, because of their ability to influence the committee, even appropriations committee staff members exercise command over certain virtually defenseless bureaucrats. If the officials did protest, their programs would suffer.

Unfortunately, congressional oversight of executive programs tends to be chaotic, uncoordinated, and frequently confused. There is no doubt that Congress has the potential to be a powerful force in promoting sound and effective administration, but it rarely lives up to this potential. There are numerous instances in which Congress fails to check the most flagrant examples of mismanagement of programs because of personal whims of members or staff personnel. In order to realize beneficial—and much needed—checks on the administration. Congress not only would have to improve its present structure and make better use of the GAO, but would be required to provide itself with sufficient qualified staff and research resources to be able to deal with a monstrous and technically sophisticated executive branch.

OTHER FUNCTIONS

The Scandinavian countries have developed an office to protect the citizen against arbitrary and unfair actions of government agencies. The official holding this office is known as the *Ombudsman*, and it is his or her duty to listen to citizen complaints and to investigate to determine whether or not they are justified. This office not only aids the citizen but serves to protect government agencies and officials from unfair complaints. Civilian review boards exercise similar functions locally in a few American cities by reviewing citizen complaints against the police.

To a limited extent, the Congress performs an ombudsman function, but only on a hit or miss basis. The individual member of Congress, if he or she is so inclined, may hear citizen complaints and investigate them. The effectiveness varies, not only with the ability of the member, but with his or her position in Congress, the kind of complaint, and the agency against which it is directed. Many agencies will go to great lengths to avoid offending any member of Congress; others exhibit great nonchalance in the face of congressional criticism unless the critic is especially powerful or is on appropriations or another relevant committee. Also, if the citizen's cause is just but unpopular, the member of Congress may be intimidated by public pressure and refuse to give more than token assistance, if that.

Related directly to the ombudsman function and much more central to the duties of legislators is the offering of services to constituents in the district, powerful factions in the district, or individual voters in the district. Whether the member truly performs this function or not, it is important for him to convince these persons and groups that he is performing it well if he is to be reelected. Catering to these interests may result in something as significant as the introduction of legislation or something as trivial as arranging for a constituent to receive a flag that has "flown" (probably for not more than a few seconds, because attendants continually run flags up and down the Capitol flag pole to satisfy such requests) over the nation's Capitol.

Another vitally important function of the Congress and the state legislatures is conducting investigations, debates, and otherwise contributing to public information. Legislatures must have adequate information if they are to legislate wisely. The investigative power can be abused so that it improperly harms individual citizens or groups and creates or contributes to a climate of fear, as was the case with the investigations of the late Senator Joseph McCarthy and those of the old House Committee on Un-American Activities; or it can be used with great discretion and complete propriety as it often is, the most notable recent example being the House Judiciary Committee's investigations pertaining to presidential impeachment. In any event, an investigation provides information not only to members of the legislature but to the public, as do legislative debates and many other activities. In this way, the legislature in a democracy assists the ongoing democratic process by encouraging a free flow of information about the government, and to and from the government.

In our political system, wrongdoing is to be punished by the courts, but the legislatures may participate in the process in cases in which public officials are involved. At the federal level the House of Representatives may impeach an official by majority vote, at which point the Senate sits as a court and tries the impeached person. A two-thirds vote is required to convict, and conviction results in removal from office. This is the only way in which the Congress can remove officials from the executive branch, and the procedure is used only under extraordinary circumstances. It has been successfully invoked less than a dozen times. The same procedure applies in most of the states, where it also is rarely used. Similarly, since the United States does not operate under a parliamentary system, the legislature does not participate in the selection of the elected executive. One exception on the federal level occurs when the Electoral College fails to give a majority vote to a candidate for President or Vice President. In this case, the House of Representatives makes the choice of President, with each state having one vote; the Senate would choose the Vice President.

The legislature, however, participates very definitely in the selection of appointive officials, both executive and judicial. Nationally, participation is limited to the Senate. Article II, Section 2, of the Constitution requires that the Senate give its "advice and consent" before the President may appoint the major officers of government. As a rule, as noted previously, the Senate turns down very few nominees, but this power can be potent, as is illustrated by the refusal of the Senate to confirm two of President Nixon's nominations to the Supreme Court, Clement Haynsworth and G. Harrold Carswell.

The need for Senate confirmation of certain other nominations permits the practice known as *senatorial courtesy*. By custom the President must consult with any senators of his party from the state in which these officials would be serving to obtain their consent before he makes the nomination. If he nominates a person to serve in a senator's state and the senator does not approve, the senator has only to announce that the nominee is "personally abhorrent" to him, and the Senate will extend senatorial courtesy to that senator and refuse to confirm the President's nomination. Senatorial courtesy applies only if the senator is of the President's party and only to certain offices within his state such as judgeships in federal district courts and U.S. marshals. An individual senator may sometimes be able to force the defeat or withdrawal of a nomination because of animosity that he feels for the nominee even when that person would not be serving within his state, but this is not senatorial courtesy and ordinarily the senator could not count on success. In the states, outside of cabinet-level officials who usually are elected separately, the customary practice is for state senates also to approve executive appointments to policy-making positions (often including the judiciary). Frequently, too, the same considerations of senatorial courtesy apply.

Certain high-ranking officials who are in the Executive Office of the President traditionally have been considered to be presidential aides and assistants rather than "Officers of the United States," as Article II, Section 2, puts it. Despite the fact that the Director of the Office of Management and Budget (OMB) is one of the most powerful officials in the government, with direct authority over the budgets of the Cabinet agencies, he originally was not subject to Senate confirmation because the OMB (formerly Bureau of the Budget) is in the President's Executive Office. Top presidential advisers, however powerful, still escape this requirement. In the Nixon administration Henry Kissinger (when he was White House adviser on foreign affairs and the architect of much of the Nixon foreign policy), John Ehrlichman (domestic adviser to the President), and H. R. Haldeman (Nixon's chief of staff who had virtually complete control over access to the President) were never confirmed by the Senate. In mid-1973 Congress passed legislation requiring these and other policy-making officials to have Senate confirmation as the Constitution specifies for Cabinet officers and others, but the act fell victim to a Nixon veto and the House could not obtain a two-thirds vote to override, even though congressional power was at stake. Early in 1974 an act succeeded in requiring confirmation of new OMB Directors, but exempted the incumbent. Carter's designation of Vice President Mondale as his

Chief of Staff for the first time put an elected official in this key position and avoided questions of senatorial confirmation.

The Powers of Congress

Article I, Section 8, of the Constitution sets forth a list of the formal powers of Congress. The list is extensive and includes, among other things, the power to lay and collect taxes, borrow money, regulate commerce, provides rules for naturalization and bankruptcies, coin money and fix standards for weights and measures, establish a postal system, create a judicial system, declare war, raise and support an army and navy, provide for a militia, create a federal district, and regulate copyrights and patents. Additionally, Section 8 grants Congress the power to adopt all laws "which shall be necessary and proper" in order to exercise the powers granted in this and other sections of the Constitution. This provision establishes the basis for the doctrine of implied powers, as discussed in Chapter 3.

Although Congress has broad powers, they are subject to limitations. The Constitution specifies certain prohibitions. The First Amendment, for example, provides that Congress shall make no law abridging freedom of speech or of the press, and Article I, Section 9, forbids Congress to pass *bills of attainder* (those laws that permit legislative rather than judicial punishment of citizens) and *ex post facto laws* (laws providing for punishment of an action that took place before the law was passed). Moreover, the courts have insisted that Congress must adopt clear standards to guide the executive officials who are to administer the laws. Too great a grant of discretion to the administration would be a delegation of legislative power and therefore unconstitutional.

Congressional Structure and Organization

In order to carry their beliefs in checks and balances into the national legislature itself, the Founding Fathers provided for a bicameral Congress. To a degree, this form was required by the nature of a federal system. With the states represented equally in the Senate, the federal structure was secure, and the House of Representatives could be based upon population. Just as the legislative, executive, and judicial branches can check one another, so too can one house of the Congress check the other because the approval of both houses is required to adopt legislation. Originally the House of Representatives was to be the democratic, or "people's" branch, and the Senate (which initially was selected solely by state legislatures, not the voters) was to dampen the presumed excesses of democracy and represent elite interests. In recent years the situation has changed. Both the House and the Senate are essentially conservative bodies, with extraordinarily conservative traditions and institutions that make it appear virtually impossible to challenge the status quo success-fully. Partly because of the greater influence of urban areas in the Senate, however, at present that body is inclined to be more open to social pro-grams and other innovations than is the House. Because the senator's constituency is an entire state, he or she is likely to be oriented toward urban needs if the state is predominantly urban. Urban states are nevertheless likely to have substantial rural and small-town areas. Be-cause members of the House are elected by districts rather than at large, even predominantly urban states may have one or more representatives whose constituencies are essentially nonmetropolitan, thereby giving the House still less of an urban flavor than the Senate. However, elections of the last few years have reduced this tendency to some extent by electing more young and reform-minded representatives to the House.

The two houses are presumed to be equal in power, and members of the House of Representatives often insist that the House is equal in honor and prestige to the Senate. Nevertheless, a senator has great advantages not available to the typical representative. As one of only one hundred members, even a freshman senator is likely to have some national visibil-ity and be a sought-after guest on the Washington cocktail circuit; few persons anywhere are so anonymous as a freshman representative. Until he or she becomes prominent in the House, the representative is lost among a large group of 435. Moreover, a senator has considerable inde-pendence because of a six-year term, whereas a representative must spend considerable time getting reelected every two years. Regardless of the pretensions of many representatives, they frequently retire from the House in order to run for the Senate when they think that they have a good chance to win; however, it would be unthinkable for a modern senator to resign in order to run for the House.

Today most political scientists and political reformers as well seem strongly to favor unicameral legislatures. There appears to be some pres-sure developing in California for a switch to a unicameral legislature, partly because of resentment over the cost of operating two houses, each with extensive research staff and other duplications. The arguments for bicameralism center largely upon the desirability of checks and balances, which many no longer take for granted, and in any event there may be many checks within one house. Additionally, since bills may be intro-duced into either house (with the exception, on the national level, of revenue bills, which the Constitution requires to originate in the House, and appropriations bills, which originate there by tradition), some argue that a bicameral arrangement permits a legislature to handle a greater volume of work than if it were unicameral. One chamber may conduct the necessary investigations and do the essential spadework on one group of bills while the other chamber performs similarly with another group, thereby saving one another considerable effort. In practice, it rarely works this way. The House and Senate are reluctant to take one another's word for anything and usually insist on going through the entire process for each bill, regardless of what the other house has done, whether in Congress or a state legislature.

Most of the literature tends to favor unicameralism as being more efficient and less expensive. There is a possibility, also, that unicameralism could increase the quality of a legislature. Some have noted a tendency in the Congress for the House to pass ill-considered and unwise legislation, which the representatives know full well should not become law but which they also know the Senate would kill. Frivolous conduct such as this would be too serious to exist in a unicameral body. It is difficult to determine accurately which form is better because there is so little experience with unicameral legislatures in the American setting. To be sure, virtually all city councils in the United States are unicameral, but the governance of cities is so different from the governance of states and nations that the experience is not directly comparable. Except for the state legislature of Nebraska, all American legislatures at the state level or higher are bicameral. Nebraska's experience seems to indicate that neither the high expectations of the reformers nor the dire predictions of traditionalists were justified. There are differences in the performance of bicameral and unicameral legislatures, but each can work reasonably well.

CONGRESSIONAL ORGANIZATION

The life of a Congress is two years, beginning in January under the terms of the Twentieth Amendment. Article I, Section 4, of the Constitution requires Congress to assemble at least once each year, and the President is empowered by Article II, Section 3, to convene Congress on "extraordinary occasions" when he deems it necessary. The only time that a President may adjourn Congress would be if the two houses could not agree on a date of adjournment, but this has never occurred. A bill lasts as long as a Congress. If it is introduced into the first session, it may be considered in the second, but if it is not acted upon in the second, it has to be reintroduced in order to be considered by a future Congress. According to the Legislative Reorganization Act of 1946, Congress is supposed to adjourn each yearly session by July 31, but the pressure of work is such that the sessions continue for most of the year. The practice tends to be different in the states because state constitutions frequently include rigid restrictions upon the number and length of legislative sessions.

Each new Congress assembles in January of odd-numbered years and organizes itself. Because the six-year terms of senators are staggered so that only approximately one-third face the voters during any given election, the Senate is considered to be a continuing body with the majority of its members carrying over from one Congress to the next. This means that Senate rules continue through succeeding Congresses, preventing the Senate from adopting new rules every two years. Frequently, at the opening sessions of new Congresses, liberals from both parties put forth the claim that the Senate is not a continuing body and can adopt new rules at the beginning of any new Congress by a simple majority vote.

Although the Senate has never accepted this argument, and it still requires a two-thirds vote to change Senate rules, the liberals made a gain in March 1975 when they succeeded in amending Rule XXII, the major point of controversy. Rule XXII permits senators unlimited debate unless halted by a motion to close off debate, the so called *cloture motion*, which traditionally has required a two-thirds majority of those present and voting. This freedom for unlimited debate permits the practice known as *filibuster*, in which one senator, sometimes in cooperation with others, continues debate for a prolonged period with the intention of defeating a bill by so tying up the Senate's business that its backers surrender in order to proceed. Although liberals generally work to eliminate the filibuster or to reduce the vote required for cloture on grounds that it is undemocratic to permit a small minority to prevent the Senate from acting, and it is true that the most notable use of the filibuster has been to defeat civil rights bills, it should be noted that liberals, too, resort to the filibuster when it is to their advantage to do so. The revision that they finally succeeded in passing in 1975 made cloture possible with a smaller majority, three-fifths, or sixty senators when all are present and voting. In order to adopt the change, the Senate invoked cloture to end a filibuster by Senator James Allen of Alabama, the first time that cloture had succeeded upon a question dealing with the cloture rule itself. The vote to revise Rule XXII was substantial, ten more than the two-thirds required, and even on the motion to end Allen's filibuster, more southern Democrats voted to invoke cloture than against it. Clearly the time for some reform, however minimal, had come.

Rule making for the House of Representatives is somewhat different. Because every member is subject to election every biennium, the

from *Straight Herblock* (Simon & Schuster, 1964)

**"YOU SEE—FIRST WOMEN, THEN NEGROES,
NOW CONGRESSMEN AND SENATORS."**

House is not considered to be a continuing body, even though most of the members are returned every election. Consequently, it adopts its rules at the beginning of each Congress. The new rules are generally the same as those in force in preceding Congress. Because of the size of the House (set by law at 435 representatives distributed among the states on the basis of population), there is no freedom for unlimited debate as there is in the Senate, and there is correspondingly less controversy over the rules.

Both the House and the Senate go through the ritual of selecting their leaders in each new Congress. Although there is very little discipline in either party, this vote to organize each house is the one time at which all members can be expected to vote the straight party line. The majority party of the House puts forth its candidate for Speaker, who is routinely elected. The Speaker of the House is not only the chief of his party in that chamber but also the presiding officer and retains the right to vote. He will be a representative with prestige and seniority, but many factors enter into the selection; the Speaker is never chosen on seniority alone. His powers are great and may be enhanced by personal skills. In a body such as the House, with rigid limitations on debate, the Speaker's power to recognize those wishing to speak is highly significant. Other prerogatives of the office include the power to interpret the rules, appoint members to conference and select committees, and refer bills to committees with the advice of the Parliamentarian.

In the Senate, the presiding officer is the Vice President of the United States, who also has the title of President of the Senate. Since he is imposed upon the Senate from the outside and may even be a member of the minority party, he has little power or influence within that body. He cannot vote except in case of a tie. The power to preside is of little consequence because of the unlimited debate that the Senate permits. The Senate does elect a President *Pro Tempore*, who has the right to preside whenever the Vice President is absent and who is chosen, as is the Speaker of the House, by a straight party vote. The President *Pro Tem*, however, is the member of the majority party with the greatest seniority, so that the position is almost entirely honorary. The power to preside is so nearly meaningless in the Senate, in fact, that freshmen senators often occupy the chair temporarily in order to gain experience, and the President *Pro Tem* rarely presides despite the numerous absences of Vice Presidents.

In state senates the presiding officer usually is the lieutenant governor. Contrary to the national practice, he or she may have real power, even equal to that of the Speaker of the House, as in Texas or California. In some states, such as Missouri, the power may lie with the senate's president *pro tem*, which, again, is in sharp contrast to the practice in the U.S. Senate.

Nationally the party offices are similar in both houses. There are majority and minority leaders, and majority and minority "whips," a term taken from the British legislature. The whips are assistants to the leaders. As with the selection of the Speaker, seniority is important in the selection of these officials but is not determining.

THE COMMITTEE SYSTEM

One factor of congressional organization that can hardly be exaggerated in importance is the committee system. Although not mentioned in the Constitution, that structure has evolved to the point where it is fundamental in the functioning of the political system. In order to achieve greater efficiency in handling the overwhelming number of bills, Congress has provided for *committees* to divide up the labor and permit a certain degree of specialization. There are four kinds of committee: select, joint, conference, and standing. Select committees are *ad hoc* bodies created for a specific purpose and for a specific length of time. When their function is completed, they are eliminated, although if they appear to be of permanent value they can be transformed into standing committees.

Joint committees are those composed of members of both houses. Standing (i.e., permanent) joint committees are not widely used by Congress, nor do they generally have the prestige of the standing committees within each house. The Joint Committee on Atomic Energy was the only one that considered legislation, but recently has been stripped of this power. As a rule, joint committees are used to coordinate policy between the House and Senate on relatively routine matters. Examples are the Joint Committee on Printing and the Joint Committee on the Library. Greater use of joint standing committees could well lead to greater efficiency in a bicameral legislature by eliminating the duplication of function that occurs when committees in each house separately consider a proposed piece of legislation. Joint select committees, on the other hand, are more extensively used, largely in the form of conference committees.

Congress uses conference committees to settle differences between the two houses whenever one house passes a bill that is not identical in all respects to the same bill passed by the other house. This happens in a majority of nonroutine cases. Unless both chambers pass a bill in exactly the same form, it cannot be forwarded to the executive for action. Each house appoints from three to nine members who serve as conferees. (The standing committees involved select the conferees from their own membership, the procedure differing according to the committee.) The conference committee may adopt the House version of the bill, the Senate version of the bill, or a compromise version. Although theoretically they are not supposed to do so, conference committees may upon occasion completely rewrite a bill, especially if the original House and Senate versions were radically different. In order to issue a report, a majority of the conferees from each house must agree. If they cannot agree, the bill fails even though it has passed both houses. The conference committee report goes back to the two houses for adoption without amendment, after which it is sent to the President for his action. Usually each house will accept a conference committee report routinely, but if either house refuses to do so, the measure dies.

The possibilities for the sudden death of a bill are almost unlimited.

The most lethal arena is the standing committee. Standing committees are the heart of the committee system. They are permanent units that each house establishes within its rules, and theirs is the task of considering proposed legislation and recommending action. Generally, standing committees are established on the basis of subject matter, with each committee having certain subjects under its jurisdiction. As a rule the committee's action is the major factor in determining the future of a bill. When a committee reports a bill favorably to the House or the Senate, the chances are good that it will be adopted, especially if the committee has been strong in its endorsement and it has acted by a large majority. It is extraordinarily rare for a bill to succeed without committee approval.

The majority party in either house always selects all committee chairmen, and always has a majority on all committees in the chamber (see Tables 4 and 5 for the current House and Senate committee heads). It is in the selection of chairmen that the famous, or infamous, seniority system may come into play. Although there have been changes in the last few years that have substantially eliminated the seniority system as a formal procedure, in most cases seniority still determines the choice of committee chairmen. The system guaranteed that the member of the majority party with the most consecutive years of service on a given committee became its chairman unless he elected to step aside. It guarded against bitter intraparty struggles in selecting leaders and also insured that chairmen would be persons of experience (though not necessarily of competence). It guaranteed as well that there would be no discrimination on the basis of race, religion, sex, or ability. Most attacks on the seniority system came from liberals, usually younger liberals. As members grew in seniority and worked into positions of power, they frequently came to be supporters of the system, whether they were liberal or conservative, on the ground that seniority had sufficient advantages to compensate for its disadvantages.

It is easy to exaggerate the shortcomings of selection by seniority. The system did work and to some extent still does. Selection by the leadership alone (once a practice of Congress and still in operation in many states) has its own, equally serious, shortcomings. Nevertheless, many flaws in a rigid selection by seniority are obvious. In addition to ignoring competence, the system offended many advocates of strong party organization and leadership. Many persons who rarely supported the position of their own party attained committee chairs, and only in the most flagrant cases was a member stripped of seniority for such actions. The system also was abhorrent to those who advocated more democracy within the houses of Congress. As a rule seniority's greatest enemies were liberals and for the simple reason that the system tended to work to the advantage of conservatives. As the liberals were well aware, less urban

TABLE 4 Standing Committees of the House as of April 30, 1977

House Committee	Sub-commit-tees	Chairman	State
Agriculture	10	Thomas Foley	Washington
Appropriations	13	George H. Mahon	Texas
Armed Services	7	Melvin Price	Illinois
Banking, Finance and Urban Affairs	10	Henry Reuss	Wisconsin
Budget	8	Robert Giaimo	Connecticut
District of Columbia	3	Charles C. Diggs	Michigan
Education and Labor	8	Carl D. Perkins	Kentucky
Government Operations	7	Jack Brooks	Texas
House Administration	7	Frank Thompson, Jr.	New Jersey
Interior and Insular Affairs	7	Morris Udall	Arizona
International Relations	9	Clement Zablocki	Wisconsin
Interstate and Foreign Commerce	6	Harley O. Staggers	West Virginia
Judiciary	7	Peter W. Rodino	New Jersey
Merchant Marine and Fisheries	5	John Murphy	New York
Post Office and Civil Service	7	Robert Nix	Pennsylvania
Public Works and Transportation	6	Harold Johnson	California
Rules	0	James Delaney	New York
Science and Technology	7	Olin Teague	Texas
Small Business	6	Neal Smith	Iowa
Standards of Official Conduct	0	John Flynt	Georgia
Veterans Affairs	5	Ray Roberts	Texas
Ways and Means	6	Al Ullman	Oregon

conservative states and districts are more likely to be politically "safe" for incumbents—that is, to present them with little challenge at elections—than are the districts and states that are more urban and therefore likely to be more liberal. An incumbent from a safe district is, of course, likely to build seniority, hence, power. Thus, the majority of committee chairmen in both houses had come from the South, and generally from the most rural districts. This tendency has lessened somewhat in recent

TABLE 5 Standing Committees of the Senate as of April 30, 1977

Senate Committee	Sub-committees	Chairman	State
Agriculture, Nutrition, and Forestry	7	Herman E. Talmadge	Georgia
Appropriations	13	John L. McClellan	Arkansas
Armed Services	8	John C. Stennis	Mississippi
Banking, Housing, and Urban Affairs	8	William Proxmire	Wisconsin
Budget	0	Edmund Muskie	Maine
Commerce, Science, and Transportation	6	Warren G. Magnuson	Washington
Energy and Natural Resources	5	Henry M. Jackson	Washington
Environment and Public Works	6	Jennings Randolph	West Virginia
Finance	10	Russell B. Long	Louisiana
Foreign Relations	9	John Sparkman	Alabama
Governmental Affairs	7	Abraham Ribicoff	Connecticut
Human Resources	8	Harrison A. Williams	New Jersey
Judiciary	10	James O. Eastland	Mississippi
Rules and Administration	0	Howard W. Cannon	Nevada
Veterans Affairs	3	Alan Cranston	California

*This table reflects the reorganization of the Senate committee structure pursuant to S Res 4 adopted on February 4, 1977, the first major revision since 1946.

years, but because it contains so many safe districts the South always has considerably more power in both houses than its relative size would warrant on a basis of strict equality, as have rural areas in general. The seniority system thus tends to give a great deal of power to a fairly small number of states with very similar, and often sectional, interests.

These shortcomings would have been less important if committee chairmen were less powerful. The chairman may call or refuse to call meetings or hold hearings, he may reward committee members with choice subcommittee assignments or deny them, and his power over committee procedure tends to be so great that in many cases he has the power to kill any bill that he fails to favor. Partly this is the result of the American congressional committee system itself; if the committees were less powerful, the issue of seniority would have been less critical because chairmen would have been less important. Most legislatures elsewhere, although they make use of committees, have nothing resembling the powerful American committees with their virtual life and death power over legislation. Instead they do what is considered here to be impossible, that is, they handle most legislative detail in the full chamber. Encouraged by weak party discipline and no executive control over the legislative schedule, the American committee system was a natural, but not an inevitable, development.

In 1971 the House Republicans led the way to reform of the seniority system by providing that committee chairmen (or, to be more precise, the ranking minority members (since Republicans were and are in the minority) were to be chosen by the Republican members of the chamber; the Democrats followed with the same reform in 1973. That same year the Senate Republicans changed their procedures to select the ranking minority members by vote of the Republicans on each committee, and the Senate Democrats in 1976 finally agreed to an election of chairmen by the Democratic Caucus (composed of all Democratic senators) and even provided for a secret ballot vote if requested by one-fifth of the Caucus members.

The new procedures probably came about both from internal pressures within Congress and widespread publicity from citizens' groups such as Common Cause and Ralph Nader's organization, among others. The reforms provide a way to remove a chairman under ordinary procedures, but in most cases those chosen are those who would have been selected under strict seniority. In early 1975, however, the House Democrats did depose three committee chairmen—Wright Patman of Banking and Currency, Edward Hebert of Armed Services, and W.R. Poage of Agriculture. The results of such reforms appear nevertheless to be mixed, when one notes that Wayne Hays, one of the most arbitrary, high-handed, and consequently disliked chairmen in the House retained his command of the Administration Committee. The sex scandals that surfaced in 1976 and forced him from power accomplished what the reformers had not, the removal of Hays and the curtailment of the dictatorial powers that he had built for himself and his committee.

In any case, even reformers almost never suggest changes in the basic system that would make the introduction and passage of laws more efficient. They want only new methods of selecting the leaders of the established mechanism. Certainly, members of Congress could change the institutions considerably if they wished. At present, the entire structure of both houses is biased against reform. It is too early to assess the impact of those reforms that have come about during the last few years, but many reforms in congressional history have made little difference in the actual operation of the legislative branch. There is little doubt that things are as they are because this is the way that most members wish them to be.

The way to become a committee chairman is still to be assigned to a committee and continue to be elected to Congress, assuming that when the member outlasts the opposition his party will be in the majority. Only a select few manage to land choice spots such as those on the Appropriations, Ways and Means, or Rules committees in the House or the committees on Appropriations, Finance, or Foreign Relations in the Senate. For a time, representatives held positions on only one committee and senators on two, although there were exceptions. The tendency now is for representatives also to serve on two, except for those who are assigned to certain committees, such as Appropriations, Agriculture, Ways and Means, Rules, and Armed Services, for which single assignments are customary.

The procedures for assigning members to committees differ according to party and chamber. The House Democratic Caucus officially assigns Democratic members, but it follows the recommendation of the Democratic Steering and Policy Committee, which includes the House leadership along with members appointed by the Speaker (if he is a Democrat, as is usually the case) and others elected by the membership from geographic zones. This arrangement was itself a 1975 reform.(Earlier the power to recommend Democratic committee assignments was given to the Democratic members of the House Ways and Means Committee.) The House Republicans employ a Committee on Committees composed of one representative from each state that has a Republican representative. Each member can cast as many votes as there are Republican representatives from his or her state, and the committee is dominated by an executive committee that includes members from the states with the largest Republican representations, such as Michigan, Illinois, California, New York, Ohio, and Pennsylvania.

In the Senate the Democratic floor leader selects a Steering Committee to make the assignments, and the chairman of the Republican Conference appoints a Committee on Committees for the same purpose. The Democrats follow the principle called the "Johnson Rule" (adopted in the 1950s when Lyndon Johnson was Majority Leader), which, stipulates that all Democrats should have one major committee assignment before any Democrat is given more than one. The Republicans make their initial assignments generally on seniority, but they follow a rule that they adopted in 1965 that no Republican can hold a seat on more than one of the four most powerful committees (Appropriations, Finance, Foreign Relations, and Armed Services) unless each Republican senator has had a chance for such an appointment.

All of these methods provide for almost complete domination by the senior members, who are unlikely to reflect changes in the political sentiment of the general electorate. Various criteria dominate the assignment process, and they change constantly. But here, as elsewhere in Congress, the emphasis is strongly upon maintaining the status quo, because those who get the key assignments tend to be those whom the leaders believe will not rock the boat.

Congressional Procedures: The Rocky Road to Legislation

The view that the House or the Senate engages in open debate and action on the floor, as reflected in the pages of the *Congressional Record*, is an illusion. In fact, most of the business of Congress takes place in committee; also, much of the action that the *Congressional Record* reports borders on fiction. The Constitution requires each house to keep a journal of its proceedings, but the proceedings within the committees, which are vitally important, are not included. A member of Congress may insert material in the *Record*, perhaps making it appear that there has been vigorous debate and that he or she has participated extensively when in reality little if anything has been said on the floor. The *Record* can be changed by a member asking unanimous consent (which is always granted) to "revise and extend" his or her remarks. Members may also insert virtually any material that they please in the rear section of the *Record* labeled "Extensions of Remarks." Debate does occur, and sometimes (though too rarely) at a high level, but the pages of the *Record* are not a perfect reflection of what happened. Members receive copies of their remarks on the floor, which they may edit to remove illiteracies or otherwise revise before they appear in the *Record*. This means that each member will apppear in the pages of the *Record* to maximum advantage as he or she sees it. If a member has failed to edit the copy and get it back in time to make the printing deadline, that portion will be deleted, and it will be noted that so-and-so's remarks will appear hereafter in Extensions of Remarks. Despite these shortcomings, the *Record* is still the best picture of congressional proceedings that exists for those who wish to follow the day-to-day workings of Congress. It is a valuable resource and one of the publishing marvels of the world, routinely appearing the day after a session under conditions of pressure that make it remarkable that it is printed at all. On occasion the *Record* may also serve as comic relief to the ponderous business of government, both in the accounts of debates and in the recipes, poems and jokes that members choose to immortalize in its back pages.

Another illusion is the stereotyped view that members of Congress sit in Washington, passing laws indiscriminately, throwing away "the taxpayers' money." In order to appreciate the difficulty of enacting legislation, let us trace the path of a bill from its introduction until it becomes law (diagrammed in Figure 3).

Only a representative or a senator may introduce a bill. Except for revenue bills, which the Constitution requires to originate in the House, a bill may begin in either the House or the Senate or simultaneously in each. By tradition, appropriations bills also originate in the House, but this is not a legal requirement. For our illustration, let us follow a bill, originating in the House, to establish a program of tuition subsidies to college students for which the introducing representative desires to authorize a total appropriation of $200 million. Because he is not likely to be able to draft so technical a bill without assistance beyond that available on his staff, the member of Congress probably would supply the outlines of the proposal to specialists in the U.S. Office of Education, who, as a matter of courtesy, would prepare the draft regardless of their opinions of the program. This procedure, of course, permits the executive to have some influence on the proposed bill, even in its initial stages.

After introduction in the House, the bill is referred to the appropriate committee, which for this bill would be the Committee on Education and Labor. That committee then refers the bill to the subcommittee having jurisdiction over the subject matter involved (in this case, probably the Subcommittee on Postsecondary Education). The subcommittee examines the bill, perhaps holds hearings and invites witnesses to testify to its virtues and shortcomings, and makes recommendations to the committee. If the subcommittee recommends against a bill, or if it fails to act, the bill usually dies. If it recommends the bill favorably, the committee may report it favorably; if, for whatever reason, the committee fails to report a bill favorably, it usually is dead. The committee may add amendments of its own, or it may completely rewrite the bill so that what comes out bears no resemblance to what went in. In our hypothetical example, the Education and Labor Committee clears the bill and reports it favorably, although with an amendment to provide a program of only $100 million.

Having survived thus far, the bill is placed on a calendar and must be cleared through the Rules Committee, which controls much of the traffic on the floor of the House. The Rules Committee does not control all matters reported from the other committees because much of the action in any session is noncontroversial and is handled in routine fashion, and certain other matters, such as those reported from the Committees on Ways and Means or Appropriations, are "privileged." Generally,

FIGURE 3. Typical Path from Bill to Law for Major Bill Originating in House

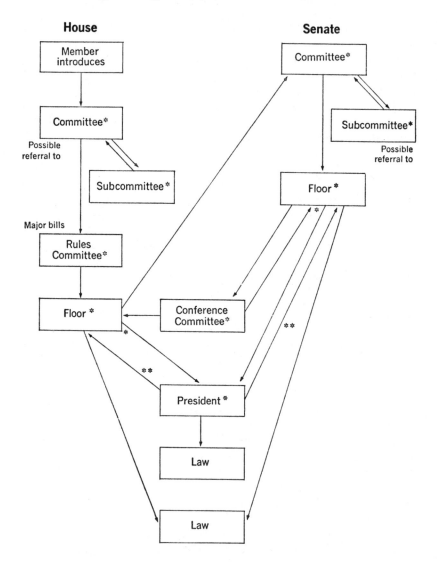

Note: Bill may originate in either House or Senate, except for revenue bills which must originate in House, or appropriations bills which originate there by custom

   * Points at which bill may die

  ** If vetoed while Congress is in session

however, most controversial measures must receive clearance by the Rules Committee before the House can act. If the Rules Committee bottles up the measure or fails to act, the bill usually dies. It is possible to force a bill out of a reluctant Rules Committee, but it is difficult, and effort in this direction is often futile. This committee has long been a graveyard for legislation, especially progressive social programs. President Kennedy spent the better part of his influence in the Congress attempting to influence an expansion of the size of the committee in order to appoint more liberally-minded members; he succeeded, but with disappointing results.

In our example, however, the Rules Committee acts favorably, and the measure goes to the floor of the full House with a "rule" permitting a certain amount of time for debate. At this point there is debate and parliamentary maneuvering; there may be efforts to table the bill or to send it back to committee that, if successful, would almost assuredly kill it. If the House votes down the bill, it is dead. Our bill survives these hurdles, and receives a favorable vote from the House, which sends it on to the Senate.

In the Senate the bill then goes to the Human Resources Committee, which has jurisdiction over educational matters. Here, everything begins again. The committee processes the bill as did its counterpart in the House. As in the House, the committee can revise or rewrite the bill, and a favorable committee report is a virtual requirement for final Senate passage. Let us assume that the committee restores the original amount of $200 million and reports the bill favorably. It then can be taken up on the floor of the Senate. Note that there is no counterpart in the Senate to

ONLY TWO MEN IN WASHINGTON FULLY UNDERSTAND THE CAUSES OF INFLATION —

UNFORTUNATELY, THEY DISAGREE —

Reprinted by permission of Washington Star Syndicate, Inc.

the House Rules Committee (there is a Senate Committee on Rules and Administration, but this is more or less the counterpart of the House Administration Committee, not the Rules Committee). Since passage by both the House and the Senate is required for all legislation, a negative vote by the Senate would kill the bill, as would Senate inaction. As in the House, a successful motion to table or to refer it back to committee would also likely spell its doom. In our example, the Senate votes favorably. Although both houses have approved it, it still is not an act of Congress because the two houses did not pass it in identical form. If there is the slightest difference between the House and Senate versions of a bill, it must go to a conference committee. Here, the House passed a bill calling for a $100 million program, but the Senate's bill called for $200 million, so it goes to conference.

The purpose of a conference committee, as discussed above, is to smooth out differences between the two houses. If a majority of the House conferees and a majority of the Senate conferees fail to agree, the bill dies even though each house had previously acted favorably. For purposes of illustration, let us assume that the conference committee approves our bill, and agrees upon a compromise figure of $150 million. The conference committee report then goes back to the two houses for final action. Usually they accept the report, but in case either does not, the bill dies. In our illustration they adopt the report by favorable vote on the floor of each house, and it becomes an act of Congress and goes to the President.

The President receives the new act and has to decide whether to sign it into law or to veto it. If he should veto it while Congress is still in session, it goes back to Congress for reconsideration, and it dies unless each house can manage to repass it by a two-thirds vote. If Congress has adjourned, a veto kills the act with no possibility of overriding the President's action. In the event that the President should do nothing, the act becomes law in ten days unless Congress has adjourned in the meantime, in which case the act is dead (the so called *pocket veto*). In the case of our hypothetical program, the President signs it into law.

It is obvious that there are many pitfalls along the way, and it is no wonder that few bills that are introduced make it through to final passage and signing. In this illustration, as complicated as the procedure has been to this point, it still is only half completed! The law merely *authorizes* the appropriation of money; it does not actually provide it. In order for the program to get underway there must be another act, an appropriations act, that also goes through the entire procedure. One difference is that this bill must travel through the appropriations committees in each house, not the legislative committees that handled the original measure, thus confronting new points of possible hostility.

A great part of the legislative process also involves bargain and compromise. In many cases personal relationships and favors owed are as important as political issues. No brief discussion can convey adequately the complexity of the entire procedure.

Only in cases in which Congress is of almost a single mind on an issue can it act quickly, and these cases are rare. In the mid-1960s Congress, with great haste, made it a federal crime to burn a draft card, and President Johnson signed it into law with equal speed. However, it took Medicare more than twenty-five years to gain passage, and it took almost one hundred years for the adoption of anything resembling an effective civil rights program.

The Future of Congress

Until recently, the numerous inadequacies of Congress as a representative institution prompted reformers to suggest measures that would make it more amenable to executive leadership and direction. In the 1970s the manifest dangers of runaway executive power have encouraged many to change their minds and to suggest reforms that would enable Congress to reassert its own power in opposition to an increasingly powerful and decreasingly controlled executive. Very likely there will be some changes. The basic structure of Congress, of course, is such that changes generally come grudgingly, if at all. Nevertheless some of the most stodgy institutions in the world have changed dramatically in the last twenty years, and it is conceivable that Congress could follow their lead; not probable, but possible.

Suggested Readings

Stephen K. Bailey. *Congress in the Seventies*. 2nd ed. New York: St. Martin's Press, 1970.*

————. *Congress Makes a Law*. New York: Columbia University Press, 1950. One of the earliest, and still one of the best, of the legislative studies.

Richard Bolling. *Power in the House*. New York: Dutton, 1968. A critical treatment by a member of the House.

Jimmy Breslin. *How the Good Guys Finally Won: Notes from an Impeachment Summer*. New York: Ballantine, 1976.* Excellent for revealing power relationships in Congress as well as for presenting insights into the background of Watergate.

Joseph S. Clarke. *Congressional Reform: Problems and Prospects*. New York: Crowell, 1965. A former senator's suggestions for reform.

————. *Congress: The Sapless Branch*. New York: Harper & Row, 1964. A critical treatment of the Senate by the former senator from Pennsylvania.

Lewis A. Dexter. *The Sociology and Politics of Congress*. Chicago: Rand McNally, 1969.* Excellent analysis of Congress as an institution.

Richard F. Fenno, Jr. *The Congressional Process: Strategies, Rules, and Procedures.* Boston: Little, Brown, 1967.*

Mark J. Green, James M. Fallows, and David R. Zwick. *Who Runs Congress?* Ralph Nader Congress Project. New York: Bantam, 1972.* One of the most revealing studies of Congress.

Donald R. Matthews. *U.S. Senators and Their World.* Chapel Hill, N.C.: University of North Carolina Press, 1960. A classic study.

Eric Redman. *The Dance of Legislation.* New York: Simon & Schuster, 1973.* One of the best studies of congressional procedures—written by a former Senate staff member.

Donald Riegle. *O Congress.* New York: Popular Library, 1972.* Reflections of a young representative.

Randall Ripley. *Congress: Process and Policy.* New York: Norton, 1975.

Alan Rosenthal. "The Effectiveness of Congress." In *The Performance of American Government,* edited by Gerald Pomper. New York: Free Press, 1972.

Arthur Schlesinger, Jr. "Presidential War: See if You Can Fix Any Limit to His Power." *New York Times Magazine,* January 7, 1973.

Frank Sorauf. *Party and Representation.* New York: Atherton, 1963.

Arthur G. Stevens, Jr., Arthur H. Miller, and Thomas E. Mann. "Mobilization of Liberal Strength in the House, 1955–1970: The Democratic Study Group." APSA, LXVIII, No. 2 (June 1974), 667–681.

John Wahlke, Heinz Eulau, William Buchanan, and Leroy Ferguson. *The Legislative System: Exploration in Legislative Behavior.* New York: Wiley, 1962.

*Available in paperback.

6 THE JUDICIAL PROCESS

Justice in America?

Nothing but the infinite number of our laws and what is quoted as authority in our courts, together with the perplexity and confusion, gave these gentlemen their importance, or indeed any importance at all.

Christopher Gadsden

In common with many animal species, human beings engage in conflict, which appears to serve a function that is fundamental in the ordering and development of a society. Where man diverges is in the degree of violence that marks so many of his groupings. Ethologists have pointed out in recent years that one factor producing this difference is the ritual behaviors that other species use to limit internal aggression and control and direct conflict. Man shares some of these behaviors in rudimentary form, but his main solution to this problem of channeling aggression involves use of language and culture. The judicial process in its many forms is the human cultural answer to the problem of conflict management. Much of man's political history may be summarized as a struggle to develop alternatives to violence in human society, first between individuals and then between small groups and the larger groups called nations.

Institutionally the judicial process is, in a sense, the heart of the political system. Even in the most simply organized societies, with few specialized roles, the role of the leader in settling disputes is perhaps the most important and most frequently performed. As the organization of society becomes more complex, the leader takes on other responsibilities in his role as judge. Eventually with increased complexity, and the acquisition of sufficient economic resources, a specialized institution, the judiciary, may emerge to settle disputes. Regardless of what form the judicial system takes, its basic political role is the same—enabling the society to control (but *not* eliminate) conflict. The system may employ violence, or the threat of violence, to support its decisions, but only in the last resort. If compliance is not voluntary for most decisions, then the system is not functioning well, and if violence is the only sanction, the costs in social development may be very high. When public acceptance of the judicial system declines and each person assumes the role of judge once again, the stability and legitimacy of the political system vanish. Respect for law is the life of the political order.

The American Judicial System

Like other parts of the American political system the judicial subsystem resulted from both colonial experience and revolutionary design. The systems in the colonies drew upon English law and institutions in the main, but other sources such as Dutch custom in New York, left their mark as well. The pressure of colonial circumstances and needs reshaped the Old World models into very different institutions. In the colonies judicial functions had been closely intertwined, often even fused, with legislative and executive ones. The highest court in the colony was usually the royal council, which was also the upper house of the legislature. The colonists rejected this fusion of powers after the Revolution and created a separate set of courts, following their understanding of the doctrine of separated powers. They staffed both state and national courts with independent judges. The Constitution established the Supreme Court at the top of the national system and left the creation of other federal courts to the Congress. State courts were to be established under state responsibility. With the passage of time, these systems have become more elaborate, and efforts to design new kinds of courts within them still continue.

The Ground of the Law

TYPES OF LAW

Courts in the United States are guided by four main sets of rules in the resolution of disputes. The most fundamental is the Constitution itself. All courts—federal, state or local—are to uphold the Constitution and may rule on any matter arising under its provisions that is within their particular jurisdiction. The Supreme Court has the power of final judicial resolution of federal constitutional questions (though Congress and the states may act to overturn a Supreme Court decision by constitutional amendment). The national Constitution takes precedence over other charters. State constitutions must contain no provisions forbidden by it, and city and county charters, in turn, must be consistent with the constitution of their state as well as the federal Constitution. The judges of state and local courts have the power to rule on cases concerning interpretation of these lower constitutions, and the high court of the particular state has the final say on these matters.

This general power to interpret constitutions and require laws and other actions of public officials to conform with them is known as *judicial review;* the basis of the political power held by American courts. Judicial review enables the courts to act as interpreters of the national Constitution itself, thus insuring its longevity and vitality. It also allows courts, using the Constitution as a measure, to weigh public acts, even those of coequal branches. The Supreme Court may thus scrutinize actions of the Congress and the President, as it did in the Watergate decisions. By exercising their power to measure politics against the Constitution, particularly the Bill of Rights, the courts become—even against their will— the conscience of the nation, upholding the values they see in the Constitution and reminding government and governed of those values from time to time. Other nations have rarely given their courts such power, allowing them to interpret laws but not constitutions. Judicial review is found in other federal systems, and to some extent in a number of countries—many of which adopted it from the American model—but its fullest application is in the United States.

Besides the Constitution the courts must also enforce obligations incurred by a *treaty,* a formal agreement between nations. A treaty may not be enforced domestically if it requires acts that are inconsistent with the federal Constitution, and, in turn, legislation that conflicts with a valid treaty cannot be enforced. For example, any treaty that entails violation of freedom of press or speech would not be enforceable in the United States. And if state fishing regulations conflicted with a treaty granting an Indian nation fishing rights in perpetuity the treaty would be given precedence.

The bulk of the judicial system's work is based upon the third and fourth sets of rules the courts must enforce—common and statutory law. The American system is part of a great legal tradition, the common law, which spread from England to its colonies in the New World, in Africa, and in Asia. In England it had its beginnings a thousand years ago in the creation of a legal system by the early kings and their nobles. Essentially the *common law* is based upon the idea of bench-made or judge-made law, grounded in community norms and history. Judges may rule upon the basis of these communal patterns, following or interpreting past decisions as well as specific statutes or rules; they may choose to overthrow those precedents, even their own. Thus the California Supreme Court ruled against capital punishment in part because it found that the consensus of the community was against the penalty. Because of this emphasis on the judge's interpretations of community beliefs, other cases, and changing circumstances, the judge has great flexibility in his decisions, and his personality and background become correspondingly important. The powerful hand of established tradition is a restraining force, yet a judge is free to take account of changes in society, to find another precedent, to note the sense of the community—in short, to keep the law a living thing. Another basis for decisions, equity, helps here as well. Once a separate system, but now essentially merged with the common law, *equity* is a system of rules by which disputes can be resolved on the ground of fairness, to prevent irreparable harm being done before a decision on the merits can be made. (For example, in *Monty Python* v. *American Broadcasting Companies, Inc.*, the creators of a television show asked for both a temporary and a permanent injunction, or order, against the ABC-edited version of their work being shown.)

Louisiana is the only state with a legal system that is not founded on the common law. This is a result of its French heritage. It is interesting to note that Louisiana leads the other states in the number of enactments struck down by the Supreme Court.

At present the growing body of *statutory law,* written law passed by legislatures, is more important as a basis of decisions than common law, based on judicial precedents. Today there are well over 1 million statutes on the books, in addition to many more millions of administrative regulations. This complex body of prohibition, regulation, and command gives judges new sources of authority and responsibility. It confronts the citizen with a vast array of obligations as well as rights and gives rise to ever growing numbers of controversies, increasing the level of judicial acitivity. The entire body of enacted law, including statutes in force in the states before the ratification of the Constitution, may be called upon by litigants and judges. Even though a law has not been enforced for decades, it is not thereby invalid, although its application may be challenged as discriminatory. Unless a statute contains an expiration date, it remains in force indefinitely, dying only when voided by the courts or purged from the books by legislative action. Thus, federal laws regulating the use of navigable waters by private persons, passed in the 1890s, were resurrected in the 1960s by ecologists to tackle industrial pollution. Legislatures rarely purge the laws, and judicial invalidation affects only a few laws, case by case.

"Crime does not pay at your level."

The exponential growth of statutes gives rise to another problem. With increases in legislation intended to regulate, police and prosecutors are forced to use more discretion as to which laws to apply, and to whom. The statute books contain a vast number of prohibitions and commands. Forgotten laws and ordinances may forbid persons who present a "disgusting" appearance to expose themselves to the public gaze. Ridiculing a public building, parading a goose on Main Street, leaving puddles in your yard longer than twelve hours, kite flying, and topless bathing suits for men have all been forbidden by law in one community or another in the past. Most of these laws are not enforced, and no one expects them to be. However, from this huge catalog of regulations, the government can find ways to prosecute almost anyone it wishes, and therein lies the problem of discretionary justice. Did the government prosecute kite flyers in Washington because it objected to this threat to the public safety, or because it objected to their previous participation in an antiwar demonstration? Why are so few prosecuted for tax evasion compared to drug offenses? As long as the statutes are so numerous, discretion in prosecution—the power to determine whether to arrest or to place on trial—remains a necessity. In those cases in which the defendant is in some way an opponent of the government, the motivation for prosecution becomes clouded. Prosecutorial discretion may be a way to make up for failure in an earlier effort to convict; thus, when it proves impossible to win conviction on charges of organized crime activities, the government need only wait until the suspect is seen spitting on the sidewalk or violating hunting regulations. More dangerous, perhaps, than petty harassment is the political trial, in which the judicial system is the background for a struggle over the possession and maintenance of power or the assertion of political supremacy by one part of the community over another.

TYPES OF LEGAL PROCEEDINGS

In most Western systems there are certain basic distinctions between various types of legal actions, although categories inevitably overlap. One distinction commonly made is between private and public suits. *Private suits,* as the name implies, are intended to settle a point at issue between private parties (e.g., with regard to marriage and inheritance). *Public suits* are undertaken in disputes over the operations of the state (e.g., the daily operations of various government agencies, covered by administrative law).

Legal scholars and lawyers also distinguish between criminal and civil actions. In a *criminal action* the government, speaking for the community as a whole, prosecutes an offense against the public order; the government accuses and tries the offender. *Civil actions* lie between private parties (or government agencies acting as private persons), and the state serves only to provide the arena for the contest, even though the outcome may have public effects. An example of a civil action with public consequences is a suit by a private interest group against car manufacturers who fail to meet antipollution standards.

Any variety of proceeding may serve as the basis for a *political trial,* although most frequently the issues are constitutional or criminal. All constitutional questions are political in some way, and dramatic power shifts may result from such political issues as the right of college students to register to vote in their college town and the legality of public campaign financing. Criminal law has a subcategory of acts that are specifically political in nature, those in which the state is inherently involved. The conduct of campaigns and elections, for example, recently has led to the courtroom. More traditionally political are offenses such as treason, sedition, malfeasance in office, and assassination, all of which have been the subject of dramatic political trials in America in the last three decades. Even ordinary criminal offenses may take on political overtones, as mentioned earlier. Much of our recent political history, and that of other nations, is reflected in trial records, though the charges at first might not seem political. Alger Hiss, for example, was charged with perjury, Spiro Agnew with accepting bribes, and Patricia Hearst with robbery.

The Courts

Laws are merely statements of intention that remain paper promises until some agency interprets them and applies them to specific problems. American courts deal only with actual cases or controversies; they do not, as some courts do, issue advisory opinions on hypothetical legislation or events. (On occasion this rule is bent, as it was in the recent Supreme Court hearing on the disputed Federal Election Campaign Act of 1974, discussed in chapter 8. The disadvantages of this practice are very great.)

The parties involved must have standing to sue—that is, each must be personally affected. A suit cannot be brought merely because the plaintiff does not like some law or act, or thinks it could be improved. The degree of injury required varies. In some instances a suit known as a *class action* is permitted when a litigant has only a minor personal interest but is acting for all persons in a particular situation. An example is a suit against an industrial polluter, in which individual damages are quite small but in sum are substantial. In some categories of suit state or federal legislation has established a right to class action; in others, however, the privilege may be varied by the courts. In 1973 the Supreme Court, decided, in *Zahn* v. *International Paper Co.*, to restrict suits in federal courts by requiring that all beneficiaries of the suit be notified by the plaintiff—a very expensive and very difficult task.

In most of their work the courts perform the basic function of resolving a dispute over the meaning of a norm in a specific case involving only a few persons directly. Did A beat up his wife? Did B sell worthless goods to C? Taken as a whole the pattern of decisions in such cases has certain policy implications, for example, concerning the rights of women or the fairness of contracts. In a series of such cases, or occasionally in one major trial, the courts act in a quasi-legislative way by establishing a new norm or reaffirming an old one. This is not judicial usurpation of the legislature's role but rather is implicit in the nature of judicial activity in this country.

There are many constraints on the courts' role as legislator. Most important, courts are passive. They do not initiate action on their own but must wait for others to bring problems to them, no matter how strongly judges may feel as individuals. If no one brings a case to the Supreme Court concerning the location of low-cost housing, the Court can issue no ruling on that matter. In addition, once the courts are engaged, the process of decision involving a major problem is likely to be a long one. A suit brought on the location of housing (*Gautreaux* v. *Hills*, 1976) took a decade before the final decision by the Supreme Court, during which time the original plaintiff died. Finally, the courts are essentially powerless to enforce their decisions, and few decisions are self-enforcing. Enforcement is up to the other branches. The executive provides the mechanism for enforcement if necessary, and the legislature must provide funds or new legislation. (In fact, the legislature often controls the finances of the courts themselves, their number and structure, and even their existence.) Implementation of the housing decision thus will require substantial cooperation from suburban officials, as well as federal agencies. In short, the courts are the weakest branch. The "nine old men" of the Supreme Court, as they were once referred to by Franklin Roosevelt, are not likely to overthrow the other branches.

On the other hand, the acceptance of courts by the public as the rightful arbiters of disputes does endow the courts with substantial authority. As long as most people, however reluctantly, regard as unlawful what the courts say is unlawful, the courts can exercise a strong influence over public issues. And in the United States there is a remarkable tendency to resort to the courts. As the nineteenth-century French observer of American life, Alexis de Tocqueville once commented, virtually every political question becomes a judicial question at some point.

THE DUAL STRUCTURE

The courts of the United States are a very complex set of institutions. Federalism has created a dual system of courts, state and federal, partly but not entirely hierarchical (see Table 6). The two subsystems are more intertwined than are the executives and legislatures of the federal and state governments. The nature and extent of this overlapping of activity lead to conflict and confusion on many occasions.

Jurisdiction often overlaps. Although there are fairly specific rules governing jurisdiction, litigants in certain civil cases may have a choice, as may prosecutors in a criminal case, concerning which court and sys-

TABLE 6   The Dual Court System*

Federal Courts	State Courts
U.S. Supreme Court (1) 9 justices	*High Courts* (52) Generally called the state Supreme Court; Texas and Oklahoma have double high courts, for criminal and civil appeals
U.S. Courts of Appeals (11) 97 judges	*Intermediate Courts of Appeal* (15) May be called appellate court, superior court, or the like
U.S. District Courts (94) 400 judges 143 full-time and 350 part-time magistrates	*General Trial Courts* County court; district court; circuit court; superior court, and so forth; also courts of special jurisdiction—divorce, probate, juvenile court. These are courts of record (i.e., they establish a record that would form the basis of any appeal).
	Inferior or Petty Trial Courts Municipal court; traffic court; justice of the peace; night court; small claims court; commissioner's court; magistrate court

*Figures as of February 1976.
Arrows indicate appeal channels; a solid line indicates a right of appeal, and a dotted line indicates judicial discretion to grant appeal or review if judges so desire.

tem to invoke. This choice may have practical consequences for one side or the other. Different courts have been shown to have different records in support of certain points of view involving management versus labor, wife versus husband, government versus opposition, and so forth. The first decision in many lawsuits must therefore be the choice of federal or state court if both have jurisdiction, and then the choice of a particular court within the system if such an option exists. In criminal law, the number of actions covered by more than one jurisdiction is smaller than in civil law, but a single act can violate both federal and state law. Prosecutors must then decide, if both are interested, who will undertake prosecution first, following certain rules of procedure. The defense may also attempt to relocate the case by having it removed to another court on grounds of local prejudice or bias on the part of the judge. In the Angela

Davis trial, several such motions were made and granted. Where prosecution in one system fails and a charge is possible in the other system, the defendant may have to stand trial again. The Fifth Amendment prohibits *double jeopardy*—retrial on the same charge after an acquittal. Originally this applied only to the federal government, and many states did not follow the rule. In 1969 the Supreme Court ruled that the states were included in the prohibition. However, the Court has not interpreted trial in both a state and a federal court as constituting double jeopardy.

STATE COURTS

The state systems vary widely in organization, depending upon the size, social environment, and wealth of the state. All states have a final court of appeal, or supreme court (generally so named). Texas and Oklahoma split these appeals between a criminal and a civil high court. The larger and more urban states have an intermediate level of appellate court as well. The workhorses of the state judicial systems are the petty and trial courts, which are divided according to jurisdiction and powers.

Inferior, or petty trial courts handle minor civil or criminal matters. A small claims court, for instance, hears civil cases in which the value in dispute is less than a certain sum, usually around $500 to $800. A justice of the peace may also have jurisdiction in minor civil cases (generally less than $200) and in cases involving misdemeanors (minor criminal matters), as well as authority to preside over marriages and sentence traffic infractions. Justices of the peace are generally poorly educated and have gained a reputation as "hanging judges"; recent studies have shown conviction rates of nearly 96 percent of cases tried. The association of the JP with an unthinking and rather sleazy kind of justice is regrettable because American society badly needs reputable and attractive minor courts. In many developing countries the need for efficient minor courts has been met by creating lay courts of limited powers (customary courts).

One possibility is to develop the existing local courts into more useful agencies. These courts, such as the small claims courts, are usually headed by those with legal training. Their jurisdiction is limited, but not as severely as that of the JPs. Given careful attention, such courts could fill the gap in judicial services, although many of them now function almost exclusively for the benefit of the advantaged. Landlords and ghetto stores, for instance, may take over the small claims court and turn it into a collection agency. The original purpose of providing a forum for small problems not requiring legal counsel is thus cynically undermined. The absence of the right of appeal from most of these courts makes their failure even more disturbing.

The trials courts of general jurisdiction handle the great bulk of criminal and civil cases in the United States. The exact number each year can only be guessed because most states do not publish collected statistics, but the figure is probably many millions. Only a small number of these cases will ever be appealed or heard by the highest state court. The quality of justice dispensed in the states' general trial courts is therefore crucial for the quality of justice in America. In most of these courts the increase in the number of cases has stretched their capabilities almost to the breaking point. The 1960s were full of the rhetoric of a "war of crime," but now that the smoke has cleared, the battle of the courts—civil or criminal—remains for the 1970s.

FEDERAL COURTS

The federal courts are not yet so overburdened, although certain of these courts may be very busy in comparison with others. The caseload is not as great because there are fewer federal statutes than state laws. At the lowest level, corresponding to the state general trial court, is the district court, where most federal trials originate. Congress established these courts in the Judiciary Act of 1789. Each state has at least one, some as many as four; the number of judges varies from one to twenty-four, according to the workload of each court. Judges are assisted in the preliminary stages by federal magistrates. The total workload of all the federal courts has risen substantially over the years, and Congress may increase the number of courts and judges.

Above the district level are the federal appellate courts—the Courts of Appeals (sometimes called circuit courts) and the Supreme Court. The 1789 Judiciary Act established the intermediate courts, each headed by a Supreme Court justice who literally "rode circuit." In 1891 the present system of appeals courts was established. Currently there are ten geographical circuits plus the District of Columbia. The Supreme Court justices have little circuit work now, except that each is responsible for a particular circuit in matters such as granting a stay of execution in that region. Appeals from a district court go to the appellate court for that circuit. The exception is the ruling of a three-judge district court; these are convened when the question is the constitutionality of a federal, state, or local law when an injunction (or court order of restraint or constraint) is sought. An appellate judge will be one of the three, and so the case will go directly to the Supreme Court, if appealed. The Burger Court has been very critical of such cases, preferring that they be heard by state courts where possible. In most cases the decision of the circuit court is the final one; the Supreme Court agrees to hear very few of the cases that come to it.

The United States Supreme Court is primarily the chief appellate court, though it has original jurisdiction (i.e., authority to hear cases not yet tried elsewhere) as well. Most original suits involve a state suing another state, which Court must hear. Suits by a state against the United States, suits by one state against aliens or citizens of another state, and those involving ambassadors and other diplomatic personnel may also originate here, but the lower courts may hear them first. Since the founding of the Supreme Court only a hundred-odd original suits have been decided. Most of the Court's work involves reviewing state and local cases or resolving appeals from federal decisions. Litigants from either state or federal courts may request the Court to review any case, i.e., may request a "writ of certiorari," and the Court has discretion to grant or refuse the request. Theoretically, there is appeal by right when a federal statute or state law has been declared in conflict with federal law, a treaty, or the Constitution, or when a state law has been upheld against such a challenge. Yet the Court has many technical grounds on which to refuse a hearing. It may find that the federal question raised is not "substantial" or was not raised early enough in the proceedings, or it may call the entire issue a "political question" that should be left to the other branches (the "hot potato rule"). Such a political question may become a judicial question when the Court is ready. For example, the Court refused to hear cases involving the apportionment of state and federal legislative districts for many years and then suddenly issued rulings on these points. The constitutionality of American involvement in Vietnam, on the other hand, is a matter that the Court is still reluctant to touch.

Congress has also established a group of special courts through its legislative authority. The Court of Military Appeals, head of the military judicial system, and the Tax Court are two such special courts. All of these courts were created primarily to administer certain specified laws. Their decisions are as much law as those of the regular courts. (Because these specialty courts were created under the legislative authority of Article I of the Constitution, they are sometimes called "legislative" courts, distinguishing them from the major federal courts, the so-called "constitutional" courts, created by the judicial authority of Article III. With the exception of the Supreme Court, however, all federal courts are legislative in the sense that Congress has created them and may abolish them if it chooses.)

ORGANIZATION OF THE COURTS

State and federal judicial systems are hierarchical in form, but the powers of the higher courts over the lower are rather limited. Depending upon the state, the state supreme court may or may not exercise some supervision over judges, transferring them where needed, or even removing them from the bench for cause. In other states judges are independent of any power except impeachment or defeat in the polling booth.

The decisions of state high courts are binding on the lower courts, but lower courts may resist, and nothing can prevent them from continuing to make decisions that are inconsistent with high court rulings. The upper courts have no enforcement powers of their own. Each court is essentially an entity unto itself. With few exceptions there are no uniform requirements of evidence and procedure, each judge determining the admissibility of evidence, when his or her court will sit, for how long, and so forth.

The Supreme Court was given authority by Congress half a century ago to set federal rules of procedure. Some of its recent rules, however, have been set aside by Congress as actually involving questions of substance, and procedure may vary widely within the general guidelines. For example, twelve of the districts do not follow the practice of the other districts in using a civil jury composed of six members. Higher federal courts have no controls over lower federal courts, other than reversing their decisions; appointment and removal are not within their powers. Even the Supreme Court cannot enforce its decisions, which may be ignored or opposed by force. A classic and much studied example is the ruling against school prayers. In many schools across the country the day still begins with prayer or Bible reading. The opponents of this decision have failed to amend the Constitution to permit such a practice, but it continues despite its present unconstitutionality. Similarly, a very strong minority objects to the decision on the constitutionality of abortions and made it a political issue in the 1976 campaigns. Lower federal courts themselves may ignore current rulings or rehear a remanded case and come to the same conclusion for slightly different reasons. This process may consume many years, as it did in the protracted segregation cases of past decades. When the battle is finally over, the original litigant may have passed the point of benefitting from the decision or even be dead.

The Judiciary: Recruitment and Roles

RECRUITMENT

There are two major ways of selecting judges in the United States—appointment and election. A third involves some combination of these, in which an appointed judge must be approved by the electorate at least once. (A fourth possibility, a career judiciary with special training, is not found in this country.)

Federal judges are all appointed, as spelled out in the Constitution, to serve during "good behavior." This is, effectively, lifetime appointment because impeachment is the only means of removal. Nine federal judges have been impeached and eight others resigned in the face of imminent impeachment; of the thousands who have held office since 1789 only four have actually been removed following impeachment (the last in 1936). In addition, the Constitution provides that their salaries may not be reduced while they serve. Thus, although the judges are chosen by a political process—nomination by the President and confirmation by the Senate— they are relatively isolated from further political pressures once on the bench. Even though Presidents have picked nearly all of their nominees from their own party, and from political persuasions congenial to them, those they have put in office have often surprised—and pained—their sponsors as they grew or changed to meet the requirements and opportunities of the bench. Accidents of history may give one President more appointments than others. Franklin Roosevelt made nine, Richard Nixon four, and Gerald Ford only one appointment. Long after a President leaves office, his judicial appointments, particularly to the Supreme Court, have an impact on the political process. It is clear now, for example, that the most lasting imprint of the Nixon administration will be its Supreme Court appointments (see p. 137 for a discussion of this point).

Critics of lifetime judicial appointment maintain that the practice may result in courts headed by those whose political views no longer reflect a national consensus, and who cannot be held accountable to the electorate. Proponents argue that this judicial independence is necessary to enable judges to rule on controversial matters, particularly constitutional ones, without fearing that they will be unseated by an unpopular decision. The old adage that Supreme Court judges "never die and seldom retire" indicates the problem and a partial solution. If retirement can be encouraged, as it is in the lower federal courts, the worst aspects of lifetime appointment can at least be controlled.

The elected judiciary originated in post-Revolutionary movements for popular control of all branches of government, and it survives in forty-five states. The details of the practice vary: all or only some of the judges may be elected; terms served may be as long as eighteen or as short as four years; candidates may run on partisan or nonpartisan tickets. Adherents claim, as did the originators, that the effect is greater democracy and greater access to the bench by those whose backgrounds are more representative of the population. Opponents point to public apathy about judicial elections, the difficulty and conflict of interest in finding campaign funds, and the possible miscarriages of justice that can result. In some states this debate has led to a composite means of selection, in which the judge is chosen by the executive—possibly in conjunction with the legislature or a special committee of lawyers and interested laymen— and is later confirmed by the electorate. Curiously, despite the longstanding argument over this issue, there has been very little research on the differences between the three methods of selection. What evidence there is indicates that the differences are slight but real. Whether they are elected or appointed, judges are part of the *political* system; a judgeship may be an important piece of patronage for a party or executive.

Whether elected or appointed, judges may take an attitude that is liberal or conservative, strict or loose constructionist, active or passive. Does the judge have a liberal or conservative philosophy of society and politics? When he is confronted with a constitutional question, does he assume that the Constitution must be interpreted flexibly in order to allow political and social change, or does he work on the basis of a literal reading of its words, despite their frustrating generality? Finally, does he think that his role should be to seek out, or to resist, opportunities to exercise policy-making powers? Each judge may show any combination of these inclinations. A liberal is not necessarily an activist judge, nor a conservative a strict constructionist.

ROLES

Judges are increasingly required to be first of all administrators. The judge must oversee his own court, including its physical plant; he may have to draw up its budget and become a lobbyist, seeking the funds and personnel needed. He and his clerks must establish procedures that will allow the court to keep track of cases filed and to keep them moving as smoothly as the course of justice will permit. Where there are a number of judges working in the same court, they must coordinate their activities or the docket will become hopelessly backlogged. Some states, and the federal system, provide management staff to assist in this job, but the judge's responsibility is always fairly substantial.

Second, the judge is a negotiator and an umpire of negotiations. The great majority of cases, civil or criminal, end in settlement without trial; civil litigants agree on a solution, prosecutors offer defendants attractive inducements to plead guilty. The judge may preside over these discussions in his chambers or simply confirm them later. Either way, he is a participant, helping to weed out those cases that do not require a trial to reach a fair settlement from those matters where the facts or law are unclear or positions are too solidly opposed for agreement. This sorting in itself helps to keep the caseload to a manageable level and also contributes to the management of conflict. The oft-discussed problem arises when the pressures of the caseload or the prosecutor's office lead to a settlement when a trial should in fact be held (see the discussion of plea bargaining below).

Third, the judge presides when a trial is needed. In the common law system he is the neutral party or umpire, regulating the combat of the two adversaries in the dispute. When there is no jury, the judge will decide issues of both law and fact, and then determine the civil settlement or the criminal penalty (unless this is specified by law). In jury trials he shares some of his authority. The jury determines the facts and may determine the penalty, with instructions on law from the judge. He will still have considerable control over the jury, through his summing up and his instructions. Under some circumstances judges may alter or set aside a jury decision on penalty or damages.

In both trial and negotiation judges act as law enforcers, applying norms to particular trouble situations. Most decisions have few overt policy implications. Cases begin and end in the trial court, and there is no published opinion other than the decision itself. However, there may be much controversy when such cases are a concealed means of political struggle, as, for instance, when employers seek injunctions against striking employees. Prosecuting attorneys may try to build political records on their successes in obtaining convictions, and judges may also have eyes on the elections. Beyond this, the general role of norm enforcer allows, or compels, enormous discretion. Over the years judges may emphasize certain aspects of the law and neglect others—in essence, making policy. This is, particularly obvious in the different sentencing patterns of judges.

The trial judge may occasionally have opportunities to engage in direct and immediate policy making in his decisions. More often it is the appellate judge (always without jury) who does so. Through interpretation of statutes and of constitutions, assessing claims against the language of the laws, judges can direct public policy in many ways. This may be forced upon the court by the legislature's deliberate vagueness in the language of a statute or by laws that conflict with each other. And regardless of legislative intent or the purpose of the framers, situations arise that were not clearly envisaged in laws or constitutions. By necessity the courts must engage in the development of public policy. The possibilities for such decisions have not been lost on the politically active. Courts have been channels for interest groups seeking to improve their own positions, particularly groups that have found the other branches of government unresponsive, such as civil rights organizations in previous decades or welfare recipients now. Particularly when a great constitutional question is at stake, the political power of the courts rests with their ability to use their policy-making opportunities wisely, thereby serving as the "conscience" of the country.

The Judicial Role of the Executive

The executive is actively involved in the judicial system. The selection of the judges, as we have seen, is one aspect of that participation.

More important, the executive provides policing, prosecution, and punishment—major components of the criminal justic system.

POLICE

The police are in the front line of the criminal justice system. Police work is essentially a local government responsibility. Although state and federal governments maintain some forces, such as highway patrols or narcotics bureaus, the bulk are in municipal departments and sheriffs' offices. Expenditures on police may constitute a quarter or more of a city's budget. These funds are spent under the authority of elected heads of the force (sheriffs), or by police chiefs appointed by the local chief executive. Whether accountable directly to the electorate or not, police chiefs and their departments eventually find themselves held responsible for public order by both the public and politicians.

The first responsibility of the police is to make arrests, primarily as the result of complaints and information from citizens, though the police themselves seek out some crimes, such as vice offenses. Enormous discretion is exercised in the course of police work, in arrests, investigations, and decisions to invoke prosecution. Such discretion makes police work and control an inherently political problem. The executive branch controls these agencies, at least indirectly, because sending in police or federal marshals or altering police procedures is ultimately in the hands of mayors, governors, and Presidents. Thus the enforcement of judicial decisions is an executive power.

Police are also norm enforcers. In their decisions to enforce certain laws severely and ignore or play down others, they give preference to certain norms, which may have definite class overtones. Crimes committed by upper-class whites may go unnoticed while the street crimes committed by lower-class minorities are attacked. The attitude of the public to the entire judicial system may flow from the manner in which police operate.

In addition, the police are often the most visible part of government to the people. Their presence itself symbolizes the maintenance of order. Increasingly the public expects social services from them as well. Police departments are the only public agencies likely to be open twenty-four hours a day, every day of the year. In their workday the police may encounter many requests that are only marginally related to law and order (e.g., finding a lost person, taking a sick person to the emergency ward) and that no other agency is seen capable of handling. In the end such services may contribute to the maintenance of the public peace. Order is more probable when minor difficulties are resolved or minor crises such as family fights prevented from getting out of hand. The quality and quantity of police services is likely to remain an important general political issue on both the national and local levels and a bone of contention within the judicial system, as it has been for centuries.

PROSECUTION

The executive also provides the prosecution in criminal matters. The prosecutor's post may be filled by a general election, even at the level of the state attorney general, or by appointment, as it is in the case of a federal district attorney. The decisions made in departments of justice, or public safety, and prosecutors' offices are, like police decisions, inherently political. Whether to investigate, what charges to bring, how to conduct the trial—all may have substantial political overtones in the immediate case and affect the general direction of law enforcement. The most graphic illustration is the conduct of investigations in the Watergate episode. Here a special prosecutor was appointed, outside normal channels, to insure that partisan pressures would not hinder the investigation of highly placed executive officials, including the former Attorney General and even the President (nominally the superior to federal prosecutors). A struggle to control the special prosecutor's office ensued, ending in the "Saturday Night Massacre" in which the first appointee to that post was fired after a string of resignations by Department of Justice officials who refused to give the order. A massive public protest quickly led to the appointment of another special prosecutor with guaranteed independence. There have been subsequent proposals for legislation establishing special prosecutors in cases where executive control of prosecution raises problems. (This is not a new issue; during the Truman administration a special investigator became entangled in controversy and was dismissed, to public outcry.)

PRISONS

Prisons and jails, and other correctional services, are another major responsibility of the executive branch. Once sentenced a convicted defendant is no longer under the control of a judge. Probation officers supervise those not sent to prison (although revocation of probation usually requires another hearing). Prisons and jails are operated by executive agencies at various levels. Release is determined by parole boards appointed by state or federal executives. The conditions in the nation's penal systems are under judicial supervision to some extent. Some prisons and jails, including the entire prison systems of Arkansas and Alabama, have been found to be so barbarous as to constitute cruel and unusual punishment, forbidden by the Eighth Amendment. The main remedy available to judges is to stop sending people to the prisons or to order them closed unless reforms are made. It is then up to the board of corrections and the legislature to act. Some reform, notably in Alabama, has been achieved in this way. However, no prison has yet been closed by judicial action, and the daily operation of the penal system, whether punitive or rehabilitative, remains outside normal judicial oversight. Public attitudes, including fear of crime, will largely determine the character of the penal system.

The Legislative Underpinning of the Judicial System

The legislature's primary role is—with executive approval—to determine the statutes by which most courts operate, thereby providing both the structure and the tools of judicial action. On the federal level Congress determines how many federal courts there will be, other than the Supreme Court. It may create new levels of courts or special courts as it wishes. Congress determines how many judges there will be. The Supreme Court has had as many as ten and as few as five, although the figure has stood at nine for a century and will probably remain there. Action to raise the number of other federal judges has been pending in Congress for several years without result. In addition, the appellate jurisdiction of the circuit courts or the Supreme Court can be varied, and Congress has done this on occasion, as well as directing that the original jurisdiction of the Supreme Court be shared with lower courts. Congress fixes salaries and other expenses of the judicial system. By 1975 there were almost 10,000 federal court employees, including judges, with a budget of $308 million. (As Chief Justice Warren Burger has pointed out, the entire judicial system costs little more than a C-5A carrier or a new bomber.) Funds and other administrative aspects of agencies and programs affecting the courts, such as the Justice Department, the Law Enforcement Assistance Administration, or the border patrol, must also be provided by Congress. These executive agencies may spend far more than the courts; the Justice Department budget, for example, was over $2 billion in 1975.

Similar comments apply to funding and structuring at the state level. Although some state legislatures have delegated some of their power of control to the judiciary, this power can always be revoked.

The Role of the Public: Lawyers and Laymen

The public is involved in the judicial process in a number of ways. Most obvious is the role of initiating judicial action. Nearly all civil suits are brought by private citizens who invoke the aid of the state in settling an argument. Most criminal cases also originate in a complaint or information from a private citizen.

LAWYERS

Over the centuries the legal profession has acquired a pervasive role in the judicial process. The legislatures that make the laws and the executives who enforce them are heavily dominated by lawyers. This has been true throughout the history of the United States and has helped to shape American politics and distinguish it from other nations'.

Lawyers also argue the majority of cases today. Only a lawyer is legally entitled to argue for another person, and it is not yet certain whether a defendant in a criminal trial may insist upon representing himself. The complexities of legal proceedings make counsel a practical necessity, and courts are reluctant to rule otherwise (although there are some courts, including most of the inferior trial courts, where lawyers are not often present and may even be barred). Recent Supreme Court decisions have expanded the right to counsel in criminal cases to include any case that might result in a prison term, no matter how brief. The government must now provide a lawyer for those who cannot afford one in nearly all criminal trials, and the government itself uses a lawyer—the prosecutor—to present its case.

Lawyers fill most of the benches. Even though there is no statutory requirement that judges hold law degrees in the federal system, no federal judge has ever been without one, not even at the Supreme Court level where the decisions are often based as much upon a knowledge of history, society, and politics as upon legal technicalities. Rarely are nonlawyers appointed or elected in state systems, except to inferior courts with sharply limited powers.

Lawyers and law schools provide the law reviews which judges often rely on in writing their decisions. Articles in the reviews may have an influence on the outcome of a whole class of cases such as segregation or environmental issues.

OTHER PROFESSIONS

Among the other private persons whose work affects the courts are expert witnesses, such as forensic medicine specialists, process servers who deliver the papers notifying a person of a suit, bail bondsmen, and private detectives. The process servers and bail bondsmen in particular have an important impact. Many instances have been discovered of process servers who earn their fees for delivering papers by discarding them and reporting to the court that they were served. The reasons range from

simple greed to fear of entering some neighborhoods. Whatever the cause, the person sued will automatically lose the case when he does not appear to contest it; the first hint he may have of the situation is when his belongings are repossessed.

Similarly, the bail bondsman's role is critical for those who cannot win release simply on their own recognizance (i.e., standing in the community) or who cannot pay the amount of bail set. The bondsman guarantees the appearance of a defendant in court and pays his bond if he fails to appear. He is not obligated to take anyone as a client. Those who cannot secure the services of a bondsman have to remain in jail for trial. Their chances of winning acquittal are less because they are not free to assist in the preparation of their defense while awaiting trial, and they may plead guilty rather than wait for trial longer than the probable penalty. In addition, the bondsman's usual 10 percent fee is not refundable if the accused does return for trial, whereas the person who posts his own bond is charged a much smaller fee. Private enterprise thus affects both civil and criminal proceedings, and the effect is discriminatory since those who suffer from these practices are mainly persons of low status. In recognition of this inequity, some projects have been set up by both government and foundations to work on the problem of the accused who cannot make bail from his or her own resources but who is likely to return for trial. The largest and most successful project is run by the Vera Institute of Justice in New York. Suit is now pending in several states seeking an end to the professional bonding system as an impediment to the constitutionally protected right to bail.

THE JURY

The Sixth Amendment to the Constitution requires that an accused person have the right to confront any witnesses against him, and to have assistance in obtaining witnesses for his defense. In all federal criminal cases, and in most federal civil cases, he may insist that this confrontation be judged by a jury. In 1968 the Supreme Court interpreted this Sixth Amendment requirement to apply to the states in major criminal cases; all of the states already had some provisions for jury trial. In the federal system these *petit,* or *trial juries,* are composed of twelve persons (as they have been in England for over 1,000 years). In the states they may be as small as six, and the Supreme Court, in a much criticized decision, has ruled that—unlike federal juries—state criminal juries may decide by the opinion of "the preponderance of the jurors" if state law so provides, rather than by a unanimous vote.

A second type of jury, the *grand jury,* may be either an indicting or an investigating body, and may be composed of as few as one or as many as thirty-three persons. Grand juries may sit for up to two years. All federal charges of capital offenses or other "infamous crimes" (felonies) must begin with a grand jury indictment, as required by the Fifth Amendment. (There were thirty-six federal capital crimes when the Supreme Court held in 1972 that the death penalty, as it had been applied, was unconstitutional. Four years later it upheld newly established state death penalties. It is up to Congress to determine how many of the old capital offenses should be restored.) Other federal charges and state offenses are generally brought to court today by the alternative of presenting information to the court and securing a decision from the judge that there is probable cause to hold the accused for trial. Approximately half of the states have grand juries, most of which are used for investigation of various public problems or the conduct of public officials rather than for indictment. They may issue reports that make accusations against specific persons without actually indicting them.

The jury as an institution goes back hundreds of years to the medieval period in English history. It became part of the common law system around 1172 during Henry II's reign and was recognized by the Magna Carta of 1215. From this time come the standard of twelve persons, the idea of a jury of one's peers, and indictment by grand jury. Essentially the jury is a means of admitting the public to the judicial process. The right of the state to try someone is thus filtered through a panel of citizens who decide the fate of the accused. In the beginning this meant nothing more than eliminating control by the king and aristocracy. Today we interpret "jury of one's peers" (not mentioned by the Constitution, which refers only to an impartial jury) as one composed at least in part of persons who have the same or similar social and economic background as the defendant. Both the grand and the petit jury are generally chosen by a jury clerk or committee from the voting lists of the area. Selectors may rely upon friends and prominent persons in the community to suggest names, tending to exclude the lower socioeconomic strata. Certain occupations are usually barred from service—doctors, lawyers, ministers, teachers, nurses, police; in some states a housewife, or any woman, may be automatically excused. Selectors may impose their own prejudices. In a recent Detroit challenge to the jury panel, for example, it was discovered that potential jurors were being excluded on grounds of having long hair, chewing gum, or wearing short skirts. In every case defense and prosecuting attorneys are permitted to excuse a specific number of jurors for no stated reasons, and others if they can excuse for bias. The result is that juries are almost never a representative sample of the population or of the defendant's peer group.

Today the institution of the jury, whether grand or trial, is under attack. Jury trials are disappearing. The pressure of circumstance and criticism has reduced them to about 10 percent of the trials in this country, which still represents almost 90 percent of all jury trials held in the world. There are many who argue that justice would be served by the elimination of the trial jury. Research in jury behavior has shown that members are generally controlled by the judge and strongly disposed to believe that the defendant is probably guilty. The grand jury is being questioned as well, particularly after the heavy-handed use of it during the Nixon administration to harass dissidents and political opponents and the introduction of "use immunity," which allows for forced testimony of an individual before a grand jury (under the threat of imprisonment for contempt if he remains silent) without promising him complete immunity from prosecution. Also assailed are the grand juries' secretive procedures, which forbid the presence of lawyers to assist, their power to issue reports without indictments, and their tendency to surrender their independence to the prosecutor; all are held as proof that they are merely another weapon of the executive against the individual. These problems are real and serious.

Yet the waning of the jury system is in some respects a blow against democracy. The colonial revolutionaries saw the grand jury as a defense against inquisitions, and given proper reform, and the repeal of "use immunity," the grand jury can so serve. Additionally, in many instances grand juries have been the means of eliminating corruption in government through their investigative powers. And finally, the trial jury remains an important defense against bias among court officials. The end of the jury would mean the closing of another avenue of public participation in the political process.

OTHER PUBLICS

Private interest groups and the general public play a role in the courts. Pressure groups may use the courts as a means of influencing public policy. Suits are often brought by individuals with the backing of a group that helps to prepare the case and provide financial support. Where an important question is at stake, the court itself may ask private and public agencies to file briefs on the law or the facts (see chapter 7).

Under the provisions of the Sixth Amendment, which guarantees a public trial, the public at large is entitled to be admitted to a trial, subject only to considerations of seating space. Only in rare instances are closed hearings held, at the discretion of a judge, in matters such as a paternity or divorce suit where publicity is a threat to the parties in the case. Some evidence may be taken in secret if considerations of national security are held at stake.

People attending trials may be friends and relatives of the parties, or they may simply be interested in the courts. Many courtrooms are filled with retired persons who find their days enlivened there. The press covers some routine cases, and the exciting cases draw hordes of reporters. Finally, in some courtrooms there may be observers who work for court reform groups such as the Equal Justice Council in Detroit and gather information on the quality of local justice.

Criminal and Civil Justice: Some Political Problems

There has been more attention to the problem of fairness in criminal trials than in civil trials. The criminal trial by its nature is "out of balance" because the state has inherently more resources than the individual. The Constitution itself contains some provisions for securing a fair trial. Five of the ten amendments in the Bill of Rights are concerned with judicial proceedings and four of those with criminal trials. At first these rights applied in the main only to federal courts, but in the last thirty years the federal courts have been extending them gradually to the states.

When headed by Chief Justice Earl Warren, the Supreme Court was zealous in guarding the rights of accused persons. The major cases dealing with that subject, summarized in Table 7, have had the effect of strengthening the constitutional ban on cruel and unusual punishment and involuntary self-incrimination, and they have extended the rights of the accused to legal counsel and to the confrontation of a hostile witness. The most controversial and misunderstood case by far was *Miranda* v. *Arizona* (1966), which set standards for admissible confessions. The reconstituted Court, now headed by Chief Justice Warren Burger, has acted to restrict the impact of some the Warren Court rulings (see again, Table 7). Although it has upheld the right to counsel in serious criminal cases and the right to a speedy trial, it has overruled many restrictions on admissible evidence, largely negating the *Miranda* decision.

What remains untouched by the Burger Court is the extension to state courts of the due process requirement of the Bill of Rights. But the prohibitions against unreasonable searches and seizures and involuntary self-incrimination have been weakened. To many, the exclusion of incriminating evidence appears to contradict the fact-determining character of a trial. And yet it is critical to understand that the only protection for the innocent and the majority is the guarantee of procedural rights even for the guilty. Unfair prosecutorial and police tactics can only be eliminated by making them unproductive. In this respect there has been a regression in the 1970s.

TABLE 7   Major Supreme Court Rulings Regarding Judicial Proceedings

Case	Relevant Amendment	Effect
Mapp v. *Ohio* (1961)	Fourth	Evidence obtained by unreasonable searches and seizures inadmissible in all courts
Robinson v. *California* (1962)	Eighth	Constitutional ban on cruel and unusual punishment extended to states
Gideon v. *Wainwright* (1963)	Sixth	Counsel must be provided to indigents in all major cases
Malloy v. *Hogan* (1964) and *Murphy* v. *Waterfront Commission* (1964)	Fifth	Right of no self-incrimination extended to states
Escobeda v. *Illinois* (1964)	Fifth and Sixth	Confessions obtained when no counsel present inadmissible
Pointer v. *Texas* (1965)	Sixth	Defendants in state trials entitled to confront adverse witnesses
Miranda v. *Arizona* (1966)	Fifth and Sixth	Standards for admissible evidence set
Washington v. *Texas* (1967)	Sixth	Defendants must be provided assistance to obtain favorable witnesses
Klopferer v. *North Carolina* (1967)	Sixth	Speedy trial must be guaranteed in all courts
Duncan v. *Louisiana* (1968)	Sixth	Jury trial guaranteed for all major offenses
Benton v. *Maryland* (1969)*	Fifth	Prohibition against double jeopardy extended to states
Harris v. *New York* (1971)	Fifth	Use of inadmissible evidence to impeach the veracity of an accused person allowed

*This and prior decisions are those of the Warren Court.

Case	Relevant Amendment	Effect
Argersinger v. *Illinois* (1972)	Sixth	Counsel must be provided in criminal cases that might result in prison sentences
Strunk v. *U.S.* (1973)	Sixth	Cases must be dismissed if speedy trial denied
U.S. v. *Robinson* (1973)	Fourth	General searches (without warrant) permissible in some cases
Michigan v. *Moseley* (1975)	Fifth and Sixth	Some *Miranda* standards for inadmissible evidence struck down

The rights of criminals are generally not deliberately and cynically violated, although there are exceptions, and heavy caseloads and poor facilities only aggravate the problem. The use of the *Miranda* warnings in particular was rarely complete, according to a number of studies. Police bias against certain groups, whether identified by skin, language, or opinion, has been shown conclusively in studies affirmed by the Presidential Commission on Crime established by Lyndon Johnson. The prosecutor's office may increase this bias when it determines which cases to pursue. The process known as *plea bargaining*, in which a defendant pleads guilty to a lesser crime for a reduced sentence, then begins. Increasing caseloads, which overburden the capacity of the courts, have resulted in this resort to bargaining rather than trial to settle cases, a procedure recognized as legal in several Supreme Court decisions (e.g., *McMann, Brady,* and *Parker*). The guilty win in this process because they are penalized less severely than they should be. Those who suffer are the innocent—both the one who pleads guilty from fear or despair and the community that is subject to the early return of criminals (and possibly also to acts of revenge by those who go to prison unjustly).

The solutions to this problem are not easy. Half of the criminal cases are crimes without victims—involving drunkenness, prostitution, drug abuse, gambling, homosexuality, and the like—and these could be removed from the courts, lessening the pressure on both the courts and the police. More judges and courts could be provided. The penal system could be made truly rehabilitative, rather than trying to provide both revenge and rehabilitation and often failing at both. Social problems that help engender crime seem to be increasing instead of diminishing, and they must be dealt with.

Changes are occurring. For instance, many states, including Maine, have struck the crime of public drunkenness from their books, and the expansion of sexual freedom has eliminated many other offenses. During the 1960s there was great improvement in the criminal justice system. Yet the resistance to change remains, and in the mid-1970s the tide is clearly beginning to run in favor of a tougher approach to crime. Large portions of society hold that a particular code of morals must be enforced by the criminal statutes, that judges are lazy and should work harder, that the penal system is already too soft, and that society has no responsibility for crime. This mood is expressed in the Criminal Justice Codification, Revision, and Reform Act now moving through Congress, which would stiffen the penalties for most offenses, restrict many of the rights of the accused won through court action, introduce the idea of an "Official Secrets" Act severely limiting freedom of speech and of the press, and in general increase the powers of the government to spy upon its citizens and force upon them its own views of the correct way of life.

The critics of this legislation are also concerned about crime but propose other solutions. First, they note that the hard-won improvements in standards of fairness in criminal trials are desirable. (That measurable improvements have been made is evident if one compares contemporary standards with those prevalent at the founding of this country, when the accused had no right to counsel, even provided for by himself, capital crimes encompassed such acts as petty thievery, and death by ordeal was common.) Reformers, recognizing that the advances made have been socially beneficial, are also cognizant of the fact that imbalances have developed that endanger both reforms and social order. Concern with the rights of the accused to the exclusion of concern with effective punishment and prevention of crime, and effective restitution to the victim, is self-defeating. Accordingly, there is rising interest in improving the standards of justice for the community. This means, first, that there must be efforts to insure that those who *are* guilty of criminal offenses will be discovered and sentenced swiftly and certainly as well as fairly. Second, it means that experiments in sentencing must be encouraged. In California, Michigan, Florida, and New York, for example, judges have ordered defendants to work in hospitals, schools, and other public agencies. Many states have some provision for compensation to the victims of violent crimes, which could be expanded to include contributions by the offender. Countries around the world have extensive experience with compensation and community service. Great Britain, for instance, has changed its penal laws to allow for such sentences at the discretion of the judge, and New Zealand has a very substantial system of compensation, supported by the state and the offender. When these ideas do not work, (e.g., if the crime committed is serious or violent and the offender is a repeated violator), stronger and punitive sentences to protect the community must be supported. In this way the balance between the rights of the accused and the community, the innocent and the guilty can be maintained.

Civil trials are also in need of reform. In this area, too, great improvements have been made since the days of imprisonment for debts. But the myth persists that civil trials are a match between private parties alone, and the state need not concern itself with assistance, despite the realities of a legal system that clearly favors the advantaged. In matters such as landlord-tenant or creditor-debtor relations, the poor, the minorities, and the uneducated have little chance against the wealth and the corporate power they confront. In matters of public concern the whole community may be at a disadvantage as well (for example, a West Virginia town opposing a strip-mining operation). If legal assistance is not made available, and the laws remain as they are, then the state has lent its weight to one part of the community against the other.

Some halting steps have been taken toward reform, but many states still leave action to private agencies; others provide help only for a few types of cases and only for the most poverty stricken. Public lawyers for the poor have been attacked at both state and federal levels, especially when they have won policy victories in court that overturn government action or law. Strong pressures exist to limit public legal aid to relatively harmless questions such as credit or divorce. The efforts of public interest law firms (a notion arising from the work of Ralph Nader, in part) have been hampered by Internal Revenue Service restrictions on their tax-exempt status.

Ironically, many of these programs themselves contribute to the problem of law and justice. In this century nearly every area of life seems to be covered by legal restriction and regulation, making it nearly impossible to cross the street without a lawyer at one's side to give advice. One critic has called this the problem of "legal pollution." Whatever name it is given, clearly many of the solutions offered to restore balance to the legal system carry with them the necessity for still more legal help. The solution to the problem of civil injustice is not, therefore, a simple one, but the effort is critical if inequality is to be reduced and democracy increased in America.

Suggested Readings

Henry J. Abraham. *The Judicial Process.* New York: Oxford University Press, 1973.*
   A good introduction, with a substantial bibliography. .
———. *The Judiciary: The Supreme Court in the Governmental Process.* Boston: Allyn & Bacon, 1969.*

————. *Justices and Presidents*. New York: Oxford University Press, 1974.*

Theodore L. Becker and Vernon G. Murray, eds. *Government Lawlessless in America*. New York: Oxford University Press, 1971.* The impact of government disregard for law on the political process.

Tom Bethell. "Criminals Belong in Jail." *Washington Monthly*, January 1976.

Paul Chevigny. *Police Power*. Garden City, N.Y.: Anchor, 1969.*

Anthony D'Amato and Robert M. O'Neill. *The Judiciary and Vietnam*. New York: St. Martin's Press, 1972.* Efforts to influence the war policy through the courts.

Leonard Downie. *Justice Denied*. Baltimore: Penguin, 1972.*

Richard E. Ellis. *The Jeffersonian Crisis: Courts and Politics in the Young Republic*. New York: Oxford University Press, 1971. The politics of court reform and the origin of the elected judiciary.

Lawrence M. Friedman. *A History of American Law*. New York: Simon & Schuster, 1973.*

Henry Robert Glick. *Supreme Courts in State Politics: An Investigation of the Judicial Role*. New York: Basic Books, 1971.

Richard Harris. *The Fear of Crime*. New York: Praeger, 1972.* The impact of crime statistics and the congressional response.

————. "The Fifth Amendment." *New Yorker*, April 5, 12, and 19, 1976.

————. "Trial by Jury." *New Yorker*, December 16, 1972.

Morton Hunt. *The Mugging*. New York: Atheneum, 1972.* The criminal justice system in a single case study.

Herbert Jacob. *Justice in America: Courts, Lawyers and the Judicial Process*. 2d ed. Boston: Little, Brown, 1972.*

E. J. Kahn, Jr. "Be Just and Fear Not." *New Yorker*, February 6, 1971.

James R. Klonoski and Robert I. Mendelsohn, eds. *The Politics of Local Justice*. Boston: Little, Brown, 1970.*

Robert Lefcourt, ed. *Law Against the People*. New York: Vintage, 1971.* A radical view of law in America.

Leonard W. Levy. *Against the Law: The Nixon Court and Criminal Justice*. New York: Harper & Row, 1974.*

Anthony Lewis. *Gideon's Trumpet*. New York: Vintage, 1964.* The story of the right to legal counsel in criminal trials.

Norval Morris and Gordon Hawkins. *The Honest Politician's Guide to Crime Control*. Chicago: University of Chicago Press, 1970.*

Albert J. Reiss, Jr. *The Police and the Public*. New Haven: Yale University Press, 1971.*

Jerome Skolnick. *Justice Without Trial: Law Enforcement in Democratic Society*. New York: Wiley, 1967.*

Robert Paul Wolff. *The Rule of Law*. New York: Simon & Schuster, 1971.*

*Available in paperback.

A NOTE ON SUPREME COURT DECISIONS: For a summary of the decisions of the Court in any session, consult one of the major law reviews, such as that of Yale, Harvard, UCLA, Michigan, and so on. Each year these reviews publish an extensive review of the previous term. The decisions of the state court are covered in the law reviews of a state's law schools.

7 INTEREST GROUPS

The System Under Pressure

> Government is instituted for the protection, safety and happiness of the people, and not for the profit, honor, or private interest of any man, family, or class of men.
>
> Mercy Warren

America has been known since the days of Alexis de Tocqueville as a "nation of joiners." Average Americans tend to form voluntary associations for nearly every conceivable purpose, and the United States has nearly every conceivable kind of interest. The associations help to bind individuals in this society in a network of close connections. When group activity takes on political coloration it ties people to the political system as well. This nation is thus made up not only of a great mass of individuals acting on their own politically, but of interest groups that link the citizen and the system and alter the shape of politics in important ways.

Interest Groups Defined

Interest groups are associations of individuals on some common ground. There are two general types of interest groups. *Primary associations* are the most basic, built on characteristics of birth or family background, such as sex, religion, region, and ethnic or racial traits, that generally cannot be changed. In the main such groups are unorganized, and many are unlikely to form the basis of any organization in the future (blondes, Westerners). However, recently some of these groups (notably blacks, Hispanic-Americans, and women) have coalesced to influence political life. Moreover, even unorganized primary groups tend to affect members' perceptions of their political interests.

More important to the political process are the voluntary *secondary associations*—organized groups with which the individual chooses to affiliate (although the choice may be limited, as, for example, membership in a labor union as a prerequisite for certain jobs). Some of these groups may have been formed for mainly political purposes, such as achieving new consumer legislation or opposing nuclear power. Others may undertake political action to obtain their real organizational goals, as do labor unions that support political candidates to protect their main economic purposes. Politically active interest groups are also called *pressure groups.*

Interest groups may be wholly private, such as the Friends of Earth, the American Medical Assocation, the National Women's Political Caucus, the United Mine Workers, or Consolidated Coal. They may also be entirely public. Certain segments of the government, for example, form interests that pressure other segments; state highway bureaus, the National Conference of Cities, and the Pentagon all have reason to influence members of Congress. Some groups are built on both public and private memberships: the highway interest brings together private companies and those local, state, and federal agencies that share their views. Whatever their makeup, nearly all interests are forced into the political arena, seeking to realize their goals by winning concessions from some part of the system. Not all groups are active all of the time, but few are able to function effectively in pursuit of their ends without some political means at some time.

Groups enable people to concentrate their resources on a common purpose perceived to be important enough to invest some energy and some wealth in its promotion. The interest group theory of politics is accordingly based upon an assumption that, other things being equal, interests supported by organization are more likely to succeed than those that are not. Success is likely to depend upon effective organization, the kind of resources that are available to the group, and the efficient use of those resources in the right places.

Assuming this theory to be true for American politics, certain questions are raised. If interests are more successful when organized, we must ask first: What interests are so represented? Who belongs to interest groups, who assumes their leadership, and how do they compete among themselves for resources and membership? Second, we must examine the techniques available to interest groups for influencing the political system and determine which groups are more likely to be able to use these techniques successfully. Finally, the findings on these points raise further questions on the relationship of group power and democratic politics.

Who Joins?

Membership in interest groups in America is widespread, particularly in comparison with some other Western nations. Roughly two-thirds of Americans belong to at least one group, compared to about half the British and German population, less than one-third of Italians, and barely one-fourth of all Mexicans. Ours is a respectable showing, although it looks somewhat different from the other direction: one-third of the population is not represented in any organized group at all. When the total is broken down, more disturbing facts appear. Men are far more likely than women to be part of a group. Occupation, income, education, and age also cause the membership rate to very substantially. Membership increases with age, probably because the older persons become, the more new roles (as worker, parent, and spouse) they must assume, and the more the new personal interests that go with these roles can be advanced by various groups. A rise in standing in occupation, income, and education also produces greater organizational involvement.

Simply stated, membership in groups is related to class. The middle and upper classes are particularly apt to join groups. This tendency holds true in all societies, including the United States. Membership rises dramatically with increased education in this country, from less than half of primary-school leavers to more than three-quarters of those with some postsecondary experience. The same relationship applies to income and to job status, which, taken together, may mean that a teacher is more likely to belong to a group than a janitor, and a well-paid janitor (say a San Francisco custodial worker) is more likely to join than a poorly paid janitor. Membership in more than one group also rises with social class standing.

The strong class bias in representation in interest groups that are politically motivated is less marked here than in some other Western societies. Nevertheless, it remains true that lower-class persons, women, the young, and minorities are likely to be only marginal participants in organizational politics. In addition, many of these people are also on the fringe of electoral politics; they come from the great mass of nonvoters in most instances. Consequently their influence is minimal, and their needs draw little attention unless they riot or in some other way demand a hearing.

Within interest groups there are additional class biases. Active leadership is generally confined to a tiny section of the whole body, drawn from the more advantaged section of the particular group. Very few interest groups are organized on a democratic basis. Those that are so structured have been singled out for study to determine how this occurs and by contrast why it does not occur in most situations. Many political scientists favor the explanation offered by Robert Michels. His "iron law of oligarchy" holds that all groups, regardless of size or purpose, will in the end be dominated by a small elite that may or may not be benign. If this explanation is true (and it is certainly descriptive of most American groups), then the policy of any particular group will be a clearer reflection of the needs of its leading elite than of the general membership. That fact would tend to intensify the effect of inequitable representation of all interests in organized groups.

To state the matter concretely, most existing organizations of the United States—far more than a simple majority—are concerned with advancing the demands of powerful minorities, especially the dominant economic interests. An even greater proportion of those actively engaged in influencing legislation come from the vested economic interests. The "owners" of America—those in control of commerce, manufacturing, and raw materials production—have the overwhelming advantage in the struggle for influence.

Yet another factor undercuts the representational effectiveness of groups. Association with a group may not mean support for its political activity. Membership in a union, for example, may be a requirement for employment and may not indicate any basic political agreement with the leadership. Many people may simply be unaware of the political side of a group's life. Some join when a group is essentially nonpolitical and fail to realize that a shift has later occurred, or they may take up membership in a service organization and pay no attention to its political positions, which may not be widely publicized. Social advantages accruing to membership in certain groups may lead some to join who dissent from the group's main goals. Thus, the early member of the once politically inert Sierra Club, the American Automobile Association driver, and the American Medical Association physician all lend their weight to the environmental, transportation, or health-care views of these groups in political action, whatever they may think or know of them.

The exceptions to this general rule are unipurpose, exclusively political groups such as Common Cause, the John Birch Society, the National Women's Political Caucus, and the People's Lobby. These groups exist only to exert pressure on the political system in support of specific policies (which all members may or may not support completely), or to express generalized discontent with the status quo from a point on the political spectrum. The policy-oriented groups form a part of the normal political system but are committed to fundamental changes in the way it works. Extremist groups fall outside established politics. They are committed to a view of the present system as fundamentally evil and may derive a perverse satisfaction primarily from their failure to achieve their goals, thereby demonstrating that they are right.

In summary, far from providing channels for the public to work for its views, the pressure group in fact serves primarily as a tool for the elites of American social life, and it strengthens whatever influence they may hold as individuals. By acting as leaders of groups, such elites acquire the resources of others—numbers, money, time—to use for their own purposes, consciously or not.

In recent years, a countervailing trend has appeared in the growth of organizations representing—often for the first time—the interests of migrant farm workers, welfare recipients, tenants, poor consumers, ethnic parents in the schools, and the like. On the one hand, these groups do add a new dimension to the world of interest group politics by bringing many people into the political arena who have been completely outside it in the past. On the other hand, such groups are subject to special difficulties, and they are not immune from influence by an elite. Mainstream groups may try to absorb the newly organized once the innovative group has done the arduous work of mobilization, as the Teamsters have crudely done in the battle for the migrant workers organized initially by Cesar Chavez. The leadership of new groups may also turn out to be autocratic. In this process a new and possibly undemocratically minded elite gains access to power on the strength of its constituency—still out in the cold. Despite these dangers the expansion of the universe of pressure groups is an encouraging sign, and the ability of new groups to press their members' needs successfully will be an important factor in strengthening democratic politics.

The Tools of Influence

Any interest group must muster one or more of three basic kinds of resources in order to exert political influence: financial power, numerical strength, or knowledge. The wealthier groups can, of course, rely most heavily upon the first. Even in its reformed condition, American politics still offers a wide space for the flexing of financial muscles. Corrupt use of money is also still extant, and not all such illicit influence is uncovered or punished; even when discovered, the specific policies bought by corruption may not be revoked. The temptation to take the most direct way to the prize is therefore still very strong. Much more reform is needed before corruption ceases to be the "American connection."

The less well-heeled must look to their membership lists for success. A consumers' group may not be able to match corporate moneybags but may carry the day by a cohesive organization that delivers large numbers of votes and hosts of willing and able campaign workers. Mass membership associations thus have some advantages in the contest against wealthy but small interests, at least where votes count, *if* the leadership is able to mobilize this resource.

Pressure groups of both kinds can offer organizational help and special knowledge to government officials in their particular areas. Much of the work of drawing up bills and revising existing regulations is done by interest groups. Often the most basic information about a subject at issue is supplied to government by those who will benefit most from the government's decision. This is particularly true for the economic "haves." State air pollution boards, for example, may base their programs on data supplied by industrial polluters; indeed, as in Texas, some of these boards may be filled with executives of polluting industries, appointed by state officials. And, despite a heating-oil shortage in the winter of 1972–1973, a general fuel crisis in 1974 and early 1977, and the strong probability of further energy problems, the government agencies that set policy in these matters—the Federal Power Commission and the Federal Energy Agency—continue to rely on the "seven sisters" of oil and their gas and coal relatives to tell them even the most basic facts about supply, demand, and cost. Corresponding examples of influence by the "have nots" are very hard to find, although some individual politicians may turn to nonvested interests to help them develop bills on national health care or migrant worker labor rights. The wealthy have an advantage in greater ability to gather substantial amounts of technical information (which may also be carefully concealed from the "have nots"), and they usually find attentive listeners in government. As a result the political system turns a deaf ear to other appeals. However, in a number of fields enthusiastic amateurs have begun to challenge the information monopoly of the great interests, and in areas such as environmental standards and consumer problems they are beginning to have some impact.

The possibility of disruptive action such as a strike, riot, or demonstration may also serve as a powerful weapon for the powerless enabling concessions to be obtained in the absence of money or organizational resources. Making such concessions permanent, however, requires more regular tactics, which helps to explain the essentially temporary benefits of the upheavals of the 1960s.

The Techniques of Influence

The basic resources discussed above may be used for a wide range of activities: marshaling public opinion, promoting campaigns, undertaking

court actions, dispensing legislative advice, endorsing candidates, publicizing opinions, serving on advisory committees, sponsoring testimonial dinners, and so forth. What a group actually does depends partly upon its resources and partly upon the target chosen. The general term for seeking influence is *lobbying*, which refers primarily to action directed at the legislature, although no branch of government is immune. In addition, reform may favor certain forms of influence rather than others. For example, the 1976 campaign laws will certainly promote "independent" advertising on behalf of politicians supporting issues favored by the group that pays the bill, as well as advertisements aimed specifically at issues.

JUDICIAL TECHNIQUES

A matter of public policy is often greatly affected by court action. Pursuing this hope, many groups work through the judicial system when it seems at all responsive. Although such tactics generally require considerable patience, an immediate change in policy is also sometimes possible by persuading a single judge, or a few appellate judges, to make a decision. Such a tactic is often far faster than fighting for legislative consideration. The resources required are much smaller in most instances than those needed in other arenas. Arguing a case in the Supreme Court costs many thousands of dollars but is usually far less costly than campaign expenses of sufficient size to open up dozens of legislative doors. No membership of any great size is needed because judicial decisions are not expected to reflect considerations of majority preference. (Judges, even elected judges, are more independent in this respect than legislators). The primary resource required is information in the form of legal briefs. The dramatic success of men such as Ralph Nader and John Banzhaf in suits against automotive giants and cigarette advertisements on television is testimony to the effectiveness of a single, well-informed, and determined individual.

The tactic by which these men won decisions was the *class action suit,* or test case brought on behalf of a large number of citizens, necessary to "trigger" policy statements from courts. Because a favorable decision in one case may determine general policy, careful choice of the particular suit is critical. Once the right example is picked, it must be supported with persuasive written briefs and oral arguments. Other groups may request, or be invited by the appellate courts, to submit supporting *amicus curiae* (friend of the court) briefs. Such requests on the part of government agencies are automatically honored, but others may be rejected by the court. Additional support may be sought through the law reviews in the months prior to the hearing.

The groups that have initiated test cases or served as *amici curiae* most frequently in recent years have been the NAACP, the American Civil Liberties Union, the AFL-CIO, the American Bar Association, the National Lawyers Guild, veterans groups, educational associations, and the government itself. Certain parties have been exceedingly successful. The NAACP and the government, in particular, have won most of the cases in which they took an interest. It is clear from the opinions handed down that supporting briefs often have a major impact on the formulation of an appellate decision.

Articles in law reviews, particularly those of the prestigious law schools such as Michigan, Harvard, and Yale, can also weigh heavily in the balance of the decision. Judges may openly cite such articles as help-ful, and Supreme Court opinions have done so in one of every four decisions. The landmark desegregation decision *Brown* v. *Board of Educa-tion* (1954) leaned heavily upon scholarly literature, both in law and social science, much of which had been contributed by academics and activists in anticipation of the suit.

Groups that essentially speak for the disadvantaged—civil rights groups, minority movements, homosexual organizations—have also turned to the courts, especially federal courts, in recent years. Such groups are not likely to have the financial resources or the status neces-sary to influence the legislature or the executive. Instead they appeal to the language of the Constitution and to established principles of govern-ment, and the courts often uphold that appeal. The success attained, however, is limited by the necessity of obtaining compliance from the rest of the political system. Judicial lobbying thus may eventually require lobbying in the rest of the political arena, either to influence the choice of judges—the dramatic fights over the proposed appointments of Carswell and Haynsworth to the Supreme Court are examples—or to influence the executive and legislative reaction to judicial rulings.

LEGISLATIVE TECHNIQUES

The most familiar form of pressure in the political arena is that of lobbying to influence legislatures. Like efforts aimed at the judicial sys-tem, legislative pressure is essentially a skilled use of situations and infor-mation, but very different in specifics. Pressure groups seek to mobilize the public to communicate with legislators. They often have staff working part or full time for their interests in city, county, state, or national legislatures. Both of these methods require substantial funds and a large enough membership or a status high enough to be impressive.

The available techniques of direct contact are much more extensive than those permissible in the judicial arena. Judges in the American system are not supposed to discuss cases with interested parties. Their role is thus the most isolated and formally impartial of any American political office, symbolized in the expression "the purple curtain" describing the barriers that courts throw up between themselves and the outside world. Legislators, however, are free to listen to arguments from anyone, and indeed are expected to. The lobbyist may be either a full-time advocate who works for one group or a free lance who takes on work for different groups at different times.

One of a lobbyist's jobs is to develop friendly contacts to assure access to legislators. This is known as "wining and dining." The lobbyist is always ready to take a legislator to lunch, to get tickets to the Superbowl, to provide a trip home in the organization's plane, or to provide a relaxing weekend at the organization's hideaway. Staff members of a committee or legislator's office may also be included because the approval of these people may be critical to the success of a proposal. Such efforts are not necessarily bribery, although they may become so, despite federal and state prohibitions against the acceptance of gifts from lobbyists in exchange for votes. Simply because of proximity and perhaps persuasiveness, legislators come to give more attention and respect to the positions supported by their friends—lobbyists and others. Legislators may scoff at the idea that their vote is bought by trivia such as golfing trips—and they are right; but they cannot deny that such favors win their attention and possibly even their respect.

Former legislators, and their staff, are ideal candidates for lobbying work, as long as their departure was not marked by scandal. Not only do they already know their way around the legislature, but they enjoy established friendships with many of those still in power. Their influence also derives from the fact that they represent the possibility of a job should those in power be defeated and unemployed in the future. Even if legislators can return to their former homes and occupations, many politicians seem to find it difficult to tear themselves away from the scene of their former glory, and large numbers become free-lance or regular lobbyists. In the twenty years after World War II, for instance, twenty-three senators and eighty representatives stayed on in Washington as lobbyists, and others offered their services as consultants on various aspects of politics.

Campaign contributions are still another means by which lobbyists influence legislators. The potential for corruption in this area is great, and it has become the target of criticism and reform. Contributions of any kind are forbidden if they are given specifically in exchange for a particular vote. Corporations and labor unions are also forbidden to contribute directly. These restrictions have easily been evaded over the years by the establishment of educational and promotional committees by industry, business, and labor interests, which channel funds and workers to campaign committees. Indeed, there were 1,000 political action committees in 1976. It is the job of the lobbyist to insure that candidates know who has earned their gratitude. The borderline of legality is often crossed in the process. Those in government may be able to protect themselves. Current examples are the abortive investigation into the illegal contributions distributed over many years through a committee under Senator Hugh Scott, abruptly adjourned by a Senate committee on campaign practices, and the inattention paid to the gifts given to many officials by the lobbyist from South Korea. However, those who make suspicious contributions may not get off so easily. In the case of agencies whose funding is controlled by Congress, an argument over "wining and dining" may end in budget cuts.

A final means by which lobbyists seek to influence legislators is by collecting, dispensing, and publicizing information. Some, in the style of Ralph Nader, may rely solely on this resource. Individuals and groups must know whom to seek out in state capitals and Washington to get things done. They may thus serve as sources of legislative research for lawmakers. This means, for example, compiling the most persuasive—if not actually distorted—set of figures about energy production, health care, foreign reactions to new policies, or the environmental impact of a new nuclear power plant. Individual legislators are unlikely to be provided with staff and funds that can match those of large interests, and what staff they do have is assigned first to service jobs—helping constituents, preparing schedules, and other practical work. Committees in specific legislative areas must divide their staff work among many pending bills, and subcommittees may wind up with only one or two hard-pressed workers for a stack of proposals. Information from the interest groups is accordingly very valuable. In state and local legislatures this outside research can be credited with improving the quality of legislative output. Many such assemblies have virtually no staff at all; for example, Alabama's legislature has four assistants for the entire body. Legislators could increase their staff assistance, but many choose to rely on outside help rather than attracting public disfavor over additional expense, particularly since legislative allocations for their own salaries and expenses have become the target of public anger. As a result, lobbies may shape the laws in the most direct fashion of all—by actually writing them.

EXECUTIVE TECHNIQUES

Within the executive branch itself, individual departments and the Executive Office of the President act as lobbyists themselves, even establishing formal liaison offices with Congress from funds specially appropriated by Congress. Mayors, governors, and other executive heads must also try to build good relations with their legislatures and with Congress. Some executive agencies are among the most powerful lobbies in any level of government. The FBI, the Pentagon, and the police have all had remarkable success in pursuit of their own institutional enrichment. Courts or legislatures have far less corresponding influence on the executive, although particular individuals who head powerful committees may find easy access to an executive agency. In part lack of influence results from a failure of the two branches to give much attention to executive liaison (although Chief Justice Warren Burger has greatly increased the federal judicial efforts in both executive and legislative lobbying).

Because the other branches are not very systematic in lobbying, the way is clear for private groups to influence the executive. Very important and sophisticated tactics have been developed as the scope of executive power and discretion has widened. Again there is a broad range of methods, often greatly favoring the highly placed and the well financed because the threat of the vote is not particularly strong against the executive. Only a few executive officers at any level are directly elected. Many are appointed, and even more secure their jobs through Civil Service and are beyond electoral control. Those who are elected are normally responsible to a much larger constituency than are legislators at the same level. Although this may mean that those elected are less subject to pressure from any one group, it may also mean a greater need for campaign funds than legislators have. Accordingly the problems of contributions and corruption are magnified in the executive branch. In 1973, for example, the press revealed that several Nixon campaign contributions were illegal. Some contributions were returned, but others were not, although they had been illegally obtained by the Nixon reelection committee. The corporate executives accused were subsequently prosecuted and some convicted, while the beneficiaries were generally left untouched. Because the executive is the prosecutor, this branch can protect itself from the law as readily as the legislature can.

The skilled use of information remains the basic means of influencing the executive. Executive work everywhere is built upon processing vast amounts of information for possible legislative proposals or administrative work. Groups that can assist in this data collection can turn government regulation to their aid. For example, the now controversial U.S. Department of Agriculture's decision to permit the sale of hotdogs and similar products that are constructed largely of meat derived from grinding up the bones left after butchering came about as a result of consultations by the Department of Agriculture with meat producers. No consumer groups provided information. It required court action to halt the implementation of this new standard until the opposing evidence could be assessed. The independent regulatory agencies are particularly notorious for having developed information links and ties of friendship with the interests they are supposed to regulate, to the virtual exclusion of the public interests they were established to protect. Shrewd businessmen in the past century—the fabled railroad and steel magnates—understood long before anyone else how easily these departments of the "fourth branch of government" could be captured and still serve as a front for reform, dampening demand for more fundamental change.

SPECIAL TECHNIQUES

In twenty-one states, interest groups can act through the *initiative*, which permits voters to petition for proposals on the ballot, and the *referendum*, which permits the electorate to vote on legislation. A great deal of money and organizational effort may be expended to defeat or to ratify a proposal. The 1976 California proposals on farm labor union rules and the nuclear power initiatives in California, Colorado, and Oregon drew attention from a wide range of permanent and ad hoc groups. Mass membership counts because large numbers of signatures are needed to qualify proposals for the ballot. Money counts too in the effort to win mass public support or to turn it away. Occasionally a group that begins with neither numbers nor finances can gather support by moral appeals—as the farm workers for a time did in California. The work of lobbying itself has been the subject of recent initiatives, which would affect all interest groups. The present reformist mood is likely to produce more battles of this kind.

Reform

One model for reform in lobbying is the initiative passed by California in 1974, which also attempted to regulate and enforce morality in the areas of campaign finance, conflict of interest, and pressure group influence. Twenty other states have also enacted similar but milder legislation in the post-Watergate years. In 1976 Congress finally undertook reform of the toothless and outdated federal lobbying law of 1946. These efforts have arisen from the recognition that existing legislation, which dates to the 1930s in many states, has entirely failed to control the excessive influence of wealth and status, often indistinguishable from outright corruption. Under weak statutes, riddled with loopholes, lobbyists generally did not even have to register, much less carefully report their expenses and activities—whether in regular sessions or in election seasons.

The new laws, which are more stringently drawn, are under the direction of independent commissions, such as the Federal Elections Commission and the California Fair Political Practices Commission. Most of these agencies are too new to have demonstrated how effective they will be in enforcing the new standards fairly and reasonably. The equalization of access to government for the many interest groups in this nation will rest heavily on such effective enforcement in the forty-one states that now require lobbying disclosure. In a related reform forty-eight states through 1976 passed *sunshine laws* requiring open meetings in legislatures and executive agencies. Such laws are designed to make backdoor influence more difficult.

The Impact of Pressure Groups on Politics

The existence of groups attempting to influence politics on a large scale within the American political system has a number of effects. One very important result is the shift of focus from the individual to the group. The overwhelming advantage of organization in winning influence means that participation must be channeled through groups. This may be the only way to organize political life in an urban, mobile, and complex society, but it does alter the basic nature of politics since most of our thinking still tends to be in terms of the individual's role in the political system.

Interest group activity in the United States appears to support the competitive elite model of American politics. This view holds that, unlike some less socially diverse nations, the United States has produced a political elite that is divided among itself on many specific questions and openly shows this division. On the basic organization of the economic and political system, however, most of the elite agree; the dominant groups in the system are working only for incremental changes, such as tax reform, rather than a radical reshaping. This means that all interest groups are essentially moderate and support the politics of "what is" and "slight change."

The system has tended to favor the smaller, more cohesive interests, which have a greater chance to obtain more concrete results than the less cohesive mass groups. Groups that are disadvantaged in our society have had little more than rhetorical rewards for their efforts. The majority of lobbyists are representatives of the corporate interests of the nation, known variously as the oil lobby, highway lobby, energy lobby, dairy lobby, and so forth. These groups are usually coalitions of powerful corporations and government agencies. Their anonymity is neither accidental nor a barrier to success, and they have achieved their aims to a

remarkable degree. Other huge interests such as labor unions are also well served by the system. The public interest groups, which are newer and speak to a whole range of concerns at once, have made gargantuan efforts with little to show in return by way of change. It is primarily single-minded groups such as the National Rifle Association, touching some deep-seated fear, or Common Cause, riding a wave of public disgust with politics, that have joined the small club of high achievers in pressure politics.

The alternate view of the American political system, the pluralist model, regards interest groups not as an elitist means of maintaining control but as a channel for mass influence on leadership, a way of participating that goes beyond voting and so contributes to democracy, despite the upper-class bias. Critics, however, think that the price is too great, that the unrepresentative character of interest groups seriously detracts from democracy in America. Such critics would prefer to see pressure groups brought under stricter controls and made as open to public scrutiny and participation as possible.

Both the elitist and pluralist views may exaggerate the importance of pressure group activities and the extent of their influence. It is unlikely that any single policy in Washington or in the states can be attributed solely to such activities. Accidents of history can help or hinder; one person can overturn the practice of decades if he or she manages to tap latent public support. And political parties play important roles in the formulation of policy. Interest groups accordingly have to compete for influence in the parties and may even try to gain favor in both major parties, but this places a strain on most groups.

Having said this, it is nevertheless the case that interest groups are important forces in American political life. The main thrust of interest group activity, in reinforcing rather than disrupting the status quo, helps explain why American politics is so stable—too stable, some would say. In the coming years their influence will probably rise as a result of the campaign reforms of the mid-1970s—an unintended and little understood effect of these reforms, as we shall see in the next chapter.

Suggested Readings

Stanley D. Bachrack. *The Committee of One Million*. New York: Columbia University Press, 1976. The China lobby.

Lynton K. Caldwell, Lynton R. Hayes, and Isabel M. MacWhirter. *Citizens and the Environment*. Bloomington: Indiana University Press, 1976.

Robert A. Caro. *The Power Broker: Robert Moses and the Fall of New York*. New York:

Random House, 1974.* A fascinating study of one man and the interests that enabled him to control much of New York for more than forty years.

Martha Derthick. *Uncontrollable Spending for Social Services Grants.* Washington: Brookings Institution, 1976. The politics of federal grants.

Murray Edelman. *The Symbolic Uses of Politics.* Urbana: University of Illinois Press, 1967.*

Phillip S. Foner, ed. *We, the Other People: Alternative Declarations of Independence.* Urbana: University of Illinois Press, 1976.* Disadvantaged interests in America.

F. Chris Garcia. *La Causa Politica: A Chicano Politics Reader.* Notre Dame, Ind.: University of Notre Dame Press, 1974.*

David Hapgood. "The Highwaymen." *Washington Monthly,* March 1969. The highway lobby.

Ira Katznelson. *Black Men, White Cities.* Chicago: University of Chicago Press, 1976.* Ethnic politics.

Richard J. Krickus. *Pursuing the American Dream: White Ethnics and the New Populism.* New York: Anchor, 1976.*

Edgar Litt. *Ethnic Politics in America.* Glenview, Ill.: Scott, Foresman, 1970.*

Lester Milbrath. *The Washington Lobbyists.* Chicago: Rand, McNally, 1963.

Jack Newfield and Jeff Greenfield. *A Populist Manifesto.* New York: Paperback Library, 1972.* A critical examination of economic power in the United States.

Michael Novak. *The Rise of the Unmeltable Ethnics.* New York: Macmillan, 1972.

Jeffrey L. Pressman. *Federal Programs and City Politics.* Berkeley: University of California Press, 1975.

Armando B. Rendon. *Chicano Manifesto: The History and Aspirations of the Second Largest Minority in America.* New York: Collier, 1972.*

H. Jon Rosenbaum and Peter C. Sederberg, eds. *Vigilante Politics.* Philadelphia: University of Pennsylvania Press, 1975. The formation of unpredictable new groups in social disorder.

Robert H. Salisbury. *Interest Group Politics in America.* New York: Harper & Row, 1970.

Walter Shapiro. "The Two Party Pork Barrel." *Washington Monthly,* November 1975.

Clement Vose. "Litigation as a Form of Pressure Group Activity." *The Annals of the American Academy of Political and Social Science,* September 1948. The classic analysis.

Harmon Zeigler and Wayne Peak. *Interest Groups in American Society.* Englewood Cliffs, N.J.: Prentice-Hall, 1972.*

Harmon Zeigler. 2nd ed. *Interest Groups in the States.* Boston: Little, Brown, 1965.

*Available in paperback.

POLITICAL PARTIES IN AMERICA

Winning Friends?

If I could not go to heaven but with a party, I would not go
there at all.

Thomas Jefferson

Like American football teams, American political parties are essentially organizations designed for winning. This sharply distinguishes them from many European parties that are primarily concerned with the refinement and presentation of an ideology or political philosophy, and it affects most aspects of the party system in the United States, including organization, campaigning, and policy making. Political parties are also organizations designed to achieve and keep political power for those who control them, and this too affects most aspects of the party system. Quite often these two purposes of American political parties—winning and keeping power—coincide, but they are not the same; when they clash one or the other must give way. The Democratic presidential campaign of 1972 stands as an object lesson on this point. Given a choice between winning the presidency and losing control of the party, the dominant figures in the Democratic party chose, nearly unanimously, to pursue defeat. This dichotomy of purpose lies at the heart of many seeming paradoxes in American party life.

The Establishment of the System

In common with most American political institutions, the present party system developed by trial and error. The framers and early supporters of the Constitution hoped that there would be no parties, or "factions," as they perjoratively described them. They thought the new nation needed consensus and considered parties essentially divisive elements, as Jefferson's comment at the beginning of this chapter illustrates. As a result, the Constitution itself made no mention of parties, and the branches of government were designed to operate in their absence. The inevitable development of parties then led to certain stresses in these constitutional mechanisms, which did not always smoothly adjust to party politics.

In the first national election the Electoral College turned unanimously to George Washington, a charismatic leader whose prestige and influence were so great that he was virtually beyond criticism. Known as "the Greatest of Good Men and the Best of Great Men," Washington stayed in office for two terms and then retired, setting a fortunate precedent for stable and peaceful succession in office—a precedent not enjoyed by many other new nations. While he was President, Washington presided, reluctantly, over the development of the first parties: the Federalists, who coalesced around the leadership of the aristocratic Alexander Hamilton, and the anti-Federalists, or Democratic-Republicans, who looked to the multitalented young Thomas Jefferson for guidance. In many respects these two parties represented the same division of interests that exists in the nation today and that is found in slightly different forms in almost all new nations. The Federalist party was made up of local elites, who tended to be older than their opponents and more conservative, and who were opposed to the expansion of popular participation in the government and were convinced of their "natural" right to rule. The Federalists saw little need for change. The Democratic-Republicans, on the other hand, attracted a large popular following by their more democratic proposals and their opposition to the growing wealth of the manufacturing class. They were ready for radical reforms everywhere, suspicious even of the Constitution and its conservative uses, as they saw it.

The Federalists won the presidency in 1796, but by 1800 the Democratic-Republicans were strong enough to put Jefferson in the White House, and the Federalists began to collapse. They retreated to the northern states and never won control at the national level again; in another decade they were virtually gone. In their alarm and bitterness, some New England Federalists attempted to bring their states to secede, but this first crisis of union was swept away by Democratic-Republican hegemony.

The Democratic-Republicans ruled the nation for a quarter of a century, but the internal cohesion of the party began to crack even during that reign. By 1824 it split into warring factions, which organized in

B.C. by permission of Johnny Hart and Field Enterprises, Inc.

1828 as the Democratic party, under Andrew Jackson, and the National Republican party, under John Quincy Adams. (In 1832 the first of many third parties, known as the Anti-Masons, emerged; its narrow advocacy of a single issue was characteristic of the third parties that would follow it.) The National Republicans joined with some disaffected Jacksonians in 1836 to form the Whig party, which remained until 1856 as the second major party. It adopted, in less arrogant fashion, many of the conservative attitudes of the Federalists. The Whigs lacked a strong leader, and the growing tensions of the slavery issue eventually tore the party apart. The Democrats were also divided on this question and finally turned against their Jeffersonian heritage when the southern wing took control and attracted the majority of Whigs to the party as well. The turmoil over slavery gave birth to the Republican party, composed of disaffected Democrats in the North, the abolitionist movement, the small Free Soil party, and the Whig progressives. In 1856 the party nominated its first presidential candidate, and in 1860 it put Abraham Lincoln in the White House, while the Democrats staggered under the first of many self-inflicted defeats. The major lines of party competition were now drawn. Republicans and Democrats would dominate political life for the next century and beyond.

The Civil War left a mark on the two parties and created many of the difficulties of twentieth-century politics. The assumption by the Democrats of the slaveholder's heritage clashed with the liberal ideals of both Jefferson and Jackson (although the words and deeds of these two men contained the seeds of this inconsistency). Eventually the party took on a split personality, one character representing the conservative states of the Old Confederacy and the other, the more liberal and urban North. Republicans too were divided. Their role as the saviors of the Union and emancipators of the slaves gave them an image of liberality that fitted poorly with the Republican record of favoring enormous concentrations of economic and political power in the hands of the great trusts of the late nineteenth century. Urban workers and farmers were represented by neither party. Their grievances produced the Populist movement. The Populist attempt to take over the Democratic party was largely successful in 1896, but they sealed their own fate by nominating the florid William Jennings Bryan, who was to be defeated for the presidency three times. The Populists collapsed after Bryan's first defeat, and the Democrats went into eclipse; the conservatives and southerners were masters of the party again. The Republicans continued to support their business associates, and even the much praised trust busting of Theodore Roosevelt was not a populist, nor even liberal, policy. The election of 1896 marked the end of any enthusiastic participation by the disadvantaged in American politics. Figures for voter turnout show a marked decline after that, continuing to the present day.

The political fortunes of the Union sweep in the Civil War and the subsequent convulsions in the Democratic party gave the Republicans effective control of national politics from 1856 to 1932, with only minor episodes of Democratic resurgence. Then the Republican failure to respond to the Great Depression with more than platitudes led to a substantial realignment of forces across party lines. The minorities and the poor returned to the Democrats, drawn by Franklin D. Roosevelt's more liberally oriented national policy of greater government intervention in economic and social affairs. In turn, the Republicans solidifed their stand as the party of big business and the champion of rugged individualism, entailing minimal government. In an increasingly complex and interdependent world, the Republican view of politics was doomed to minority status. It has controlled only two Congresses since 1932, and in 1977 held only 12 governorships and 5 state legislatures. Additionally, Republican party affiliation has been in continual decline since the New Deal, falling to around 21 percent in 1976.

The rise and fall of the two parties over the past 120 years reflects the fact that there are differences in their basic programs, which the voters perceive and act upon. However, the gap between the two parties' views seems inconsequential to many, in or out of party life, who call for a fundamental restructuring of the parties in order to reflect opinion to the right and the left. Although survey work has shown that the leadership of the two parties differs widely in ideology, activists and officeholders in both are predominately members of the upper social strata, reflected in the similarity of their campaign offerings.

The lack of clear differences between the parties has been heightened by the absence of strong third parties. Since the end of the Civil War there have been only four substantial national challenges by third parties. In 1892 the Populists won 8.5 percent of the votes; Theodore Roosevelt's Progressive (Bull Moose) party took 27.5 percent in 1912; and Robert La Follette's Progressives, 16.5 percent in 1924; more recently, George Wallace's American Independent party drew 13.5 percent of the vote in 1968. (The Dixiecrat party's effort of 1948 was generally limited to the Deep South, and so did not offer a national challenge.) None of these parties lasted long as national organizations, although they—and some of their less successful kin—often managed to achieve some power in local politics. On a national level, their power is best measured by the degree of influence they have had on one or both of the major parties, rather than by officeholding. Cooption, the takeover of principles, is success, but it is also defeat for it means the death of the third party. The alternatives are to die without influence, or to live on the fringe of insignificance. No third party established since the Civil War has been strong enough on its own to compete with the two major parties or to overthrow one of them.

For the two major parties, the lack of third-party competition has meant that the only real electoral threat to either comes from only one party. The process of gradually absorbing the members and aims of some third parties has also produced major parties that are conglomerates of many different interests. Like two conglomerates that control an economic sector, the two parties are able to operate without sharply defining their differences, often cooperating with each other. Voters find themselves offered policies whose main difference may be only the way in which they are packaged and advertised.

Party Systems and Organization

The absence of strong party doctrines, and the failure of the two main parties to enforce conformity even to the vague policies they do support, is known in shorthand form as a lack of party "responsibility," which the much admired European parties do exhibit. The main features of American party systems and organizations have tended to undercut any development toward strict party discipline. Unlike most European parties, the major American parties are decentralized on both national and state levels. The central party organizations—the national committees and the national conventions—have little control. Conventions choose only the presidential and vice-presidential candidates; other national offices—the congressional seats—are filled by candidates nominated by state and local party groups. There may be a broad gulf between the President and those of his party in the Congress. Some observers have described this as a four-party situation, with a congressional and a presidential party in each major party. National party officials, excepting an incumbent President, have no power over party officeholders. They can rarely deny them nomination, and although they do have some funds to disburse, most campaign funds are raised at other levels of the party or by the candidates themselves. Each officeholder is therefore essentially free of national party discipline.

Party responsibility, as a prerequisite to more clearly defined conservative and liberal parties, would require a tightening of this disjointed party structure. In the early 1970s a number of individuals and groups did shift party allegiances, which seemed to point toward greater ideological clarity. For the most part, however, these movements were not accompanied by any greater centralization or party discipline. And in 1976 groups such as labor, which had briefly flirted with the Republicans during the Nixon years, appeared to have returned to the Democrats. Nor did the 1976 contest between Ronald Reagan and Gerald Ford seem to be based on a fundamental ideological change in the Republican party. Politics is still very much a matter of personalities in a context of loose alliances.

These loose party structures reflect the style of popular participation in American parties. Most voters, although associating themselves with one party or the other, do not formally join a party. Such party "identifiers" may either consistently vote for one party or split their vote between the two parties, although voting for one more frequently than the other. A more select group of voters take the trouble to go to the polls in a primary election and are willing to register as supporters of a particular party in those states where this is a requirement for primary voting. These primary voters often influence other people's political opinions. An even smaller group are party activists, some 5 to 10 percent of the adult population, who join a party, work in a particular campaign, or run for office themselves. The party leadership constitutes a minuscule group, drawn from officeholders in the party and incumbents of government office, plus a handful of powerful personal friends and financial backers. The mix of leaders and followers varies from state to state, depending upon the different social, economic, and historical circumstances of each state.

The uniting of party identifiers, primary voters, party activists, and party leaders into one party gives the national party a somewhat disheveled look, to a large extent unavoidable—and unobjectionable—in a very plural society. In addition, each state has a slightly different party system of its own, built on local differences, which gives a base for the continuation of differences in political style and affects the character of political participation in each area.

ONE-PARTY SYSTEMS: CLOSED AND COMPETITIVE

Only a few states in American history have been ruled by single political parties that were not internally competitive. Opposition cannot be outlawed legally, but it can be done informally by men of great power. An example is Huey Long, who ruled the Democratic party in Louisiana with an iron hand in the late 1920s and 1930s and through it the state. Very few people opposed to Long were allowed, or able to take, any strong role in party or government. The Democratic party in Alabama followed a similar pattern in the 1960s under George Wallace. The late Chicago Mayor Richard Daley's Cook County organization is a contemporary urban example. In such a situation persons and groups who would normally be included—or excluded—may be brought into or kept out of the party because of their relationship with the dominant figure. Such a party system is rare in America, partly because it is a basic norm of American politics that competition and opposition are not to be suppressed—at least not openly—and partly because the normal pattern of American politics *is* competition, and uniformity goes against the grain. One-party rule under a single powerful figure resembles the situation in many colonial states after they came to independence under a single charismatic leader.

Although one-party rule under a dominant leader is relatively rare in this country, many American states, by history and by tradition, have been governed almost exclusively by one party, although there is competition within the party. The Democrats in the southern states and the Republicans in New England and parts of the Midwest are examples. The same situation prevails in many urban areas, where the "machine" has been a dominant feature for long periods: Chicago, Memphis and New York's Albany and Tammany Hall stand out. Here the other party may exist largely on paper, for the purpose of receiving patronage from the White House when that party occupies it, and it may or may not campaign for office. In this respect, it is like the closed single-party system, except that in this system genuine opposition—under the umbrella of a single party—is allowed to exist, although it may be tightly controlled.

The primary election is frequently the vehicle for such competition. In some districts only one or two persons compete in the primary, but more commonly a number of candidates run, the winner gaining only a small plurality of the vote. Particularly in the South, where this form of competition has been raised to a fine art, a *runoff election*, in which the top two or three competitors run again in another primary to determine which is the most favored, may be held. This overcomes the deficiency of the first result, in which no clear performance has been shown. The winner, facing minimal opposition in the general election (if any at all) is virtually certain of election. The minority party in such systems succeeds, on the average, less than 20 percent of the time.

The existence of many states and localities with essentially single-party government has helped to produce many oddities in the national parties. People who would normally be members of one party must run for office under the other label if they wish to win; here the purpose of winning supersedes that of maintaining principles. If a person has hopes for national power, he or she may join the local minority—as John Connally did in shifting to the Republicans in Democratic Texas. Otherwise, his or her choice is dictated by the local system.

TWO-PARTY SYSTEMS: DOMINANT AND COMPETITIVE

The majority of American states have two active parties competing with each other. However, many of these come very close to being single-party systems because one party is heavily dominant, winning between 60 and 80 percent of the contests. Thus, many political scientists take the single-party and the two-party dominant cases together and categorize the bulk of party systems in the United States as essentially lacking in competition. Some go even further in claiming this is a deliberate design on the part of party politicians, to retain their control by keeping the appearance of a lively opposition, which they need to justify their own appeals for support. While it is difficult to read motives, this is not an entirely unfair reading of behavior.

The second type of two-party system is the truly competitive one, in which the parties are fairly evenly matched, winning and losing in the 40 to 60 percent rage. Neither can be confident of success nor certain of defeat, and party affiliation need not rest simply upon joining the only game in town. In this situation the ideological lines may be more clearly drawn, and the mix of interest groups in the state can coalesce into natural associations. The larger states, such as California and Illinois, with both urban and rural sectors, industrial and agricultural interests, and highly diversified populations are likely to develop such systems naturally because it is difficult to force strongly plural societies into a single mold. Thus, these systems may not be the most numerous, but the majority of the people live in states where competitive two-party politics exist.

THREE- OR FOUR-PARTY SYSTEMS

These are rare; New York State, with its Liberal and Conservative parties supplementing the Democrats and Republicans, is one of the few examples. The Liberals and Conservatives may support the candidates of the major parties, but they will often nominate their own, and may even elect them. For example, Senator James Buckley won on the Conservative ticket in 1970. In general such an occurrence means that the candidates of the major parties were too similar and so split one segment of the vote, allowing the third-party candidate to gather all the opposition and slip in with a plurality. Thus, when an essentially two-party system was restored in 1976, and Senator Buckley ran as a Republican, he lost.

Third-party candidates may also upset the balance of forces between the major party contenders. For example, a Liberal contender may siphon liberal support from the Democratic runner, electing a Republican in the ensuing split vote. Similar situations may occur nationally as well. In 1968 the combined vote of Nixon's opponents was greater than his own. Because there are no runoff elections nationally to force a majority choice, Nixon won his first term. The problem could surface again. For a time in 1976, for instance, it was feared that third-party candidate Eugene McCarthy might draw enough votes away from Democrat Jimmy Carter in key states to throw the election to Gerald

Ford. The McCarthy challenge failed, but the threat of a third-party siphoning effect remains.

MULTIPLE-PARTY SYSTEMS

There are not many examples of this in the American political system. Some single-party states, such as Florida, have appeared to be multiparty systems in behavior because of the existence of many factions within the single Democratic party. In Europe such systems are commonly associated with coalition government because no single party is strong enough to govern alone, at least not for long. In the European form the various parties are likely to be quite clear-cut in their ideological differences, and often unable to stay very long in a coalition. The closer in beliefs two partners are, the sharper their arguments may be. As a result, governments form and re-form.

One Party, Two Party, Three Party, Four: Choice and Consequences

The two-party system (and its variations) that marks American political life is no doubt a result of history, natural propensity, and accident, but there is also an element of deliberate choice and deliberate efforts to halt the development of third parties. In this the two main parties are united.

THE CHOICE

Various constitutional and statutory arrangements give existing parties the edge over newly forming parties. Preeminent among these arrangements are the single-member districts, found in almost all federal and state electoral systems whether required by the Constitution or not. A system of *single-member districts* means that the membership of a legislature (or court) is chosen from strictly drawn areas, each area electing only one candidate. There can be but one victor and party in each district; no matter how numerous a party may be, if it is spread over several districts, it will lose every one unless it is sufficiently concentrated to win district majorities. The alternative, multimember *proportional representation*, has been used primarily in American cities. In this system, much favored in Europe's multiparty nations, each party receives a portion of the seats being filled, roughly approximate to its percentage of the vote overall. Proportional representation allows a minority to win some recognition and actually to participate in the government. Where this system has been used in the United States, conservatives, socialists, and even communists have won some recognition. In some localities a multimember executive may also reflect a mix of parties if each member is elected separately, although this is not itself proportional representation.

A third party, or an independent candidate, encounters many other obstacles, even in being placed on the ballot. The general practice is to require a new party to obtain the signatures of a percentage of the voters in the last election in order to qualify for official listing on the ballot. If this percentage turns out to be low enough to allow a third party to qualify, the state may then change the necessary percentage. For example, Pennsylvania quadrupled the requirement after the Peace and Freedom party qualified in 1968. Additional requirements may be imposed, such as the stipulation in Utah that names come from at least ten counties, or the Indiana requirement that a satisfactory loyalty oath be sworn (disqualifying both the American party and the Peace and Freedom party, even though the latter copied its oath directly from the state statutes). Only those parties that have elected a President since 1950 are listed in the District of Columbia; no matter how large a vote any other party may have drawn thereafter, it must apply for listing in each new election. Under such stringent (and readily manipulable) standards, it is a remarkable victory for any new party to win a place on the ballot in even one state. The listing of George Wallace in all fifty states in 1968, and Eugene McCarthy in thirty-five in the 1976 election, is a tribute to their determination and support. Money may be a factor as well. Filing fees tend to discourage struggling parties and independents. And the 1974 Federal Election Campaign Act may even have complicated the task of campaign financing for third parties by limiting contributions by individuals and setting certain standards of qualification for public funds (see the discussion at the end of this chapter).

Once the voting begins, a new party often finds that in many states any complaint about the conduct of the polling must go to representatives of the major parties—the legal electoral supervisors. Also, the "winner takes all" system of state by state voting in the Electoral College works against a third-party candidate for the presidency, just as the single-member district does for other elections. A substantial minority vote throughout the country may produce few, if any, Electoral College votes. This is essentially what happened to George Wallace in 1968, and his American Independent party collapsed shortly after that election.

THE CONSEQUENCES

The majority opinion among American political scientists and American politicians is that the extremely disjointed, gangling parties in the dominant two-party system have been beneficial to the nation. One writer describes the major parties as "vast gaudy friendly umbrellas," under which we all may stand. The hypothesis underlying this view is essentially that this arrangement is necessary to the politics of pluralism. The United States is a huge country, with a population representing nearly all the world's nationalities, races, religions, colors, languages, and cultures. Its socioeconomic interests range from billionaires to share-croppers, General Motors to "ma and pa" grocery stores, the "Beautiful People" to the migrant workers. Its huge natural regions are distinguished by separate histories and problems. If all these divisions were to be represented by political parties, the nation itself might become irreparably divided and the central government paralyzed. Instead, the two major parties hold out their umbrellas against the deluge. They cut across sections, socioeconomic interests, racial and national groupings, and by so doing they hold the center. It is true that a great many of the compromises that produce such a broad appeal have been motivated by the desire for office and the associated desire to keep the system going, but this has been the price of union.

The defenders of the present two-party system also point to the fact that the drive to put together a majority has had the (perhaps unintentional) effect of expanding democracy by widening the franchise as politicians sought support from young people, women, illiterates, poor people, and other disadvantaged groups. The right to vote, in turn, has led these groups to other forms of participation and to inclusion in the concerns of politicians and government agencies.

Finally, according to the system's advocates, the long historical development of the two-party system is itself evidence of its legitimacy. Clearly, the American parties became what they are because the American people preferred them that way. They developed over the centuries in response to the felt needs of the times; if they had not been satisfactory, the people would have rejected them in preference for some other scheme. Instead, time and again the people have rejected the alternatives offered by more ideological parties. For 120 years Americans have given nearly all their votes and contributions to the two major parties, an indication that change is not really needed.

Critics of the American party system disagree. For one thing, they see unity at any price as no longer a compelling argument. The Civil War, after all, is over; the Union has been preserved. No one seriously expects another conflict like the Civil War to split the Union, so why should this unlikely prospect justify the continuation of a political oligarchy that is both bland and blind? Critics also point out that the expansion of the franchise has had little to do with the actual parties. The efforts of excluded groups themselves, with assistance from dedicated supporters who believed in the principles of democracy, won the vote for blacks, women, young people, and the District of Columbia.

The strongest argument for the continuation of a two-party system, the argument from tradition, has also come under attack. The parties may have been adequate to the needs of earlier times, critics contend, but the pressures of the late twentieth century are too great to be contained within a nineteenth-century framework. The inability of the parties to present and act on clear alternatives hinders the ability of the political system to cope with the great issues in American life now. The candidacies of Barry Goldwater, George McGovern and Jimmy Carter (and the near miss by Ronald Reagan in 1976) have demonstrated the growing disaffection of the populace with politics as usual, although in themselves these candidacies have not brought about the fundamental changes that are needed. In addition, the dramatic decline of Republican registration to only one-fifth of the electorate has raised serious questions about the future of party competition in the present arrangement of forces.

One final argument against the continuance of the present two-party setup connnects the existing system with the ugly underside of American politics: the demonstrated lack of principle among many politicians, the willingness to exploit fear and prejudice in order to collect votes, the continuing failure to deal with the twin horrors of racism and poverty, the apathy and immaturity of much of the electorate, and the comfortable collusion that tolerates capricious monopoly in government and in the economy, because both parties benefit. The obsession with keeping control and with building a winning coalition sweeps all before it, including the question of "winning for what?"

The solution to the problems pointed out by critics may be either the development of a greater range of parties or the refinement of the present two into responsible liberal and conservative parties. Whichever of the alternatives is chosen, it seems certain that with greater attention to principles, a greater measure of clarity in presenting programs, and the discipline necessary to implement principled programs, the parties could bring the American goal of political freedom and economic welfare closer to fruition. From this perspective the party upheavals since 1964 (the year of the Goldwater candidacy) are evidence of party failure and of public desire for a more representative and directive system.

THE "NEW POLITICS"

In the late 1960s and early 1970s the "new politics" dominated American political commentary, if not American politics. Popular dissatisfaction with politics generated support for dissident candidates, who held virtually nothing in common except opposition to the two major parties—and to their "jointly owned subsidiary," the federal government. Both Eugene McCarthy and George Wallace, for example, attracted wide attention, which resulted in some Electoral College votes for Wallace. The movements for both men, however, were founded in grassroots support for personalities, rather than sustained organizational drives, which made bold talk of a third-party victory in the presidential races totally unrealistic.

Candidates such as McCarthy and Wallace tap a pervasive discontent with present policies and those in control that has developed in the electorate. But such candidates have not been able to channel that discontent to reach their final ends. Most have met resounding defeats, and those defeats may have served to confirm the cynicism of much of the electorate about politics in general, underlined by Watergate and other scandals in the past few years.

The 1976 campaigns perhaps generated some optimism in light of reforms undertaken in the Watergate's aftermath. But although the effects of these reforms is still not entirely clear, it is probably safe to say that increased party responsibility is not developing. The expansion of the primary system, for example, was supposed to encourage more popular participation in government and make parties more responsive to the people. Some interpret the nomination of Jimmy Carter by the Democrats and the near nomination of Ronald Reagan by the Republicans as indicative of the fact that elite groups are losing their control over parties and that the mass of voters are winning influence in politics. But this is too naive a view. The Carter candidacy, at least, illustrated that support by party regulars is still very important in campaigns. It may also be said that to some extent the primary system has opened the door to influence by single-interest groups. Moreover, the influence of the media in directing attention to certain issues or candidates has been increased by the primary system. Thus, the direction of change of this one reform has not been toward party discipline and responsibility.

Party Functions in American Politics

The post-Watergate reforms have not altered the functions that parties have served in politics over the length of this country's existence. The parties act, first, as brokers in the struggle for power, enabling various special interest groups to work together for those common purposes that also serve party needs. In exchange for support, interest groups gain access to those of the party who gain office. In the process of campaigning and in the presentation of ideas when in office, party activists carry out a second function of parties—continuing the political culture and offering the public very generalized "maps" of what happens in politics and why. Party loyalty aids in the task. Loyalty to one or the other party, although decreasing, is still strong in many families and many sections of the country, establishing continuity across generations. Although an individual may change the affiliation of his childhood as the result of later adult experiences, his early political experiences among family and friends—collectively called "political socialization"—help determine how and why he reacts to events as he does; no one can completely escape his childhood. Finally, the most immediate and dramatic function of parties is the recruitment and selection of the successive political leadership of the country.

RECRUITMENT AND SELECTION

The public participates in politics primarily through elections, which fill over 600,000 government posts. For some of the lower offices—uninteresting, underpaid, and powerless—the party is critical in finding candidates and persuading them to run. Keeping as many offices as possible in the right hands helps maintain control over both the party and the political system. More sought after offices do not need the party as recruiting agent, but those who seek them ordinarily turn to a party for campaign assistance; as a result, parties have generally selected those candidates as well. Winning an election as an independent, without the backing of party organization and funds, is rare and difficult. Even a wealthy independent finds that opponents claiming party loyalties and manpower have the advantage in most cases. (Nelson Rockefeller, after all, ran as a Republican as well as a Rockefeller in order to win.) Thus the parties are determinants of political leadership. The public selects its rulers from the alternatives offered by the parties.

Selection of the candidates may be either by primary or convention. Presidential and vice-presidential candidates, of course, are chosen by their parties' national conventions. Many of the delegates to those conventions are selected by primary elections; the remainder are selected by their state and local parties, usually in party meetings at various levels. The primary as noted above, has gained increasing favor as being more representative, but both primaries and conventions are in essence selection by the few for the many. Primary voters are generally drawn from the more active and more highly placed segment of the electorate. A convention or party caucus allows an even smaller group to select the nominees. The individual delegates who are chosen for a convention may be committed to vote for a particular person, or they may be uncommitted—and subject to various persuasive tactics when there is a close contest, such as the 1976 match between Reagan and Ford.

Certain categories of contenders have the advantage in the selection battle. The incumbent who wishes to run again will almost always be renominated, riding on his patronage and the public familiarity with his name. Most of the time he will not be opposed, and he has the resources of his office at hand if he is. In Massachusetts, for example, of the ninety-three incumbent representatives seeking renomination from 1960 to 1974, ninety-one were successful, largely because they were unopposed. Incumbents are reelected more than 90 percent of the time (e.g., only three of the ninety-one renominated representatives in Massachusetts were defeated). An incumbent must suffer an extraordinary fall from favor to lose the confidence of his party or his constituency. Nixon's resignation precipitated many such falls from favor of those who had backed the President on the Judiciary Committee. Perceptive officeholders who foresee an imminent downfall can save face by retiring from office, as Wayne Hays did following page-one sex scandal revelations about him. Only when retirement comes is the selection process normally thrown open to challengers. The parties and the electorate then must weigh the credentials of new competitors—their record in other offices, announced positions, organizing ability, and personal character, as well as their ability to wage a tough campaign if opposition in the general election seems probable.

THE CAMPAIGN AND ITS FUNDING

The major feature of American political campaigns in the last quarter century has been their cost. In Lincoln's first election the parties spent $100,000. In 1952—the last major campaign conducted with little or no television—the two parties spent $140 million, including $11.5 million on the presidential race. In 1972 some $400 million was poured into campaigning. Nixon and McGovern alone spent $94 million, with Nixon outspending McGovern by some $16 million.

The causes of this dramatic escalation in spending may be laid to several fundamental changes since Lincoln's day. Inflation and rising labor costs have contributed. Also, the population increased sevenfold, and a much greater part of it has the right to vote. Campaign techniques to reach this vast new voting public have changed as well. Direct mass mailings cost millions of dollars. The production of political broadcasts and purchase of television time cost much more, roughly a quarter of all expenditures in 1968.

Campaign costs, and the sources that underwrite these costs, came under close scrutiny in the late 1960s and early 1970s. Critics of the prevailing system contended that high costs were restricting the field of potential leaders to the rich and the friends and allies of the rich. The

reason for this, they maintained, was that the public was not involved in significant numbers in the financing of campaigns. Studies showed that only about 10 percent of the voting public—usually political activists—contributed to candidates. Moreover, the donations from this small segment of the population were generally insufficient to run full-scale national campaigns. Thus, more and more, national candidates came to depend upon large contributors to meet the high costs of electioneering.

The financing of the 1972 presidential election bore out the critics' contention. In that year the Republican Committee to Reelect the President (CREEP) collected more than one hundred contributions of $40,000 or more. One of these was a $2-million donation from an insurance tycoon, and other contributions came from executives of at least eighteen firms who used corporate funds illegally. In some cases it appears that the committee may have used duress to secure these "donations" from corporate executives. In other instances (most notably, a case involving a substantial contribution from milk dealers), corporate interests may have given in expectation of public favors later. (Indeed, milk price supports were raised in 1972.) Overall, the efforts of the reelection committee were so successful that the Nixon campaign ended with a surplus, even after financing the criminal acts of the Watergate burglars and their associates.

When the extent of corruption and abuses of power in the 1972 elections came to light, Congress responded by passing the Federal Election Campaign Act of 1974. The intention was to place limits upon spending, to restrict contributions stringently, and to require full reporting of contributions and expenditures. Additionally, the legislation established a fund, financed with income tax check-offs (i.e., one dollar from each taxpayer's taxes if he or she designated it on the tax return), to assist in financing the campaigns of the major presidential contenders; the requirements are so structured as to permit federal financing also of some of the minor candidates.

Reform ran into difficulty in January 1976, when the Supreme Court struck down several portions of the campaign finance law of 1974. The Court upheld spending limitations upon presidential candidates who accepted federal matching funds, but it eliminated ceilings upon the expenditures of congressional candidates, none of whom receives federal money. Moreover, the Court ruled that any candidate might spend as much of his or her own money as desired, and it held that no citizen could be restricted in the amount of money that he might spend to elect a candidate, so long as the expenditures were not coordinated with the candidate or his campaign organization. The overall limits on direct contributions remain: no person may contribute more than $1,000 to a candidate; the amount that a special interest group (such as political action committees formed by businesses, unions, or professional organizations) may contribute is $5,000.

It is likely that the new practices aided Jimmy Carter in winning the 1976 Democratic nomination, but it is too early to evaluate their full impact on the American political system. Possibly, that impact, combined with the newly revitalized system of presidential primaries, will be substantial. On the other hand, there are many ways in which most restrictions can be avoided. If the system of campaign finance and control cannot be rigidly supervised by some public agency, trusted by the public, in place of the generally covert and corruptible vesting of power in private hands, the foundations of the political system will be dangerously weakened. It is up to the public and the politicians who perceive the consequences of the present system to seize the initiative and present alternatives. Much of the political history of the 1970s will be written in the campaign account books.

Suggested Readings

David P. Adamany and George E. Agree. *Political Money: A Strategy for Campaign Financing in America.* Baltimore: Johns Hopkins Press, 1975.

Herbert E. Alexander, ed. *Campaign Money.* New York: Free Press, 1976.* A collection edited by the major student of campaign finances.

Angus Campbell, et al. *The American Voter.* New York: Wiley, 1964.* The major study of voting in America.

William Chambers. *Political Parties in a New Nation.* New York: Oxford University Press, 1963.* The origins of the American system.

Edwin Diamond. *The Tin Kazoo: Television, Politics and the News.* Cambridge, Mass.: M.I.T. Press, 1975.

Elizabeth Drew. "Presidential Campaigning." *New Yorker,* December 1, 1975.

William Flannigan and Nancy Zingale. *The Political Behavior of the American Electorate.* 3rd ed. Boston: Allyn & Bacon, 1975.

Bruce F. Freed. "This Time Everybody's Got a CREEP." *Washington Monthly,* November 1975.

Gerald H. Gaither. *Blacks and the Populist Revolt: Ballots and Bigotry in the New South.* University, Ala.: University of Alabama, 1976.

Arthur T. Hadley. *The Invisible Primary.* Englewood Cliffs, N.J.: Prentice-Hall, 1976.

Richard Harris. "A Fundamental Hoax." *New Yorker,* August 7, 1971.

Walter Karp. *Indispensable Enemies: The Politics of Misrule in America.* Baltimore: Penguin, 1974.* A critical view of the two parties.

William R. Keech and Donald R. Matthews. *The Party's Choice.* Washington: Brookings Institution, 1976.* Selection of candidates.

V.O. Key, Jr. *Politics, Parties, and Pressure Groups.* 5th ed. New York: Crowell, 1967.

————. *The Responsible Electorate.* Cambridge, Mass.: Harvard University Press, 1966.

Everett Carl Ladd, Jr., and Charles D. Hadley. *Transformations of the American Party System.* New York: Norton, 1975.*

Nelson W. Polsby and Aaron Wildavsky. *Presidential Elections: Strategies of American Electoral Politics.* New York: Scribner, 1976.*

Gerald Pomper. *Elections in America: Control and Influence in Democratic Politics.* New York: Dodd, Mead, 1968.* A critical view.

————. *Voter's Choice: Varieties of American Electoral Behavior.* New York: Dodd, Mead, 1975.

Milton Rakove. *Don't Make No Waves, Don't Back No Losers.* Bloomington: Indiana University Press, 1975.* The Daley machine in Chicago.

Austin Ranney. *The Doctrine of Responsible Party Government.* Urbana, Ill.: Illini Books, 1962.*

Kirkpatrick Sale. *Power Shift: The Rise of the Southern Rim and its Challenge to the Eastern Establishment.* New York: Vintage, 1975.*

Walter Shapiro. "The Two Party Pork Barrel." *Washington Monthly,* November 1975.

Frank Sorauf. *Party Politics in America.* Boston: Little, Brown, 1968.*

*Available in paperback.

DEMOCRACY IN AMERICA

Losing?

> Sometimes it is said that man cannot be trusted with the government of himself. Can he then be trusted with the government of others? Or have we found angels in the form of kings to govern them? Let history answer this question.
>
> Thomas Jefferson

Democracy is one of the most elusive concepts in American political history. In the official documents that marked the birth of this nation, the word "democracy" does not appear; instead, the founders used the term "republic," which means the public thing, a society governed by and in the public interest perhaps, but not clearly a people's government. Some years later there was an explosion of democratic sentiment in the age of Andrew Jackson, and since then democracy has come into common use rhetorically, despite much private skepticism.

Democracy literally means rule by the people; in its Greek roots it had overtones of rule by the mob. This original pejorative sense, and the circumstances that shaped it, obviously have little application today. In order to examine our own society and compare it with others, we must look for the contemporary meanings of the term "democracy."

Who Are the People?

Defining democracy as rule by the people is not very helpful unless it is clearly understood who "the people" are, that is, which Americans are entitled to participate in politics. In every society some are excluded from its political life (the polity). The dimensions of exclusion—the grounds on which people are excluded—must affect the dimensions of democracy. The archetype of democracy, the Greek city-state, excluded many inhabitants—slaves, women, and freemen who were not citizens. Even at the height of democratic rule no more than a small minority of the residents were allowed as participants, thus severely restricting the scope of popular government. Other states that are self-proclaimed democracies are also undone by statistics. For example, in the Republic of South Africa, with an ostensibly democratic constitution, some 85 percent of the adult population (mainly of black ancestry) is permanently excluded from the polity, and the methods used for enforcing this exclusion have brought South Africa to the verge of dictatorship and the brink of chaos. One significant measurement of democracy, then, is the proportion of the society that is qualified for political participation.

PARTICIPATION IN AMERICA: THE FORMAL RULES

Political participation refers to a range of activities, but basic to them all is the activity of voting. Various legal and constitutional restrictions on the *franchise*—the right to vote—exist in the United States. The two centuries of our independence have witnessed many changes in these rules, some in the form of constitutional amendments (see Table 8 for a summary of these changes).

The primary responsibility for the determination of the right to vote was given to the states in Article I of the Constitution, and eligibility for federal voting is largely dependent upon qualification for state elections. State property qualifications were the earliest restrictions on the franchise, and these began to fall in the early nineteenth century. One relic of this restriction that carried over into the twentieth century was the requirement that a fee, or poll tax, be paid to register. Generally enforced in the South, this provision effectively disenfranchised the poor, particularly the black. It took national action to kill the poll tax, in the form of the Twenty-fourth Amendment of 1964, which banned it as an impediment to voting in federal elections; two years later the Supreme Court extended the ban to state elections. Only a few special elections in some states, usually involving water boards and other special public agencies, or school board property tax millage, still require property ownership for voter participation. The Supreme Court has ruled several times, most recently in the 1971–1972 term, that such election requirements are not unconstitutional, even if they also include weighted voting on the basis of property size. This judicial view of the franchise might be called "no representation without taxation."

The extension of the franchise to the excluded black population began in the northern states and was eventually accomplished nationally

TABLE 8 Changes in the Franchise, 1789–1976

Qualifications or Exclusions	Present Status
Property	Abolished by state action and the Twenty-fourth Amendment, excepting certain special elections
Race	Abolished by state action and the Fifteenth Amendment
Sex	Abolished by state action and the Nineteenth Amendment
Age	Lowered by state action and by the Twenty-sixth Amendment to eighteen
Residence in Washington	Abolished by the Twenty-third Amendment, for the office of President only
Literacy	Abolished for national offices by the 1970 Voting Rights Act; suspended in some states by the 1965 Voting Rights Act
Citizenship	No change
Length of residence	Limited by the 1970 Voting Rights Act for national offices to thirty days; being reduced by federal and state courts for state elections
Presence at the polls on election day	Not required in some elections if advance notice given for casting absentee ballot
Good character and mental capacity requirements	Suspended in some states by the 1965 Voting Rights Act; others not constitutional
Registration	In effect in most states

after the Civil War with the passage of the Fifteenth Amendment (which applied at the time only to black men). After Reconstruction many southern states adopted restrictive means, such as the poll tax or literacy tests, to deny blacks the franchise. Such devices fell in the civil rights battles of the 1960s. The Voting Rights Act of 1965 forbade literacy tests in those states and counties that had less than half of the adult population registered. Even where they are now permitted, literacy tests do not apply for federal elections under the regulations of the 1970 Voting Rights Act. Most districts now apply no literacy test at all, and they cannot do so to exclude particular groups. The other clear ethnic exclusion, that of Indians, began to disappear in the late nineteenth century, and Indians were given a statutory right to vote in 1924, part of a long-delayed process of granting them full citizenship. By 1948 this process was completed in the main, although Indians living on federal reservations were often not admitted to state political processes.

Half of the population remained completely outside the polity for the first century of American independence. In 1890 Wyoming broke the barrier by granting women the right to vote and a few other states followed. A long struggle then ensued which culminated in the Nineteenth Amendment of 1920, establishing women's suffrage on a national basis.

Further substantive changes extending the franchise came in this century. In 1961 the Twenty-third Amendment granted the residents of the federal capital the right to choose electors in the presidential election (residents of the District of Columbia still have no voting representation in Congress, which continued to run the city itself until 1971.) The 1970 Voting Rights Act, besides abolishing literacy tests, attempted to assert federal control over age, literacy, and residential requirements for all elections. The Supreme Court ruled that it could do so only for federal contests. This left the states with the option of running two sets of polls—one for federal, one for state elections—or changing their own regulations; they chose the latter by ratifying the Twenty-sixth Amendment in 1971 to lower the voting age in all elections to eighteen. At the time of ratification, most states did have residence requirements exceeding thirty days, the new federal limit, and they clung tenaciously to them. Since then, however, some of the longer residence times have been struck down by the federal courts, which are approaching apparent a-greement on sixty days as the maximum time permitted.

A number of other exclusions still exist. Qualified voters absent from their home districts may be prevented from taking part, unless they can comply with absentee ballot provisions—frequently complicated or nonexistent. Americans living overseas, other than those in the military or foreign services, are effectively disenfranchised. Those in jail, even merely awaiting trial, do not qualify as absentees. The insane, the mentally incapable (designated as "idiots" in some states), and convicted felons (except those in California) are also not eligible to vote. Citizenship itself is required, and sometimes a waiting period after attaining citizenship is imposed. Some states enforce a qualification by "good character," which excludes a range of people—from participants in duels to paupers and servicemen dishonorably discharged. Some of these restrictions are controlled by the 1965 Voting Rights Act, and others are palpably unconstitutional even though they remain on the books. Special disqualifications exist in some states for those convicted of political offenses, such as lobbying violations.

The restriction that probably prevents more Americans from voting than any other is the requirement of registration to vote. This practice developed after the Civil War and reached full flower in the early twentieth century, when forty-two states had such a requirement. The practice started because of the rise of corrupt political machines based on electoral fraud. When voters were personally known to poll workers and parties competed more honestly, fraud was not a problem. With the growth in population and changes in social conditions, however, it became necessary to introduce some check on the possibility of multiple voting. Unfortunately, registration, in conjunction with literacy and good character requirements, also facilitated the contraction of the electorate to those approved by the power holders.

Even where fairly applied, registration requirements today constitute an enormous barrier to participation in elections. Almost two-thirds of the population is of voting age—about 140 million people in 1972. At election time only 95 million were registered, a gap of 45 million. Of those 45 million, some 5-10 percent were excluded by the various temporary or permanent disabling factors such as insanity. The remainder did not, or could not, register, and so were not able to participate in choosing their leaders.

Some critics have argued that to elevate the level of participation in American political life, most of the qualifications for voting should be abolished. That raises the question: Which requirements are legitimate and which are an unnecessary impediment to a healthy polity? Regarding some qualifications, there is not much debate. For example, few would argue that a minimum age requirement constitutes a fundamental injury to democracy, and most would agree that the age now established is reasonable. A second common requirement, sanity, seems justified in principle, although greater efforts to safeguard the rights of those whose sanity is questioned is still needed, particularly refinement of the standards for involuntary committal.

Many of the other requirements for voting are less defensible and could be eased or eliminated. They operate primarily as barriers for the less advantaged, and they often disenfranchise permanently for a single mistake, such as a bad conduct discharge or a felony. The California Supreme Court has ruled that denial of the franchise to felons after release is unconstitutional. This practice in other states should also join the discards of history.

Registration is a thorny issue. Given the size of the electorate and the history of party corruption, it is probably necessary. In its present form, however, the system is defective. Few states offer any registration by mail or set up registration booths in easily accessible places. Many states purge a voter from the rolls if he does not vote during some specified period. This practice tends to eliminate those who vote primarily in federal elections and generally works to the disadvantage of Democrats. No state makes election day a holiday, and nearly all elections occur on regular working days. The complexity of most registration procedures also discourages people, especially those who work and are pressed for time or who have little education. Finally, residence requirements for registration disenfranchise a large number of people because ours is a mobile society in which some 20 percent of the population moves every year. Proposals for national mail registration have been consistently defeated for largely partisan reasons. Until such reform is accomplished, the proportion of Americans who form this "government by the people" is likely to remain a national embarrassment.

PARTICIPATION IN AMERICA: THE INFORMAL BARRIERS

Not all of those formally qualified to vote participate to the same extent. The effects of various cultural and political encouragements or discouragements to participation produce substantially higher voter turnouts among certain segments of the population—the better educated, those who have jobs of middle or higher status, those who have jobs at all, men, whites, Republicans, city people, northerners, and older people (up to retirement age). Taken together, the figures for participation are hardly impressive. The highest turnout for a recent presidential election was 64 percent in 1960. The 1976 figures are discouraging by contrast, with only 54 percent voting, the lowest turnout since 1948.

Congressional elections, stripped of presidential glitter, routinely muster only 40 to 50 percent at best. In state and local elections the percentage may slip into the twenties or far below, with rare exceptions where a race is hotly contested on personal or ideological grounds, such as the 1969 Detroit mayoral election that pitted a black man against a white in a closely divided city. These low turnouts in local politics seem paradoxical to those who believe that governments close to the people are the most responsive and the most representative. Given such small interest, local governments are instead more likely to sink into corrupt and oligarchic politics.

Minimal participation, coupled with a depressingly low public support for democratic principles (see pp. 193–194), points to another paradox. Although political rhetoric in the United States strongly supports participation as the source of legitimacy, for both the general system

and for specific governments, a substantial number of Americans never participate in elections at all, and an even greater number participate only in presidential elections. Survey research shows a very low level of knowledge about the system among those who do not vote and a very high degree of alienation from it. Nonvoters believe that the system is unresponsive, that it does not serve their interest, and that it offers no relevant choice of candidates or policies. Backing those beliefs is the reality of their circumstances in life—low-paying jobs or none at all, little education, and low status in general as a result of sex, ethnic background, or age. Cut off from the wider society, most do not even participate indirectly through membership in pressure groups of any kind.

The long-run effects of such a huge group existing outside the polity are unknown. Members might provide a base of support for a home-grown fascism or combine to bring the prevailing middle-class order into sudden chaos. The failure of the system to activate their interest is symptomatic of a deeper failure of representative government. In the short run it may be true, as elite theorists tend to argue, that their entry into politics would upset the system. Sudden increases in participation have sometimes resulted in the defeat of programs for lessening economic inequity or in the election of demagogues. Recognition of these immediate difficulties does not excuse inaction to clear up the underlying problem. We may pay a high price in the future for ignoring the problem of reconnecting alienated citizens to the system now.

PARTICIPATION IN AMERICA: FORMS OF INFLUENCE

Citizens can exercise influence through a variety of channels, most of which flow from the power to elect government officers. There may be direct influence on officials, in campaigns or in office; these are primarily through interest group actions (examined in chapter 7). Electoral participation, based on parties, is a more public channel and, at least potentially, subject to greater public control and encouragement. Roughly three-fifths to two-thirds of the population engage in party politics or interest group activities. Beyond these basic means, individuals may become further involved in the system by encouraging others to vote or join; about one-third of the population, designated as "opinion leaders," participate in this activity. Percentages decline rapidly for greater activism. About one-tenth contribute to campaigns or groups, or engage in sustained political work, and roughly one-twentieth are involved to the extent that they can be called "activists." Only 1 percent or so of the population will ever run for office.

As the percentages drop, a significant class bias emerges. Very few people of low socioeconomic status ever work in campaigns, contribute to a candidate or party, or run for office. Fewer still are elected. Leadership in the United States has become much more representative in this century, but it is still primarily drawn from the middle and upper classes and from among white males. Blacks hold slightly less than 1 percent of elected offices, although they compose 11 percent of the population; women, over half of the population, have roughly the same representation. Other groups as well are inadequately represented. In principle anyone can be elected; in practice this is not so.

Can the People Rule?

From one perspective democracy means simply that the majority of the people consent to their government. In some respects this is too broad a view. Nearly all societies can be so defined since any government may be said to have consent in some sense by merely surviving. A more de-

"Attention out there! We now bring you an opposing viewpoint to a CBS editorial!"

Drawing by Richter; © 1975 The New Yorker Magazine, Inc.

manding definition requires that some form of popular consultation be built into the system, consultation based on choice rather than ratification of a single offering. This is usually accomplished through regular competitive elections. Finally, the determining principle for victory in such competitive elections must be majority rule; minority rule, on whatever grounds, cannot stand as democracy. The analysis of democracy in America accordingly becomes a search for the mechanics of majority rule in determining who will hold power and how it will be used.

THE LIMITS OF MAJORITY RULE

The framers of the Constitution feared tyranny of any kind. Experience with monarchy led them to make the legislature dominant in the system. Experience with virtually unchecked legislative power in the states produced a system of internal and external checks, which in time would become a powerful force against majority rule. The framers feared the tyranny of the majority more than anything else. (As Alexis de Tocqueville later pointed out, this kind of tyranny *is* the most frightening because it is so difficult to perceive and to remove.) As a result they founded a system essentially structured to make majority rule possible, but difficult.

The legislature was split into two houses, partly modeled on the two houses of colonial rule—royal council and colonists' assembly. In addition theories of the time favored a balance of interests, best achieved by representing different interests in different bodies. In the Senate the interest of the states was upheld. Each was to be represented equally, regardless of area or population. As a result the votes of a majority of Senators today may represent only a minority of the population (as little as 15 percent). This can prevent action desired by a majority and can even lead to passage of minority-sponsored legislation. The interest of the people at large was to be upheld in the House of Representatives, apportioned by population. This body can counter the undue influence of the minority in the Senate, but if the House is composed of those primarily representing locally based elites and interests, it may fail to do so. The House itself is not completely representative because each state, no matter how small its population, has one member. Otherwise, according to Supreme Court rulings in the 1960s, districts may not vary significantly in population within a state. The historical superstructure of committees and procedures discussed in chapter 5 operates in both houses as an effective check on majority opinion in many instances.

Because of the Electoral College system, the office of President may also not represent the majority. The apportionment of the College itself by state delegations corresponding to membership in Congress, and the winner-take-all election of delegations, may skew the outcome of the popular vote. On three occasions—for John Quincy Adams in 1824, Rutherford B. Hayes in 1876, and Benjamin Harrison in 1888—the Electoral College has chosen a candidate who actually lost in the popular voting. For thirteen other Presidents elected with less than a popular majority because of multiple candidacies, the College turned pluralities into majorities, even though runoff elections might in some cases have given different results.

In turn, the President chooses the federal judiciary, which is itself not expected to respond to the majority's sentiment. If a majority feel, for example, that abortion is wrong or busing is contrary to reason, that is not binding on the judiciary. The public has no means of removing a federal judge, short of the rare and difficult impeachment process.

State governments, by contrast, are more clearly based on majority rule. As a result of Supreme Court rulings, all state legislatures must apportion both houses on population, rather than by counties or other political divisions. Even though recent decisions have permitted some deviation from numerical equality in one house where related to divisional lines, the ties to majority representation are still maintained. State executives, including sometimes heads of state departments, are also elected directly. Finally, most of the states have an elected judiciary.

Below the state level, majority rule is less strong again. In many of the special districts majority rule is diluted by restrictions on voting. Additionally, the form of many city and county governments offers fused or delegated functions, based on complex systems of districting, appointed boards insulated from popular control, and so on. The impact of the Supreme Court has not yet been felt at the local level.

The failure of majority rule at the local level is particularly important because this is the level at which citizens have the most opportunity to govern themselves. The unrepresentative structures and the low level of participation at this level, however, have often produced corrupt and entrenched oligarchies. People are still attracted to the idea of participation in politics, as shown by recent demands for decentralization of local agencies, the proliferation of block clubs and neighborhood associations, and other proposals promoting greater participation in governing schools, transportation, and other basic aspects of life. Such proposals are sometimes reactionary in purpose, but there is more than that to these demands.

Long ago Thomas Jefferson suggested that one urgent requirement for the success of the American experiment was the provision of some means whereby ordinary citizens could *be* their government as well as simply *choose* their government. He advocated as the basic unit of government a system of wards, which would be linked to the upper levels and partly empowered to choose their membership. Nothing came of this idea. Instead, as the cities increased in size, the boroughs and neighborhoods ceased to have any real political autonomy, and the cities themselves were often stripped of the powers needed for significant control over their conditions. Rural areas simultaneously slid into lethargy. Local governments in all their varieties are badly in need of reform today. This level is the natural locus for direct democracy, and the lack of it here is still a sore point in the system.

THE LIMITS OF MAJORITY OPINION

One other characteristic of American politics that detracts from its representative nature is the difficulty voters encounter in trying to influence policy through casting their ballot. The policy stands of the parties are generally vague, and particular candidates may have very different views. The voter who is issue oriented must rely on campaign statements by individual candidates for information about the policy ideas held by the candidate and his or her party. Campaign statements, however, are often fuzzy, conflicting, and couched in generalities, sometimes by accident, sometimes by design. Even the voter who is shrewd enough to penetrate this smokescreen, perhaps with the aid of past voting records, is unlikely to find a nominee who supports all of his or her own views. More probably, each candidate offers both congenial and displeasing approaches, and the voter must determine which combination is most satisfactory. On occasion a single issue may become prominent enough to drive a voter away from a preferred candidate or party because of disagreement. Many Republicans deserted Barry Goldwater in 1964 because of their fears of his stance on Social Security and foreign policy. Their flight was paralleled in 1972 by that of many Democrats who were frightened of George McGovern's guaranteed income proposal.

Election results can therefore be difficult to interpret, and clear mandates on policy issues are rarely accorded candidates. The vote for Eugene McCarthy in the 1968 New Hampshire primary came from those dissatisfied with Lyndon Johnson's war policy, but some wished to end the war in Vietnam and some wished to press it more vigorously. In 1972 the voters gave Richard Nixon the second largest margin in history but simultaneously increased the number of his opponents in the Congress. Votes may be cast from dissatisfaction with the incumbent, regardless of the views of the challenger; from misunderstanding of either's views; from party loyalty; and from considerations of personality, ethnic identity, good looks, or location on the ballot (with those listed first thought to have an automatic edge). Candidates in such contests can easily feel free to take no stands at all or to present indecisive and inconsistent answers. Once in office, they may take actions opposing the expectations of a large segment of their constituencies. A voter who finds himself thus abandoned on issues may become soured on politics entirely.

The exceptions to this pattern of limited popular influence are the initiative and the referendum, discussed in chapter 7. These devices, as noted previously, are means by which the public can express its opinion on specific issues, even if the legislature, executive, and judiciary are obstinate in refusals to act. They have been most widely used in the West (as in California, where voters have secured 157 initiatives through 1974). Even though poorly written propositions sometimes blur the effectiveness of specific votes, the initiative and referendum stand as unique and valuable contributions to democracy. A California public interest lobby, with the support of Common Cause and Ralph Nader, is undertaking a major campaign to introduce these progressive devices in those states without them, and then at the federal level itself. It is a telling commentary on their own attitudes toward popular sovereignty that governments strongly resist such reforms. It is an equally telling commentary on the state of public trust in government that such reforms seem certain to be enacted in many states, if not in Washington, D.C.

MAJORITY RULE AND MINORITY RIGHTS

Regardless of the degree of majority influence, in a plural nation the problem of minority rights arises. *Plural societies* are composed of at least two groups that differ because of race, religion, nationality, language, or regional subculture. Few such societies have been democratic. Most are ruled by a dominant group or coalition, or alternatively by one determined minority that has a monopoly on the means of force. Both China and Russia are plural societies dominated by one or two large groups; South Africa's plural society is controlled by a white minority, which is itself split between the ruling class who speak Afrikaans and the subordinate class who speak English. Switzerland and Canada are members of the much smaller group of plural democracies. In such democracies minority rights and majority rule are carefully balanced.

The United States is particularly burdened with the problem of minority rights because it is subject to so many kinds of divisions. The framers of the Constitution and the supporters of the Bill of Rights placed many checks on majority rule in order to protect minority rights. These checks, on occasion, have been turned into channels of minority dominance; majority rule, in turn, has been a means of minority suppression. With the disappearance of the ideal of the melting pot in the last decade and the reassertion of difference, the always difficult job of reconciling majority and minority interests has become even more complicated. Issues such as bilingual education, community control of services, and even racial and ethnic separatism will continue to trouble our politics. Such problems are perhaps inevitable in a plural system, but the extent to which pluralist conflict results depends upon the values supported by the political culture that is its environment. What do people in the society know or believe about politics? What kind of support do they give democratic values, and how much emphasis to a confrontation style of minority rights? What kinds of policies result?

Democracy Among the People: The Environment of Politics

In the past two decades political scientists, sociologists, and psychologists have undertaken considerable research on political beliefs, feelings, and values of the various groups that make up our political culture. The discoveries so far are not particularly encouraging for democracy. Abstract statements of political freedom win support from most of the people, as they do in other Western nations such as Great Britain. However, when principles are translated into concrete problems—freedom of speech for atheists or communists, employment of homosexuals in schools, the rights of the accused rapist, the freedom of black families to live next door—support for ideals plummets. (In contrast the citizens of Great Britain respond with concrete support for abstract values.) In general people in positions of political leadership take much more tolerant positions on concrete problems than the average citizen. Even so, a substantial minority, in some cases close to a majority, of the leadership is also intolerant of democratic requirements and of minority rights.

One analyst has labeled these feelings "working-class authoritarianism." The citizen will often take liberal stands on economic matters such as trade unions, but on "noneconomic" issues such as freedom of speech he assumes a rigid posture against those he regards as holding dangerous views, especially those in a position to influence his children. Leaders are able to escape this authoritarianism to some extent because they have benefited from greater education and may have a somewhat happier personal situation: greater income, greater leisure, and greater job satisfaction often translate into a less jaundiced world view. Stated more cynically, leaders have greater personal choice in where they live, work, or send their children to school.

A second disturbing factor in the American political environment is the strong alienation from politics expressed by the majority of the people. The common view of politics is that it is a "dirty" business. A

mother does not dream of her child growing up to be a politician, even though she may think it all right for him or her to aspire to the presidency. The common referent for the government is "it" or "them"; few people speak of the government as something that belongs to them, and even fewer conceive of it as the people themselves. The outcome is a substantial sense of isolation and helplessness. On occasion this can flare into rage, ending in acts of individual destruction or group violence. In this sense a riot is a political act in which the participants are generally responding to some felt need. This latent political fury may be manipulated, but riots do not always require an agitator, and agitators cannot sow anger where the ground is not ready.

The attitudes and values about the political system that form the political culture and subcultures of the United States are passed on to succeeding generations through a process known as *political socialization*. The term refers to the way a society perpetuates itself and its political ideas by teaching those ideas to the young. The key areas of influence in this process are the family, the schools, and the experiences of early adulthood; peer groups also play some role.

Parents and the older children in a family shape the political attitudes of the young from a very early age. The patterns of authority that are established in a family, the attitudes that the parents express toward outward authority, the opinions expressed directly, and the general pattern of the parents' beliefs all form the background for the child's growing perceptions of society and his or her attempts to relate to it. The economic and social standing of the family also contributes to the environment influencing the child's developing political attitudes. By the time the child enters school, he or she has already acquired some knowledge of what the political system is all about and what the "correct" attitude toward politics is. Contacts with other children and their parents have also begun to have an influence.

Political socialization is affected considerably by the education the child receives. Here a major distinction occurs. Those who go through primary school and high school only, particularly in a vocational program, receive a different kind of education and socialization from those who are expected to go on to college, and the difference is generally reinforced by home and peer group experiences. For the group as a whole, public schools rarely offer any serious discussion of political and economic realities. It is an exceptional history course that mentions the blemishes on the American past or the acuteness of its present problems. How many high-school students have discovered the political role of the police in the development of American cities, the ugly history of Japanese-American internment of World War II, or the antilabor Red Scare after World War I, which culminated in the deportation of thousands of aliens and the trial of Sacco and Vanzetti? This lack of information coupled with an often authoritarian relationship between teacher and student leaves students with, at best, an unthinking loyalty to political symbols—the flag, the salute, the national anthem, and the Constitution. Later, if these symbols are challenged, as some in the peace and black-power groups unwisely did with the flag and the anthem, the response may be frighteningly violent. Also, although the right to participate by voting and the duty of each to exercise that right is emphasized in suburban civics classes, the value of participation is not much taught, nor absorbed, in lower-class and minority areas. When a substantial number see political rights as onerous duties, the ideal held by those who fought for an independent republic two centuries ago has been betrayed.

A third period of socialization is the post-high-school years. The college bound today number well over 40 percent of high-school graduates. The rest leave the school system for work, never to return. Many of those headed for college already have more tolerant and questioning attitudes as a result of family background—buttressed by a liberal secondary education—than do their working peers. The university has served generally to widen differences between the two groups by helping students break with the prejudices of their parents and establish their own political perspectives. Although college education has in the past been associated with conservative economic views, partly because college graduates have commanded higher incomes, this is not the conservatism identified as "working class authoritarianism." Thus higher education has traditionally produced a split *within* generations that is as great as any *between* generations.

There are some indications that this standard developmental sequence of political socialization is now breaking down. The rapid spread of college education in many new forms, ferment in the labor force over the nature of work, and the expansion of women's role in political and social life have made the future political environment very unpredictable. For the first time in history more than half of the population will soon be able to go into postsecondary education. Educated or not, working people of all ages are questioning the organization and control of the economy in general and their jobs in particular. Women of all classes are no longer content with supportive and submissive roles.

It is possible of course that all of this ferment will result simply in change without development. College education—conducted in large, impersonal classes, with a vocational emphasis for poorly trained high-school students—may simply turn into four more years of high school endured for higher wage entitlements. Worker control may lead to nothing more than increased leisure time to pursue purely private interests and a further slackening of the work ethic. Women may be content simply to join the system rather than reshaping it. But the trends visible today need not lead in that direction. People may see in education a way of enriching life, may restructure work to enhance human dignity, may seek out new roles in life to expand human possibilities. If social ferment is brewing from these new orientations, then political development of an order in keeping with the spirit of the American Revolution may be forthcoming.

Democracy Among the People:
The Effects of Politics

The interaction of the political culture and the political system itself, in the context of social and economic power, produces policy, the specific actions of government in regulating and directing the distribution of resources, under the broad outlines of general goals. Equal opportunity, full employment, work with dignity, and peace with honor are the goals of government policy making today. The question we must examine here is the extent to which government policy reduces or magnifies social and economic inequities. The answer to that question has a direct bearing on our evaluation of how democratic this nation is.

Distribution of resources may be approached as a political question in two ways. The first perspective is that of poverty in the most basic sense—insufficient food, clothing, and shelter. Such conditions eliminate the possibility of even the most minimal political participation for those who suffer them. There can be little doubt that such poverty exists in America. Senate committees, privately funded researchers, and government statisticians from many executive agencies have all testified in the past decade to the fact that grinding poverty affects millions of people—huge numbers of them children, living in a state of mental and physical retardation as a result. The political system made a partial response to front-page publicity on poverty in America, and the dimensions of poverty were reduced, at least enough to remove it from the immediate concerns of politicians, but not enough to remove it from America, one of the world's most affluent nations. As long as such basic inequality exists—and there are signs that more people are slipping to the poverty level again—the political system itself is crippled in its struggle to become democratic.

The second perspective is that of distribution above the poverty line. Statistics show that income and ownership of the nation's wealth are heavily concentrated in the upper levels of society. In the distribution of income the share of the top 5 percent is equal to that of the bottom 40 percent, and the top 20 percent take nearly eight times what the bottom 20 percent do. Wealth, the ownership of resources, is even more concentrated. The upper one-fifth of families owns more than 80 percent of the nation's wealth, and the bottom one-fifth has none; within the upper tier, less than 1 percent of the population as a whole have as many assets as the entire bottom 70 percent of the nation. These patterns have not altered much since the statistics began to be collected in the 1920s. Income distribution has become slightly more equitable, but the distribution of ownership has become less so, and at an accelerating pace, since World War II.

Government action in the form of taxation has little, if any, impact. Taxes in the United States consume about 30 percent of income, regardless of size. The progressive income tax and the taxes on wealth itself (estate, capital gains, and gift taxes) frequently can be reduced or avoided entirely by the wealthy, with the services of tax experts whose charges are themselves deductible. The government's taxation policy seems to be to set very high nominal rates and then nullify them with loopholes, producing very low effective rates for the "owners" of America. Middle- and low-income wage earners have relatively few tax loopholes that can be used to advantage. In addition there are sales taxes, Social Security payroll deductions, and property taxes that fall more heavily on the vast middle and lower classes than on the rich.

The structure of government benefits reinforces this pattern of inequity. Although the governments of the United States together make transfer payments of $170 billion in programs and payments—in welfare, Social Security, unemployment compensation, food stamp and medicare programs—the net result is not a better distribution of income and wealth. In fact, in making such payments, the governments often give more to those who have more, offsetting the intended effect of better distribution. Government subsidies also tend to defeat this policy objective because subsidy programs greatly benefit the haves (such as farm subsidies that give benefit not to the poorer farmers, but overwhelmingly to the wealthiest few). Additionally, general government services such as education, highway construction and maintenance, and police and fire protection, are of far greater quality in wealthier communities. Poorer communities may have to tax themselves very heavily to provide even minimal services, whereas the accumulated wealth in another neighborhood can support better programs at a lower tax rate.

The distribution of income affects, to a marked degree, the participation of citizens in the polity, their attitude toward politics, and their support for democracy. As long as the distribution of ownership in America is so badly skewed, democratic politics will remain equally limited and shallow. To the extent that government policies support or even encourage economic inequality, they foster political inequality and a nondemocratic political culture. More people today are willing to question policies. In the 1970s, challenges to the discrepancies of public service have been mounted in the courts and the middle class has raised a taxpayer's revolt to which both candidates in 1976 gave recognition. We have not yet answered the question that lies at the root of these specifics: In the perspective of what we would like our political system to be, what is a fair distribution of economic power, and what must we do to get it? When we do arrive at an answer, then we will know how democracy stands in America.

Suggested Readings

Larry L. Berg. *Corruption in the American Political System.* Morristown, N.J.: General Learning Press, 1976.* Historical and contemporary study.

Judith Best. *The Case Against Direct Election of the President.* Ithaca, N.Y.: Cornell University Press, 1975.

Alexander M. Bickel. *The Morality of Consent.* New Haven: Yale University Press, 1975.

Bruce Bliven, Jr. "All-Volunteer Armed Forces." *New Yorker,* November 24 and December 1, 1975.

Taylor Branch. "The Screwing of the Average Man: Government Subsidies: Who Gets the $63 Billion?" *Washington Monthly,* March 1972.

James E. Conyers and Walter L. Wallace. *Black Elected Officials.* New York: Basic Books for Russell Sage, 1976.

Robert Dahl. *Preface to Democratic Theory.* Chicago: University of Chicago Press, 1956.*

Roland Delorme and Raymond McInnis, eds. *Antidemocratic Trends in Twentieth-Century America.* Reading, Mass.: Addison-Wesley, 1969.*

Douglas F. Dowd. *The Twisted Dream.* Cambridge, Mass.: Winthrop, 1974.* An indictment of economic power in America.

Murray Edelman. *The Symbolic Uses of Politics.* Chicago: University of Illinois Press, 1967.*

Richard Goodwin. "Who Runs the Economy?" *Rolling Stone,* 1975. The influence of politics and economics on each other.

Richard Harris. "Freedom of Speech." *New Yorker,* June 17 and 24, 1974.

Robert Hess and Judith Torney. *Development of Political Attitudes in Children.* Garden City, N.Y.: Doubleday, 1968.

Penn Kimball. *The Disconnected.* New York: Columbia University Press, 1972. The nonparticipants in American politics.

Gabriel Kolko. *Wealth and Power in America.* New York: Praeger, 1962. A critical Marxist view.

Ralph M. Kramer. *Participation of the Poor.* Englewood Cliffs, N.J.: Prentice-Hall, 1969.

Andrew Levison. "The Working Class." *New Yorker,* September 2, 1974.

Seymour Martin Lipset. *The First New Nation.* Garden City, N.Y.: Anchor, 1967.* The development of democracy in America.

———. *Political Man.* Garden City, N.Y.: Anchor, 1963.*

Jarol B. Manheim. *Déjà Vu: American Political Problems in Historical Perspective.* New York: St. Martin's Press, 1976.*

———. *The Politics Within.* Englewood Cliffs, N.J.: Prentice-Hall, 1975.

Michael Novak. *The Rise of the Unmeltable Ethnics.* New York: Holt, Rinehart and Winston, 1972.

Richard Parker. *The Myth of the Middle Class.* New York: Liveright, 1972.

H. Jon Rosenbaum and Peter C. Sederberg, eds. *Vigilante Politics.* Philadelphia: University of Pennsylvania Press, 1976.

David C. Saffell. *American Government: Reform in the Post-Watergate Era.* Cambridge, Mass.: Winthrop, 1976.*

E.E. Schattschneider. *The Semi-Sovereign People.* New York: Holt, Rinehart and Winston, 1960.* A classic.

Ira Sharkansky. *The United States: A Study of a Developing Country.* New York: McKay, 1975.* An examination of the United States by areas and a comparison to the Third World.

Paul M. Sniderman. *Personality and Democratic Politics.* Berkeley: University of California Press, 1975.

Philip Stern. *The Rape of the Taxpayer.* New York: Vintage, 1975.*

*Available in paperback.

10 CONCLUSION

Considerations for the Future

> Arbitrary power is like most other things which are very hard, very liable to be broken.
>
> Abigail Adams

From the discussion of the foregoing chapters, it is obvious that the American system has many strengths, but it is equally obvious that there are weaknesses as well. Some of the weaknesses may be dealt with by tinkering with the structures and mechanisms of government. Others may require fundamental changes in the thought and reactions of the people themselves. Still others may be beyond the capability of a political system to eliminate. In an imperfect world it is essential to work for improvement, but futile to expect perfection. Without attempting to judge which weaknesses of the system may be inevitable, we can identify some of the inadequacies that present the greatest difficulties.

Institutional Shortcomings

There is much that can be said about each of the three branches of government. It is painfully obvious that Congress must become more efficient and more courageous. Either would be small improvement without the other. In order to begin to redress the present imbalance of power between the legislative and executive branches, Congress must become more assertive on important matters. In order to accomplish this, it must first equip itself in terms of staff and research resources to place

201

itself more nearly on an equal basis with the executive. All of the government must become more responsive to the people if the system is to retain its democratic basis, and this is especially true of Congress. It is not enough to be responsive, however; Congress also must pay careful attention to its function of assisting in the political education of the nation. This requires careful attention to the fundamentals of political issues and publicity to the results. Unfortunately Congress has tended in many instances to operately as quietly as possible, such as when it works to maintain tax loopholes for the benefit of special interests.

An even greater tendency to restrict the ebb and flow of information is evident in the executive branch. According to some who have been close to Presidents, the presidency provides much more leisure than the popular myth would indicate, and it is less of a "killing" job than often thought. Therefore, even that slim basis for the dangerous isolation of the President from all public contact and review is specious. It is not the Congress alone but also the President and his executive branch that need to provide more information to the public and to be more responsive to the popular will.

Executive isolation reached its peak in the bitterly secretive Nixon administration. It is too early to determine the direction that President Carter's administration will take, but a key point of his campaign was the need for less secrecy in government and more popular participation in governmental processes. Because no President has total control even over the executive branch, and because the real world of governmental administration is often considerably more complicated than might be reflected in a political campaign, the President is faced with a formidable task even if he devotes major attention to the elimination of informational and other barriers. It is interesting, however, that the President of the United States is now on record as favoring a less mystic view of the presidency itself, and that there may now be major efforts to retreat from that product of the tendencies of many decades, the "imperial presidency."

In the judiciary, the dangers are the slowness of the system, the possible impact of political considerations at the expense of justice, and, here also, the tremendous advantage that accrues to those of wealth. The greatest dangers of all are probably those least recognized by the public: the fragility of the courts themselves, of the judicial system, and of constitutional guarantees. Supporting justice when it is unpopular requires courage of the federal judiciary, with its appellate jurisdiction subject to congressional control and its inability to enforce its own decisions. A courageous judge and a much-publicized court case in which justice triumphs over great odds are likely to receive the publicity; the many instances of injustice, large and small, many of them occurring routinely, day in and day out, rarely do. And when they do, who cares?

Among other key institutions, political parties need to be more responsive to the public will. In this instance, as discussed below, much of the fault belongs to the public rather than to the parties themselves. The situation is even more complicated with regard to the institutions of local government. As pointed out previously, many are designed in such a way as to make popular control difficult, if not impossible. Nevertheless, there is more often than not little popular interest even when the public has an opportunity to participate.

Questions of Ethics

Periodically throughout American history the matter of political ethics has become a subject for popular concern; largely as a result of Watergate, we are now in such a period. This attention to ethics may take any of a variety of forms, including consideration of both the personal and the official conduct of officeholders, and matters of general equity such as tax reform. There is more at work here than a simple reaction to the political corruption of Watergate and the accompanying abuses of political power. Modern technology, a disastrous war, and the growth in size and complexity of government as well as other areas of modern life have led to greater feelings of alienation from the system; the belief that all was not well with American politics preceded Watergate. The forces that helped produce the new politics of the 1960s were ready for the new politics of the 1970s; Watergate only underlined the need for purging and humanizing a bloated and arrogant system.

There has always been more emphasis upon strict standards for employees of the executive branch than for members of Congress. Strict laws for years have governed conflicts of interest for members of the bureaucracy, whether career or political appointee. Only recently, however, has Congress even paid lip service to controlling conflicts of interest for its own members. Congressmen routinely voted upon measures in which they had personal interest, such as to subsidize an industry in which they held stock or to favor agricultural subsidies when they owned farms and would profit directly. In fact, the most glaring conflicts of interest were routinely accepted among members of Congress, conflicts that would have been the basis for immediately firing a member of the executive branch, even a civil servant. The creation of ethics committees in Congress was a welcome sign, and even more welcome is the fact that they have begun to function at least in a minimal fashion.

More important than conflicts of interest, however, are the other forms of unethical uses of power such as the use of official authority to work against political opponents. In this category, Congress cannot begin to equal the worst abuses of the executive. Changes in incumbents, and at least a temporary rise in popular attention and concern, have reduced an extraordinary level of abuse of office to a more normal one, but there is still an unresolved crisis here. A nineteenth-century reformer commented despairingly that "the people that sinks to sleep, trusting in politicians . . . for the safety of their liberties, never will have any." Already there are distinct signs that the public is dozing again. Its attention is caught by political events, but often the wrong ones. Matters of personal conduct often unrelated to official functioning are frequently more newsworthy, and certainly more entertaining, than the more abstract yet more important issues of the ethical uses of official authority. The public eagerly reads of President Kennedy's sex life, for example, but few are even aware of really substantive issues.

Questions of ethics in politics are similar to all ethical questions. They can never be answered completely, nor can they produce full agreement. Intelligent and well-informed persons of good will frequently disagree. Even highly technical questions rarely lead to consensus among experts in the field, and in matters of morality each must essentially be his own expert. It is through politics and the political processes that the answers must come, and they must be such as to avoid rigid solutions that cannot be changed to meet changing conditions; principles may be eternal, but practices in a rapidly evolving world cannot be. The function of politics is to select guiding principles and to adjust practices accordingly. At this time, there remain many things that clearly are awry.

What About the Public?

It is all too easy to document the degree to which political apathy and ignorance are prevalent throughout American society. Voter turnout alone is enough to raise danger signals. High voter turnout does not prove that democracy thrives—witness the Soviet Union, where virtually everyone votes—but low turnout is an immediate sign that democratic foundations may be shaky. Having said this, we must warn that very little can be accomplished merely by increasing the percentage of those who cast ballots. Voting is minimal involvement, indeed, and there even may be question whether it makes a difference, at least without some basic reforms. Some may argue, for example, that voting for either candidate in 1964 would have brought continuation of the Vietnam War, and that the same war continued throughout and beyond Richard Nixon's first term even though he had promised to end it speedily. Superficially, such arguments may suggest that it is futile even to vote. In reality, however, they indicate that mere voting is not enough, that concerned citizen involvement considerably beyond the casting of a vote is essential. Both the structure of institutions and the standards of political ethics are now subject to scrutiny, and in each case the basis of the concern regards the distribution of power.

Maldistribution of power is apparent whether the subject under consideration is private power versus the public interest, the power of the affluent versus the poor, the power of mainstream groups versus minorities (especially racial and ethnic minorities), or even the distribution of power within the government itself. Constitutional democracy calls for majority rule, but it sets limits to that rule where it impinges upon minority rights. The balance between majority rule and minority rights is difficult to maintain even in theory. In practice, the majority does at times overstep the boundaries, and conversely there are powerful elite minorities as well who are frequently able to constrict majority rights—perhaps even invisibly. Such distortions of a constitutional democracy are built upon majority failures: lack of concern for either majority or minority rights, lack of knowledge, or lack of concern for politics in general.

The corruptive nature of campaign financing, the power of wealth throughout the system, and the relative powerlessness of the individual citizen are some of the most obvious factors in need of change. One of the answers might evolve from party reform, but the people are the key. The parties, above all other institutions, should be the people's organizations. Both parties have made efforts at reform, but more are necessary. The Republicans historically have tended to be somewhat more democratic in their internal proceedings than have the Democrats, but in the 1972 campaign, the Democrats made a major breakthrough in attempting to reach the grass roots and gain the participation of the "man in the street." The results demonstrated that party reform alone is insufficient. The Democrats held open meetings throughout the country as the first step in delegate selection to the Democratic National Convention; in some wards, because of corrupt party officials, lack of interest, or some other reason there were no attempts to hold meetings (although delegates later appeared from some of the meetings that were not held!). In other wards, the officials were there, but no one else came. Probably the typical ward was one in which a few dozen citizens appeared but in which there were possibly a hundred times that many Democratic voters. This was not caused by lack of publicity; the meetings were announced publicly and well in advance. The situation was the same in 1976, when both parties made similar efforts to build upon grassroots foundations. In such a setting one well organized faction of the party can easily seize control of the

entire mechanism; the Goldwater and McGovern campaigns and sometimes that of Reagan are all cases in point. The lack of interest in public
affairs that this illustrates is one of the strongest indicators that all is not
well with the American political system and that its future may not be
bright.

On the other hand, we may be seeing evidence of new political
concern. Campaign reforms, the growth of the presidential primary system, interest in tax reform, and the continuing development of the new
politics have their hopeful aspects. It is possible that much of the apathy
that has characterized American politics has resulted from a feeling of
powerlessness on the part of the people, and that they may yet realize
their potential for effective political activity and work for changes. The
record of the past is not encouraging; reform movements have blossomed
forth only to dwindle. In many cases, even the reforms that have succeeded have been ironically counterproductive. Nevertheless, the potential exists for popular concern and activity to improve the lot of Americans through political action; the price, however, is not just involvement,
but intelligent and informed involvement.

We may slip back into our bad political habits that have permitted or
encouraged many of our difficulties, or we may be on the verge of meaningful developments. Certainly there have been recent changes. The
party system has been in trouble for some time. Both parties are losing
members, although Carter appears to have reinstated much of the coalition that Franklin Roosevelt created in the years of the depression. The
poor, blacks and other ethnic minorities, labor unions, and intellectuals
formed a potent partnership that dominated American politics for decades. The reforging of the alliance may or may not halt the trend toward
independent voting that for better or worse has influenced the political
system in recent years. If it does, where does that leave the Republican
party, and what are the implications for the two-party system? Whether it
would hinder or encourage party realignment no one can be sure;
whether party realignment would lead to beneficial or detrimental
changes, again, no one can be sure. One can be sure that the reforms that
are necessary will not come if the system reverts to "politics as usual."
The urgent need is to humanize and control power; beyond that, few
things, if any, are certain.

Citizens in a popular government must maintain a sense of vigi-
lance and of responsibility for the political actions of their nation if they
are to prevent the erosion of liberties and halt the decay of popular
institutions. Moreover, citizens must retain a desire for freedom and a
confidence in their ability to govern themselves. Otherwise, the burdens
of freedom will appear too difficult for them to bear. More than thirty

years ago, Erich Fromm wrote, in *Escape from Freedom*, of the manner in which many persons and nations seek the security and certainty of authoritarianism as an escape from the trials and uncertainties of the free life.*

Apathy is not the only threat to constitutional democracy, but it combines with the others to make them even more threatening. Various totalitarian ideologies contend with the ideals of freedom for the affection of the citizens. Some are obvious, some subtle. Frequently the plea of necessity will be sufficient to convince many that they should suffer unnecessary restrictions on their personal and political lives in order to advance national security or to preserve law and order. The plea of special expertise will convince many others that they should not criticize officials because they have better information. Either plea is fundamentally an argument for the subversion of constitutional democracy.

Whither Constitutional Democracy?

Constitutional democracy depends on an enlightened citizenry and a free flow of information to the government, and from and about the government. A major tendency of government is to wish to protect itself from criticism. One of the easiest ways to accomplish this, and one of the ways most destructive to a free society, is to conduct governmental operations in secrecy. Governments that are cut off from criticism tend to become arrogant, and arrogant governments consider themselves justified in treating their citizens as children, rather than as free adults. Thomas Jefferson recognized long ago that a free press was an absolute necessity if free government is to exist, yet today there is relatively little protest when reporters are jailed for refusing to divulge their sources of information.

One danger to constitutional democracy is that the right of the press to criticize as it sees fit, even unfairly, often seems to be a bigger issue than the governmental policies themselves. Many Americans seem to have lost sight of the true function of the news media in a free society. If they perform their functions well, they will inevitably irritate those in power; that is their job, "to comfort the afflicted and afflict the comfortable." All administrations, regardless of party, intention, or persuasion, need constant criticism and overseeing by an unrestricted press to encourage the degree of humility proper to the servants of the public. Unfair, even vicious, criticism, is vastly preferable to too little. No newspaper has ever overthrown a government, but many governments have over-

*New York: Holt, Rinehart & Winston, 1941.

thrown freedom of the press! Regardless of the reason, when there is a dearth of criticism, whether the lack results from apathy, inadequate searching for information, or official intimidation, it is potentially fatal to free and open government. Such considerations led Jefferson to conclude that if forced to choose, he would prefer a free press with no government to a government with no free press.

Constitutional democracy in the United States has withstood many determined assaults. It is now under much more subtle attack than, for example, the attacks from those professing totalitarian ideologies of both the right and the left during the period of the Great Depression. Neither the Communist party, the John Birch Society, the Minutemen, the Weathermen, the Ku Klux Klan, the American Nazis, nor any other extremist group has ever been the major threat to American democracy. The major threat is the insidious encroachment upon democracy in little ways, raising no alarm, destroying by attrition.

Also threatening constitutional democracy is our lack of concern with the language. Advertisers constantly tell us that every product is better than every other; politicians, similarly, more often than not speak with a view toward obtaining emotional reactions rather than seeking to enlighten or educate. George Orwell long ago wrote of the decay of language and of the deleterious effects that linguistic decay has on the quality of political life. Today, it often is difficult to tell if politicians wish to speak the truth or not. They tend to speak in formulas, saying the same things and repeating the same patterns over and over. The hearers have come to expect just this, and, far from being outraged, they accept it as normal. The extraordinary politician who speaks out tends often to offend, to enrage, or to confuse. Many office seekers, both "conservative" and "liberal," appear to believe that the quickest path to office is to repeat the same clichés and to shy away from reasoned and critical analysis. Whether they intend it or not, such speakers are engaging in deception, and often are deceived along with their listeners.

The federal system is built upon a tenuous balance between national and state power. It is important to recognize that either level of government can be a progressive force and that either can be regressive; neither an all-powerful national government that swallows the states nor a retreat to the reactionary and discredited theories of "states' rights" provides any answer to the questions posed by modern conditions. It is doubtful whether any form of organization can insure a specific result. Those who develop solutions probably will have to investigate methods of political education as well as revisions of structures. They probably also will have to be unconcerned with political labels, because the most promising solutions are likely to be those that will involve considerable innova-

tion, and those who advocate innovation often are the targets for name-calling. Arrogance in high places is destructive, regardless of the form of government, just as national arrogance is destructive on an international basis. It will require something innovative to revise the attitudes that are responsible for both kinds of arrogance.

One of the most salient features of modern America is that the citizen's life is affected more and more by decisions made elsewhere and over which he or she has no control. The pressures of increasing population, the effects of a technologically oriented industrial society, the availability of ever newer and more sophisticated techniques for the invasion of privacy, public apathy, and political ignorance and misinformation all combine to cast doubt upon the future. It is the privilege, right, and obligation of us all to see to it that constitutional democracy survives even these troubles and grows to meet the new challenges, in freedom. It can be done. The price is commitment—commitment to knowledge, and commitment to the use of that knowledge.

APPENDIX A

The Mayflower Compact
November 11, 1620

(The first constitution established by the people in the New World)

In the Name of God, Amen, We whose names are underwritten, the Loyal Subjects of our dread Sovereign Lord King James, by the Grace of God, of Great Britain, France, and Ireland, King, Defender of the Faith, &c. Having undertaken for the Glory of God, and Advancement of the Christian Faith, and the Honour of our King and Country, a Voyage to plant the first colony in the northern Parts of Virginia; Do by these Presents, solemnly and mutually in the Presence of God and one another, covenant and combine ourselves together into a civil Body Politick, for our better Ordering and Preservation, and Furtherance of the Ends aforesaid; And by Virtue hereof do enact, constitute, and frame, such just and equal Laws, Ordinances, Acts, Constitutions, and Offices, from time to time, as shall be thought most meet and convenient for the general Good of the Colony; unto which we promise all due Submission and Obedience. In Witness whereof, we have hereunto subscribed our names at Cape Cod the eleventh of November, in the Reign of our Sovereign Lord King James of England, France, and Ireland, the eighteenth, and of Scotland, the fifty-fourth. Anno Domini, 1620.

APPENDIX B

The Declaration
of Independence*

The Unanimous Declaration of the Thirteen United States of America

When in the Course of human events, it becomes necessary for one people to dissolve the political bands, which have connected them with another, and to assume among the powers of the earth, the separate and equal station to which the Laws of Nature and of Nature's God entitle them, a decent respect to the opinions of mankind requires that they should declare the causes which impel them to the separation.—We hold these truths to be self-evident, that all men are created equal, that they are endowed by their Creator with certain unalienable Rights, that among these are Life, Liberty and the pursuit of Happiness.—That to secure these rights, Governments are instituted among Men, deriving their just powers from the consent of the governed,—That whenever any Form of Government becomes destructive of these ends, it is the Right of the People to alter or to abolish it, and to institute new Government, laying its foundation on such principles and organizing its powers in such form, as to them shall seem most likely to effect their Safety and Happiness. Prudence, indeed, will dictate that Governments long established should not be changed for light

and transient causes; and accordingly all experience hath shewn, that mankind are more disposed to suffer, while evils are sufferable, than to right themselves by abolishing the forms to which they are accustomed. But when a long train of abuses and usurpations, pursuing invariably the same Object evinces a design to reduce them under absolute Despotism, it is their right, it is their duty, to throw off such Government, and to provide new Guards for their future security.—Such has been the patient sufferance of these Colonies; and such is now the necessity which constrains them to alter their former Systems of Government. The history of the present King of Great Britain is a history of repeated injuries and usurpations, all having in direct object the establishment of an absolute Tyranny over these States. To prove this, let Facts be submitted to a candid world.—He has refused his Assent to Laws, the most wholesome and necessary for the public good.— He has forbidden his Governors to pass Laws of immediate and pressing importance, unless suspended in their operation till his Assent should be obtained; and when so suspended, he has utterly ne-

* As it reads in the parchment copy

213

glected to attend to them.—He has refused to pass other Laws for the accommodation of large districts of people, unless those people would relinquish the right of Representation in the Legislature, a right inestimable to them and formidable to tyrants only.—He has called together legislative bodies at places unusual, uncomfortable, and distant from the depository of their public Records, for the sole purpose of fatiguing them into compliance with his measures.—He has dissolved Representative Houses repeatedly, for opposing with manly firmness his invasions on the rights of the people.—He has refused for a long time, after such dissolutions, to cause others to be elected; whereby the Legislative powers, incapable of Annihilation, have returned to the People at large for their exercise; the State remaining in the meantime exposed to all the dangers of invasion from without, and convulsions within.— He has endeavoured to prevent the population of these States; for that purpose obstructing the Laws for Naturalization of Foreigners; refusing to pass others to encourage their migrations hither, and raising the conditions of new Appropriations of Lands.—He has obstructed the Administration of Justice, by refusing his Assent to Laws for establishing Judiciary powers.—He has made Judges dependent on his Will alone, for the tenure of their offices, and the amount and payment of their salaries.—He has erected a multitude of New Offices, and sent hither swarms of Officers to harrass our people, and eat out their substance.— He has kept among us, in times of peace, Standing Armies without the Consent of our legislatures.— He has affected to render the Military independent of and superior to the Civil power.—He has combined with others to subject us to a jurisdiction foreign to our constitution, and unacknowledged by our laws; giving his Assent to their Acts of pretended Legislation.—For quartering large bodies of armed troops among us:—For protecting them, by a mock Trial, from punishment for any Murders which they should commit on the Inhabitants of these States:—For cutting off our Trade with all parts of the world:—For imposing Taxes on us without our Consent:—For depriving us in many cases, of the benefits of

Trial by Jury:—For transporting us beyond Seas to be tried for pretended offenses:—For abolishing the free System of English Laws in a neighboring Province, establishing therein an Arbitrary government, and enlarging its Boundaries so as to render it at once an example and fit instrument for introducing the same absolute rule into these Colonies:—For taking away our Charters, abolishing our most valuable Laws, and altering fundamentally the Forms of our Governments:—For suspending our own Legislatures, and declaring themselves invested with power to legislate for us in all cases whatsoever.—He has abdicated Government here, by declaring us out of his Protection and waging War against us.—He has plundered our seas, ravaged our Coasts, burnt our towns, and destroyed the lives of our people.—He is at this time transporting large Armies of foreign Mercenaries to compleat the works of death, desolation and tyranny, already begun with circumstances of Cruelty & perfidy, scarcely paralleled in the most barbarous ages, and totally unworthy the Head of a civilized nation.—He has constrained our fellow Citizens taken Captive on the High Seas to bear Arms against their Country, to become the executioners of their friends and Brethren, or to fall themselves by their hands.—He has excited domestic insurrections amongst us, and has endeavoured to bring on the inhabitants of our frontiers, the merciless Indian Savages, whose known rule of warfare, is an undistinguished destruction of all ages, sexes and conditions. In every stage of these Oppressions We have Petitioned for Redress in the most humble terms: Our repeated Petitions have been answered only by repeated injury. A Prince whose character is thus marked by every act which may define a Tyrant, is unfit to be the ruler of a free people. Nor have We been wanting in attentions to our British brethren. We have warned them from time to time of attempts by their legislature to extend an unwarrantable jurisdiction over us. We have reminded them of the circumstances of our emigration and settlement here. We have appealed to their native justice and magnanimity, and we have conjured them by the ties of our common kindred to disavow these usurpations, which would inevitably interrupt our connections and correspondence. They too have been deaf to the voice of justice and of consanguinity. We must, therefore, acquiesce in the necessity, which denounces our Separation, and hold them, as we hold the rest of mankind, Enemies in War, in Peace Friends.—

We, therefore, the Representatives of the United States of America, in General Congress, Assembled, appealing to the Supreme Judge of the world for the rectitude of our intentions do, in the Name, and by the Authority of the good People of these Colonies, solemnly publish and declare, That these United Colonies are, and of Right ought to be Free and Independent States; that they are Absolved from all Allegiance to the British Crown, and that all political connection between them and the State of Great Britain, is and ought to be totally dissolved; and that as Free and Independent States, they have full Power to levy War, conclude Peace, contract Alliances, establish Commerce, and to do all other Acts and Things which Independent States may of right do.—And for the support of this Declaration, with a firm reliance on the protection of divine Providence, we mutually pledge to each other our Lives, our Fortunes and our sacred Honor.

APPENDIX C

The Constitution
of the United States of America

We the People of the United States, in Order to form a more perfect Union, establish Justice, insure domestic Tranquility, provide for the common defence, promote the general Welfare, and secure the Blessings of Liberty to ourselves and our Posterity, do ordain and establish this Constitution for the United States of America.

Article. I.

SECTION. 1. All legislative Powers herein granted shall be vested in a Congress of the United States, which shall consist of a Senate and House of Representatives.

SECTION. 2. The House of Representatives shall be composed of Members chosen every second Year by the People of the several States, and the Electors in each State shall have the Qualifications requisite for Electors of the most numerous Branch of the State Legislature.

No Person shall be a Representative who shall not have attained to the age of twenty five Years, and been seven Years a Citizen of the United States, and who shall not, when elected, be an Inhabitant of that State in which he shall be chosen.

Representatives and direct Taxes shall be apportioned among the several States which may be included within this Union, according to their respective Numbers, which shall be determined by adding to the whole Number of free Persons, including those bound to Service for a Term of Years, and excluding Indians not taxed, three fifths of all other Persons. The actual Enumeration shall be made within three Years after the first Meeting of the Congress of the United States, and within every subsequent Term of ten Years, in such Manner as they shall by Law direct. The Number of Representatives shall not exceed one for every thirty Thousand, but each State shall have at Least one Representative; and until such enumeration shall be made, the State of New Hampshire shall be entitled to chuse three, Massachusetts eight, Rhode-Island and Providence Plantations one, Connecticut five, New-York six, New Jersey four, Pennsylvania eight, Delaware one, Maryland six, Virginia ten, North Carolina five, South Carolina five, and Georgia three.

When vacancies happen in the Representation from any State, the Executive Authority thereof shall issue Writs of Election to fill such Vacancies.

The House of Representatives shall

217

chuse their Speaker and other Officers; and shall have the sole Power of Impeachment.

SECTION. 3. The Senate of the United States shall be composed of two Senators from each State, chosen by the Legislature thereof, for six Years; and each Senator shall have one Vote.

Immediately after they shall be assembled in Consequence of the first Election, they shall be divided as equally as may be into three Classes. The Seats of the Senators of the first Class shall be vacated at the Expiration of the second Year, of the second Class at the Expiration of the fourth Year, and of the third Class at the Expiration of the sixth Year, so that one third may be chosen every second Year; and if Vacancies happen by Resignation, or otherwise, during the Recess of the Legislature of any State, the Executive thereof may make temporary Appointments until the next Meeting of the Legislature, which shall then fill such Vacancies.

No Person shall be a Senator who shall not have attained to the Age of thirty Years, and been nine Years a Citizen of the United States, and who shall not, when elected, be an Inhabitant of that State for which he shall be chosen.

The Vice President of the United States shall be President of the Senate, but shall have no Vote, unless they be equally divided.

The Senate shall chuse their other Officers, and also a President pro tempore, in the Absence of the Vice President, or when he shall exercise the Office of President of the United States.

The Senate shall have the sole Power to try all Impeachments. When sitting for that Purpose, they shall be on Oath or Affirmation. When the President of the United States is tried the Chief Justice shall preside: And no Person shall be convicted without the Concurrence of two thirds of the Members present.

Judgment in Cases of Impeachment shall not extend further than to removal from Office, and disqualification to hold and enjoy any Office of honor, Trust or Profit under the United States: but the Party convicted shall nevertheless be liable and subject to Indictment, Trial, Judgment and Punishment, according to Law.

SECTION. 4. The Times, Places and Manner of holding Elections for Senators and Representatives, shall be prescribed in each State by the Legislature thereof; but the Congress may at any time by Law make or alter such Regulations, except as to the Places of chusing Senators.

The Congress shall assemble at least once in every Year, and such Meeting shall be on the first Monday in December, unless they shall by Law appoint a different Day.

SECTION. 5. Each House shall be the Judge of the Elections, Returns and Qualifications of its own Members, and a Majority of each shall constitute a Quorum to do Business; but a smaller Number may adjourn from day to day, and may be authorized to compel the Attendance of absent Members, in such Manner, and under such Penalties as each House may provide.

Each House may determine the Rules of its Proceedings, punish its Members for disorderly Behaviour, and, with the Concurrence of two thirds, expel a Member.

Each House shall keep a Journal of its Proceedings, and from time to time publish the same, excepting such Parts as may in their Judgment require Secrecy; and the Yeas and Nays of the Members of either House on any question shall, at the Desire of one fifth of those Present, be entered on the Journal.

Neither House, during the Session of Congress, shall, without the Consent of the other, adjourn for more than three days, nor to any other Place than that in which the two Houses shall be sitting.

SECTION. 6. The Senators and Representatives shall receive a Compensation for their Services, to be ascertained by Law, and paid out of the Treasury of the United States. They shall in all Cases, except Treason, Felony and Breach of the Peace, be privileged from Arrest during their Attendance at the Session of their respective Houses, and in going to and returning from the same; and for any Speech or Debate in either House, they shall not be questioned in any other Place.

No Senator or Representative shall, during the Time for which he was elected, be appointed to any civil Office under the Authority of the United States, which shall have been created, or the Emoluments whereof shall have been encreased during such time; and no Person holding any Office under the United States, shall be a Member of either House during his Continuance in Office.

SECTION. 7. All Bills for raising Revenue shall originate in the House of Representatives; but the Senate may propose or concur with amendments as on other Bills.

Every Bill which shall have passed the House of Representatives and the Senate, shall, before it become a Law, be presented to the President of the United States; If he approve he shall sign it, but if not he shall return it, with his Objections to that House in which it shall have originated, who shall enter the Objections at large on their Journal, and proceed to reconsider it. If after such Reconsideration two thirds of that House shall agree to pass the Bill, it shall be sent, together with the Objections, to the other House, by which it shall likewise be reconsidered, and if approved by two thirds of that House, it shall become a Law. But in all such Cases the Votes of both Houses shall be determined by yeas and Nays, and the Names of the Persons voting for and against the Bill shall be entered on the Journal of each House respectively. If any Bill shall not be returned by the President within ten Days (Sunday excepted) after it shall have been presented to him, the Same shall be a Law, in like Manner as if he had signed it, unless the Congress by their Adjournment prevent its Return, in which Case it shall not be a Law.

Every Order, Resolution, or Vote to which the Concurrence of the Senate and House of Representatives may be necessary (except on a question of Adjournment) shall be presented to the President of the United States; and before the Same shall take Effect, shall be approved by him, or being disapproved by him, shall be repassed by two thirds of the Senate and House of Representatives, according to the Rules and Limitations prescribed in the Case of a Bill.

SECTION. 8. The Congress shall have Power To lay and collect Taxes, Duties, Imposts and Excises, to pay the Debts and provide for the common Defence and general Welfare of the United States; but all Duties, Imposts and Excises shall be uniform throughout the United States;

To borrow Money on the credit of the United States;

To regulate Commerce with foreign Nations, and among the several States, and with the Indian Tribes;

To establish an uniform Rule of Naturalization, and uniform Laws on the subject of Bankruptcies throughout the United States;

To coin Money, regulate the Value thereof, and of foreign Coin, and fix the Standard of Weights and Measures;

To provide for the Punishment of counterfeiting the Securities and current Coin of the United States;

To establish Post Offices and post Roads;

To promote the Progress of Science and useful Arts, by securing for limited Times to Authors and Inventors the exclusive Right to their respective Writings and Discoveries;

To constitute Tribunals inferior to the supreme Court;

To define and punish Piracies and Felonies committed on the high Seas, and Offences against the Law of Nations;

To declare War, grant Letters of Marque and Reprisal, and make Rules concerning Captures on Land and Water;

To raise and support Armies, but no Appropriation of Money to that Use shall be for a longer Term than two Years;

To provide and maintain a Navy;

To make Rules for the Government and Regulation of the land and naval Forces;

To provide for calling forth the Militia to execute the Laws of the Union, suppress Insurrections and repel Invasions;

To provide for organizing, arming, and disciplining, the Militia, and for governing such Part of them as may be employed in the Service of the United States, reserving to the States respectively, the

Appointment of the Officers, and the Authority of training the Militia according to the discipline prescribed by Congress;

To exercise exclusive Legislation in all Cases whatsoever, over such District (not exceeding ten Miles square) as may, by Cession of Particular States, and the Acceptance of Congress, become the Seat of the Government of the United States, and to exercise like Authority over all Places purchased by the Consent of the Legislature of the State in which the Same shall be, for the Erection of Forts, Magazines, Arsenals, dock-Yards, and other needful Buildings;—And

To make all Laws which shall be necessary and proper for carrying into Execution the foregoing Powers, and all other Powers vested by this Constitution in the Government of the United States, or in any Department or Officer thereof.

SECTION. 9. The Migration or Importation of such Persons as any of the States now existing shall think proper to admit, shall not be prohibited by the Congress prior to the Year one thousand eight hundred and eight, but a Tax or duty may be imposed on such Importation, not exceeding ten dollars for each Person.

The Privilege of the Writ of Habeas Corpus shall not be suspended, unless when in Cases of Rebellion or Invasion the public Safety may require it.

No Bill of Attainder or ex post facto Law shall be passed.

No Capitation, or other direct, Tax shall be laid, unless in Proportion to the Census of Enumeration herein before directed to be taken.

No Tax or Duty shall be laid on Articles exported from any State.

No Preference shall be given by any Regulation of Commerce or Revenue to the Ports of one State over those of another; nor shall Vessels bound to, or from, one State, be obliged to enter, clear or pay Duties in another.

No Money shall be drawn from the Treasury, but in Consequence of Appropriations made by Law; and a regular Statement and Account of the Receipts and Expenditures of all public Money shall be published from time to time.

No Title of Nobility shall be granted by the United States; And no Person holding any Office of Profit or Trust under them, shall, without the Consent of the Congress, accept of any present, Emolument, Office, or Title, of any kind whatever, from any King, Prince or foreign State.

SECTION. 10. No State shall enter into any Treaty, Alliance, or Confederation; grant Letters of Marque and Reprisal; coin Money; emit Bills of Credit; make any Thing but gold and silver Coin a Tender in Payment of Debts; pass any Bill of Attainder, ex post facto Law, or Law impairing the Obligation of Contracts, or grant and Title of Nobility.

No State shall, without the Consent of the Congress, lay any Imposts or Duties on Imports or Exports, except what may be absolutely necessary for executing its inspection Laws: and the net Produce of all Duties and Imposts, laid by any State on Imports or Exports, shall be for the Use of the Treasury of the United States; and all such Laws shall be subject to the Revision and Controul of the Congress.

No State shall, without the Consent of Congress, lay any Duty of Tonnage, keep Troops, or Ships of War in time of Peace, enter into any Agreement or Compact with another State, or with a foreign Power, or engage in War, unless actually invaded, or in such imminent Danger as will not admit of delay.

Article. II.

SECTION. 1. The executive Power shall be vested in a President of the United States of America. He shall hold his Office during the Term of four Years, and, together with the Vice President, chosen for the same Term, be elected, as follows

Each State shall appoint, in such Manner as the Legislature thereof may direct, a Number of Electors, equal to the whole Number of Senators and Representatives to which the State may be entitled in the Congress: but no Senator or Representative, or Person holding an Office of Trust or Profit under the United States, shall be appointed an Elector.

The Electors shall meet in their respective States, and vote by Ballot for two

Persons, of whom one at least shall not be an Inhabitant of the same State with themselves. And they shall make a List of all the Persons voted for, and of the Number of Votes for each; which List they shall sign and certify, and transmit sealed to the Seat of the Government of the United States, directed to the President of the Senate. The President of the Senate shall, in the Presence of the Senate and House of Representatives, open all the Certificates, and the Votes shall then be counted. The Person having the greatest Number of Votes shall be the President, if such Number be a Majority of the whole Number of Electors appointed; and if there be more than one who have such Majority, and have an equal Number of Votes, then the House of Representatives shall immediately chuse by Ballot one of them for President; and if no Person have a Majority, then from the five highest on the List the said House shall in like Manner chuse the President. But in chusing the President, the Votes shall be taken by States, the Representation from each State having one Vote; a quorum for this Purpose shall consist of a Member or Members from two thirds of the States, and a Majority of all the States shall be necessary to a Choice. In every Case, after the Choice of the President, the Person having the greatest Number of Votes of the Electors shall be the Vice President. But if there should remain two or more who have equal Votes, the Senate shall chose from them by Ballot the Vice President.

The Congress may determine the Time of chusing the Electors, and the Day on which they shall give their votes; which Day shall be the same throughout the United States.

No Person except a natural born Citizen, or a Citizen of the United States, at the time of the Adoption of this Constitution, shall be eligible to the Office of President; neither shall any person be eligible to that Office who shall not have attained to the Age of thirty five Years, and been fourteen Years a Resident within the United States.

In Case of the Removal of the President from Office, or of his Death, Resignation, or Inability to discharge the Powers and Duties of the said Office, the Same shall devolve on the Vice President, and the Congress may by Law provide for the Case of Removal, Death, Resignation or Inability, both of the President and Vice President, declaring what Officer shall then act as President, and such Officer shall act accordingly, until the Disability be removed, or a President shall be elected.

The President shall, at stated Times, receive for his Services, a Compensation, which shall neither be encreased nor diminished during the Period for which he shall have been elected, and he shall not receive within that Period any other Emolument from the United States, or any of them.

Before he enter on the Execution of his Office, he shall take the following Oath or Affirmation:—"I do solemnly swear (or affirm) that I will faithfully execute the Office of President of the United States, and will to the best of my Ability, preserve, protect and defend the Constitution of the United States."

SECTION. 2. The President shall be Commander in Chief of the Army and Navy of the United States, and of the Militia of the several States, when called into the actual Service of the United States; he may require the Opinion, in writing, of the principal Officer in each of the executive Departments, upon any Subject relating to the Duties of their respective Offices, and he shall have Power to grant Reprieves and Pardons for Offenses against the United States, except in Cases of Impeachment.

He shall have Power, by and with the Advice and Consent of the Senate, to make Treaties, provided two thirds of the Senators present concur; and he shall nominate, and by and with the Advice and Consent of the Senate, shall appoint Ambassadors, other public Ministers and Consuls, Judges of the supreme Court, and all other Officers of the United States, whose Appointments are not herein otherwise provided for, and which shall be established by Law; but the Congress may by Law vest the Appointment of such inferior Officers, as they think proper, in the President alone, in the Courts of Law, or in the Heads of Departments.

The President shall have Power to fill up all Vacancies that may happen during the Recess of the Senate, by granting Commissions which shall expire at the End of their next Session.

SECTION. 3. He shall from time to time give to the Congress Information of the State of the Union, and recommend to their Consideration such Measures as he shall judge necessary and expedient; he may, on extraordinary Occasions, convene both Houses, or either of them, and in Case of Disagreement between them, with Respect to the Time of Adjournment, he may adjourn them to such Time as he shall think proper; he shall receive Ambassadors and other public Ministers; he shall take Care that the Laws be faithfully executed, and shall Commission all the Officers of the United States.

SECTION. 4. The President, Vice President and all Civil Officers of the United States, shall be removed from Office on Impeachment for, and Conviction of, Treason, Bribery, or other high Crimes and Misdemeanors.

Article. III.

SECTION. 1. The judicial Power of the United States, shall be vested in one supreme Court, and in such inferior Courts as the Congress may from time to time ordain and establish. The Judges, both of the supreme and inferior Courts, shall hold their Offices during good Behaviour, and shall, at stated Times, receive for their Services, a Compensation, which shall not be diminished during their Continuance in Office.

SECTION. 2. The judicial Power shall extend to all Cases, in Law and Equity, arising under this Constitution, the Laws of the United States, and Treaties made, or which shall be made, under their Authority;—to all Cases affecting Ambassadors, other public Ministers and Consuls;—to all Cases of admiralty and maritime Jurisdiction;—to Controversies to which the United States shall be a Party;—to Controversies between two or more States;—between a State and Citizens of an-

other State;—between Citizens of different States;—between Citizens of the same State claiming Lands under Grants of different States, and between a State, or the Citizens thereof, and foreign States, Citizens or Subjects.

In all Cases affecting Ambassadors, other public Ministers and Consuls, and those in which a State shall be Party, the supreme Court shall have original Jurisdiction. In all the other Cases before mentioned, the supreme Court shall have appellate Jurisdiction, both as to Law and Fact, with such Exceptions, and under such Regulations as the Congress shall make.

The Trial of all Crimes, except in Cases of Impeachment, shall be by Jury; and such Trial shall be held in the State where the said Crimes shall have been committed; but when not committed within any State, the Trial shall be at such Place or Places as the Congress may by Law have directed.

SECTION. 3. Treason against the United States, shall consist only in levying War against them, or in adhering to their Enemies, giving them Aid and Comfort. No Person shall be convicted of Treason unless on the Testimony of two Witnesses to the same overt Act, or on Confession in open Court.

The Congress shall have Power to declare the Punishment of Treason, but no Attainder of Treason shall work Corruption of Blood, or Forfeiture except during the Life of the Person attainted.

Article. IV.

SECTION. 1. Full Faith and Credit shall be given in each State to the public Acts, Records, and judicial Proceedings of every other State. And the Congress may by general Laws prescribe the Manner in which such Acts, Records and Proceedings shall be proved, and the Effect thereof.

SECTION. 2. The Citizens of each State shall be entitled to all Privileges and Immunities of Citizens in the several States.

A Person charged in any State with Treason, Felony, or other Crime, who shall flee from Justice, and be found in another State, shall on Demand of the executive Authority of the State from which he fled, be delivered up, to be removed to the State having Jurisdiction of the Crime.

No Person held to Service or Labour in one State, under the Laws thereof, escaping into another, shall, in Consequence of any Law or Regulation therein, be discharged from such Service or Labour, but shall be delivered up on Claim of the Party to whom such Service or Labour may be due.

SECTION. 3. New States may be admitted by the Congress into this Union; but no new State shall be formed or erected within the Jurisdiction of any other State; nor any State be formed by the Junction of two or more States, or Parts of States, without the Consent of the Legislatures of the States concerned as well as of the Congress.

The Congress shall have Power to dispose of and make all needful Rules and Regulations respecting the Territory or other Property belonging to the United States; and nothing in this Constitution shall be so construed as to Prejudice any Claims of the United States, or of any particular State.

SECTION. 4. The United States shall guarantee to every State in this Union a Republican Form of Government, and shall protect each of them against Invasion; and on Application of the Legislature, or of the Executive (when the Legislature cannot be convened) against domestic Violence.

Article. V.

The Congress, whenever two thirds of both Houses shall deem it necessary, shall propose Amendments to this Constitution, or, on the Application of the Legislatures of two thirds of the several States, shall call a Convention for proposing Amendments, which, in either Case, shall be valid to all Intents and Purposes, as Part of this Constitution, when ratified by the Legislatures of three fourths of the several States, or by Conventions in three fourths thereof, as the one or the other Mode of Ratification may be proposed by the Congress; Provided that no Amendment which may be made prior to the Year One thousand eight hundred and eight shall in any Manner affect the first and fourth Clauses in the Ninth Section of the first Article; and that no State, without its Consent, shall be deprived of it's equal Suffrage in the Senate.

Article. VI.

All Debts contracted and Engagements entered into, before the Adoption of this Constitution, shall be as valid against the United States under this Constitution, as under the Confederation.

This Constitution, and the Laws of the United States which shall be made in Pursuance thereof; and all Treaties made, or which shall be made, under the Authority of the United States, shall be the supreme Law of the Land; and the Judges in every State shall be bound thereby, any Thing in the Constitution or Laws of any State to the Contrary notwithstanding.

The Senators and Representatives before mentioned, and the Members of the several State Legislatures, and all executive and judicial Officers, both of the United States and of the several States, shall be bound by Oath or Affirmation, to support this Constitution; but no religious Test shall ever be required as a Qualification to any Office or public Trust under the United States.

Article. VII.

The Ratification of the Conventions of nine States, shall be sufficient for the Establishment of this Constitution between the States so ratifying the Same.

done in Convention by the Unanimous Consent of the States present the Seventeenth Day of September in the Year of our Lord one thousand seven hundred and Eighty seven and of the Independence of the United States of America the Twelfth In witness whereof We have hereunto subscribed our Names,
GO. WASHINGTON—PRESIDT.
   and deputy from Virginia

AMENDMENTS TO THE CONSTITUTION

Amendment [I.]*

Congress shall make no law respecting an establishment of religion, or prohibiting the free exercise thereof; or abridging the freedom of speech, or of the press; or the right of the People peaceably to assemble, and to petition the Government for a redress of grievances.
[Ratified December 15, 1791]

Amendment [II.]

A well regulated Militia, being necessary to the security of a free State, the right of the people to keep and bear Arms, shall not be infringed.
[Ratified December 15, 1791]

Amendment [III.]

No Soldier shall, in time of peace be quartered in any house, without the consent of the Owner, nor in time of war, but in a manner to be prescribed by law.
[Ratified December 15, 1791]

Amendment [IV.]

The right of the people to be secure in their persons, houses, papers, and effects, against unreasonable searches and seizures, shall not be violated, and no Warrants shall issue, but upon probable cause, supported by Oath or affirmation, and particularly describing the place to be searched, and the persons or things to be seized.
[Ratified December 15, 1791]

Amendment [V.]

No person shall be held to answer for a capital, or otherwise infamous crime, unless on a presentment or indictment of a Grand Jury, except in cases arising in the land or naval forces, or in the Militia, when in actual service in time of War or public danger; nor shall any person be subject for the same offence to be twice put in jeopardy of life or limb; nor shall be compelled in any criminal case to be a witness against himself, nor be deprived of life, liberty, or property, without due process of law; nor shall private property be taken for public use, without just compensation.
[Ratified December 15, 1791]

Amendment [VI.]

In all criminal prosecutions, the accused shall enjoy the right to a speedy and public trial, by an impartial jury of the State and district wherein the crime shall have been committed, which district shall have been previously ascertained by law, and to be informed of the nature and cause of the accusation; to be confronted with the witnesses against him; to have compulsory process for obtaining witnesses in his favor, and to have the Assistance of Counsel for his defence.
[Ratified December 15, 1791]

Amendment [VII.]

In Suits at common law, where the value in controversy shall exceed twenty dollars, the right of trial by jury shall be preserved, and no fact tried by a jury, shall be otherwise re-examined in any Court of the United States, than according to the rules of the common law.
[Ratified December 15, 1791]

Amendment [VIII.]

Excessive bail shall not be required, nor excessive fines imposed, nor cruel and unusual punishments inflicted.
[Ratified December 15, 1791]

Amendment [IX.]

The enumeration in the Constitution, of certain rights, shall not be construed to deny or disparage others retained by the people.
[Ratified December 15, 1791]

Amendment [X.]

The powers not delegated to the United States by the Constitution, nor prohibited by it to the States, are reserved to the States respectively, or to the people.
[Ratified December 15, 1791]

Amendment [XI.]

The Judicial power of the United States shall not be construed to extend to any

---

* Brackets enclosing an amendment number indicate that the number was not specifically assigned in the resolution proposing the amendment.

suit in law or equity, commenced or prosecuted against one of the United States by Citizens of another State, or by Citizens or Subjects of any Foreign State.
[Ratified January 23, 1798]

Amendment [XII.]

The Electors shall meet in their respective states and vote by ballot for President and Vice-President, one of whom, at least, shall not be an inhabitant of the same state with themselves; they shall name in their ballots the person voted for as President, and in distinct ballots the person voted for as Vice-President, and they shall make distinct lists of all persons voted for as President, and of all persons voted for as Vice-President, and of the number of votes for each, which lists they shall sign and certify, and transmit sealed to the seat of the government of the United States, directed to the President of the Senate;—The President of the Senate shall, in the presence of the Senate and House of Representatives, open all the certificates and the votes shall then be counted;—The person having the greatest number of votes for President, shall be the President, if such number be a majority of the whole number of Electors appointed; and if no person have such majority, then from the persons having the highest numbers not exceeding three on the list of those voted for as President, the House of Representatives shall choose immediately, by ballot, the President. But in choosing the President, the votes shall be taken by states, the representation from each state having one vote; a quorum for this purpose shall consist of a member or members from two-thirds of the states, and a majority of all the states shall be necessary to a choice. And if the House of Representatives shall not choose a President whenever the right of choice shall devolve upon them, before the fourth day of March next following, then the Vice-President shall act as President, as in the case of the death or other constitutional disability of the President—The person having the greatest number of votes as Vice-President, shall be the Vice-President, if such number be a majority of the whole number of Electors appointed, and if no person have a majority, then from the two highest numbers on the list, the Senate shall choose the Vice-President; a quorum for the purpose shall consist of two-thirds of the whole number of Senators, and a majority of the whole number shall be necessary to a choice. But no person constitutionally ineligible to the office of President shall be eligible to that of Vice-President of the United States.
[Ratified June 15, 1804]

Amendment [XIII.]

SECTION 1. Neither slavery nor involuntary servitude, except as a punishment for crime whereof the party shall have been duly convicted, shall exist within the United States, or any place subject to their jurisdiction.

SECTION 2. Congress shall have power to enforce this article by appropriate legislation.
[Ratified December 6, 1865]

Amendment [XIV.]

SECTION 1. All persons born or naturalized in the United States and subject to the jurisdiction thereof, are citizens of the United States and of the State wherein they reside. No State shall make or enforce any law which shall abridge the privileges or immunities of citizens of the United States; nor shall any State deprive any person of life, liberty, or property, without due process of law; nor deny to any person within its jurisdiction the equal protection of the laws.

SECTION 2. Representatives shall be apportioned among the several States according to their respective numbers, counting the whole number of persons in each State, excluding Indians not taxed. But when the right to vote at any election for the choice of electors for President and Vice President of the United States, Representatives in Congress, the Executive and Judicial officers of a State, or the members of the Legislature thereof, is denied to any of the male inhabitants of such State, being twenty-one years of age, and citizens of the United States, or in any way abridged, except for participation in rebellion, or other crime, the basis of representation therein shall be reduced in the proportion which the number of such male citizens shall bear to the whole number of male citizens twenty-one years of age in such State.

SECTION 3. No person shall be a Senator or Representative in Congress, or elector of President and Vice President, or hold any office, civil or military, under the United States, or under any State, who, having previously taken an oath, as a member of Congress, or as an officer of the United States, or as a member of any State legislature, or as an executive or judicial officer of any State, to support the Constitution of the United States, shall have engaged in insurrection or rebellion against the same, or given aid or comfort to the enemies thereof. But Congress may by a vote of two-thirds of each House, remove such disability.

SECTION 4. The validity of the public debt of the United States, authorized by law, including debts incurred for payment of pensions and bounties for services in suppressing insurrection or rebellion, shall not be questioned. But neither the United States nor any State shall assume or pay any debt or obligation incurred in aid of insurrection or rebellion against the United States, or any claim for the loss or emancipation of any slave; but all such debts, obligations and claims shall be held illegal and void.

SECTION 5. The Congress shall have power to enforce, by appropriate legislation, the provisions of this article.
[Ratified July 9, 1868]

Amendment [XV.]

SECTION 1. The right of citizens of the United States to vote shall not be denied or abridged by the United States or by any State on account of race, color, or previous condition of servitude.

SECTION 2. The Congress shall have power to enforce this article by appropriate legislation.
[Ratified February 2, 1870]

Amendment [XVI.]

The Congress shall have power to lay and collect taxes on incomes, from whatever source derived, without apportionment among the several States, and without regard to any census or enumeration.
[Ratified February 3, 1913]

Amendment [XVII.]

The Senate of the United States shall be composed of two Senators from each State, elected by the people thereof, for six years; and each Senator shall have one vote. The electors in each State shall have the qualifications requisite for electors of the most numerous branch of the State legislatures.

When vacancies happen in the representation of any State in the Senate, the executive authority of such State shall issue writs of election to fill such vacancies; *Provided,* That the legislature of any State may empower the executive thereof to make temporary appointments until the people fill the vacancies by election as the legislature may direct.

This amendment shall not be so construed as to affect the election or term of any Senator chosen before it becomes valid as part of the Constitution.
[Ratified April 8, 1913]

Amendment [XVIII.]

SECTION 1. After one year from the ratification of this article the manufacture, sale, or transportation of intoxicating liquors within, the importation thereof into, or the exportation thereof from the United States and all territory subject to the jurisdiction thereof for beverage purposes is hereby prohibited.

SEC. 2. The Congress and the several States shall have concurrent power to enforce this article by appropriate legislation.

SEC. 3. This article shall be inoperative unless it shall have been ratified as an amendment to the Constitution by the legislatures of the several States, as provided in the Constitution, within seven years from the date of the submission hereof to the States by the Congress.
[Ratified January 16, 1919]

Amendment [XIX.]

The right of citizens of the United States to vote shall not be denied or abridged by the United States or by any State on account of sex.

Congress shall have power to enforce this article by appropriate legislation.

[Ratified August 18, 1920]

Amendment [XX.]

SECTION 1. The terms of the President and Vice President shall end at noon on the 20th day of January, and the terms of Senators and Representatives at noon on the 3d day of January, of the years in which such terms would have ended if this article had not been ratified; and the terms of their successors shall then begin.

SEC. 2. The Congress shall assemble at least once in every year, and such meeting shall begin at noon on the 3d day of January, unless they shall by law appoint a different day.

SEC. 3. If, at the time fixed for the beginning of the term of the President, the President elect shall have died, the Vice President elect shall become President. If a President shall not have been chosen before the time fixed for the beginning of his term, or if the President elect shall have failed to qualify, then the Vice President elect shall act as President until a President shall have qualified; and the Congress may by law provide for the case wherein neither a President elect nor a Vice President elect shall have qualified, declaring who shall then act as President, or the manner in which one who is to act shall be selected, and such person shall act accordingly until a President or Vice President shall have qualified.

SEC. 4. The Congress may by law provide for the case of the death of any of the persons from whom the House of Representatives may choose a President whenever the right of choice shall have devolved upon them, and for the case of the death of any of the persons from whom the Senate may choose a Vice President whenever the right of choice shall have devolved upon them.

SEC. 5. Sections 1 and 2 shall take effect on the 15th day of October following the ratification of this article.

SEC. 6. This article shall be inoperative unless it shall have been ratified as an amendment to the Constitution by the legislatures of three-fourths of the several States within seven years from the date of its submission.

[Ratified January 23, 1933]

Amendment [XXI.]

SECTION 1. The eighteenth article of amendment to the Constitution of the United States is hereby repealed.

SEC. 2. The transportation or importation into any State, Territory or possession of the United States for delivery or use therein of intoxicating liquors, in violation of the laws thereof, is hereby prohibited.

SEC. 3. This article shall be inoperative unless it shall have been ratified as an amendment to the Constitution by conventions in the several States, as provided in the Constitution, within seven years from the date of the submission thereof to the States by the Congress.

[Ratified December 5, 1933]

Amendment [XXII.]

SECTION 1. No person shall be elected to the office of the President more than twice, and no person who has held the office of President, or acted as President, for more than two years of a term to which some other person was elected President shall be elected to the office of the President more than once. But this Article shall not apply to any person holding the office of President when this Article was proposed by the Congress, and shall not prevent any person who may be holding the office of President, or acting as President, during the term within which this Article becomes operative from holding the office of President or acting as President during the remainder of such term.

SEC. 2. This Article shall be inoperative unless it shall have been ratified as an amendment to the Constitution by the legislatures of three-fourths of the several States within seven years from the date of its submission to the States by the Congress.

[Ratified March 1, 1951]

Amendment [XXIII.]

SECTION 1. The District constituting the seat of Government of the United States shall appoint in such manner as the Congress may direct:

A number of electors of President and Vice President equal to the whole number of Senators and Representatives in Congress to which the District would be entitled if it were a State, but in no event more than the least populous State; they shall be in addition to those appointed by the States, but they shall be considered, for the purposes of the election of President and Vice President, to be electors appointed by a State; and they shall meet in the District and perform such duties as provided by the twelfth article of amendment.

SEC. 2. The Congress shall have power to enforce this article by appropriate legislation.

[Ratified April 3, 1961]

Amendment [XXIV.]

SECTION. 1. The right of citizens of the United States to vote in any primary or other election for President or Vice President, for electors for President or Vice President, or for Senator or Representative in Congress, shall not be denied or abridged by the United States or any State by reason of failure to pay any poll tax or other tax.

SECTION 2. The Congress shall have power to enforce this article by appropriate legislation.

[Ratified January 23, 1964]

Amendment [XXV.]

SECTION 1. In case of the removal of the President from office or his death or resignation, the Vice President shall become President.

SEC. 2. Whenever there is a vacancy in the office of the Vice President, the President shall nominate a Vice President who shall take office upon confirmation by a majority vote of both houses of Congress.

SEC. 3. Whenever the President transmits to the President pro tempore of the Senate and the Speaker of the House of Representatives his written declaration that he is unable to discharge the powers and duties of his office, and until he transmits to them a written declaration to the contrary, such powers and duties shall be discharged by the Vice President as Acting President.

SEC. 4. Whenever the Vice President and a majority of either the principal officers of the executive department or of such other body as Congress may by law provide, transmit to the President pro tempore of the Senate and the Speaker of the House of Representatives their written declaration that the President is unable to discharge the powers and duties of his office, the Vice President shall immediately assume the powers and duties of the office as Acting President.

Thereafter, when the President transmits to the President pro tempore of the Senate and the Speaker of the House of Representatives his written declaration that no inability exists, he shall resume the powers and duties of his office unless the Vice President and a majority of either the principal officers of the executive department or of such other body as Congress may by law provide, transmit within four days to the President pro tempore of the Senate and the Speaker of the House of Representatives their written declaration that the President is unable to discharge the powers and duties of his office. Thereupon Congress shall decide the issue, assembling within 48 hours for that purpose if not in session. If the Congress, within 21 days after receipt of the latter written declaration, or, if Congress is not in session, within 21 days after Congress is required to assemble, determines by two-thirds vote of both houses that the President is unable to discharge the powers and duties of his office, the

Vice President shall continue to discharge the same as Acting President; otherwise, the President shall resume the powers and duties of his office.
[Ratified February 11, 1967]

Amendment [XXVI.]

SECTION 1. The right of citizens of the United States, who are 18 years of age or older, to vote shall not be denied or abridged by the United States or any state on account of age.

SEC. 2. The Congress shall have the power to enforce this article by appropriate legislation.
[Ratified July 5, 1971]

Proposed Amendment [XXVII.]

SECTION 1. Equality of rights under the law shall not be denied or abridged by the United States or by any State on account of sex.

SEC. 2. The Congress shall have the power to enforce, by appropriate legislation, the provisions of this article.

SEC. 3. This amendment shall take effect two years after the date of ratification.

APPENDIX D

The Gettysburg Address
November 19, 1863

(In these two short paragraphs, Abraham Lincoln summed up the principles of the American Revolution. They have endured the test of a century of change.)

Four score and seven years ago our fathers brought forth on this continent, a new nation, conceived in Liberty, and dedicated to the proposition that all men are created equal.

Now we are engaged in a great civil war, testing whether that nation or any nation so conceived and so dedicated, can long endure. We are met on a great battle-field of that war. We have come to dedicate a portion of that field, as a final resting place for those who here gave their lives that that nation might live. It is altogether fitting and proper that we should do this.

But, in a larger sense, we can not dedicate—we can not consecrate—we can not hallow—this ground. The brave men, living and dead, who struggled here, have consecrated it, far above our poor power to add or detract. The world will little note, nor long remember what we say here, but it can never forget what they did here. It is for us the living, rather, to be dedicated here to the unfinished work which they who fought here have thus far so nobly advanced. It is rather for us to be here dedicated to the great task remaining before us—that from these honored dead we take increased devotion to that cause for which they gave the last full measure of devotion—that we here highly resolve that these dead shall not have died in vain—that this nation, under God, shall have a new birth of freedom—and that government of the people, by the people, for the people, shall not perish from the earth.

GLOSSARY

Articles of Confederation The constitution of the thirteen American colonies, adopted in 1781 and replaced by the Constitution of the United States in 1789. The major weakness of the Articles was that it left most power in the hands of the states.

authoritarianism The principle that stresses obedience to authority and disregards notions of inherent rights or liberties.

authority The legitimate power to order or command as defined by the political system.

bandwagon movement A political movement that attracts increasing attention and numbers of followers.

bicameral legislature A legislative body composed of two houses or chambers.

bill of attainder An act or law that singles out a specific person for punishment. It is forbidden by the Constitution as amounting to punishment by the legislature rather than by the courts.

bill of rights A specific list of liberties to be protected from governmental infringement. In the United States, the term refers to the first ten amendments to the U.S. Constitution, or similar lists in state constitutions.

bureaucracy A system of administration based upon organizational structures designed to perform specific functions and subject to a hierarchy of authority. The term also refers collectively to the employees and officials in such a system.

Cabinet A body of presidential advisers consisting of the heads of the major executive departments, with temporary additions as determined by the President.

checks and balances A scheme resulting from the separation of federal powers into different segments (e.g. legislative, executive, and judicial branches) which is intended to prevent abuse of power by providing countervailing authority.

civil liberties The right of the people to be free from unreasonable interference, especially from the government. All rights included in the Bill of Rights are civil liberties.

civil rights The right to participate in government equally with other citizens and to receive equitable treatment from the institutions of government and society.

civil suit A suit undertaken by private individuals against others or by or against government agencies acting as private persons.

class action suit A lawsuit brought by one or a few persons on behalf of a large number of persons who may have been damaged by some action. It is frequently used on behalf of consumers.

cloture The procedure to shut off debate in the United States Senate; It is invoked infrequently, generally to halt a filibuster.

cold war The term applied to the tension between the United States and the Soviet Union, especially during the two decades or so following World War II.

committees (**congressional**) Units within Congress, and usually within one house, to divide labor and permit specialization. They recommend action to the full chamber, or, in the case of joint committees, to the full Congress.

common law A system of unwritten law, found especially in England and the United States, that is derived from tradition and precedent.

confederacy A league of independent states.

Congress The national legislature of the United States.

Congressional Record The journal that publishes the daily proceedings of Congress.

consent The principle that the only valid laws are those to which the people give their agreement, either directly or by some indirect method such as the actions of their representatives.

conservative Literally, one who wishes to preserve existing institutions. The term is generally applied to those who stress duties, tradition, and legitimate authority, and who accept society as an organic entity with claims upon the individual. It is often used in the United States, in a confusing and imprecise fashion, to mean one who opposes the expansion of the powers of government.

constitution A device to limit the exercise of governmental power and to assign specific authorities to specific agencies.

constitutionalism The situation that exists when a government abides by regularized restrictions upon its power.

criminal action A legal action undertaken by the government in the public's name for an offense against the public order.

democracy A political system in which the people are the source of authority, and in which the institutions enable the majority, at least potentially, to dictate major policy outlines. Originally, the term referred to rule directly by the people.

depression A period of economic decline characterized by low demand, low prices and business activity, and extraordinarily high unemployment.

double jeopardy Being tried twice for the same offense, that is, being brought to trial again upon a charge for which one has already been acquitted. The practice is forbidden in the United States both to federal and state governments, although the Supreme Court has held that trials in both federal and state courts on charges arising from the same alleged offense do not constitute double jeopardy.

equality In politics, the impartiality of law and government in treating all citizens by the same rules and standards.

equity The system of rules, developed in England and followed in the United States, that overcomes the limitations of the common law by providing for the resolution of a dispute "in fairness" before a decision on the merits can be made.

ex post facto law "After the fact," or a law punishing an action that took place before the law was passed. Passage of such laws is forbidden by the U.S. Constitution.

executive The person or agency that administers the laws.

executive agreement An agreement between the President and a foreign state having the force of law.

executive order A directive issued by the President or under his order pertaining to the administration of the laws.

executive privilege The presumed right of a President or his subordinates on his order to withhold information or testimony requested by another branch of government.

franchise The right to vote.

federalism A system of dividing powers territorially, so that there are strong constituent units and a strong central authority, each with powers that the other cannot abolish.

filibuster An obstructive tactic of delivering long speeches, practiced on occasion in the U.S. Senate, to defeat a proposal by allowing no other proposal to be considered.

fundamental law A constitution.

gerrymander Any scheme that establishes the boundaries of an electoral district in such a fashion that it is markedly favorable to one faction as opposed to another. The term applies especially to districts that achieve this purpose by being highly irregular in shape.

government Human institutions designed to afford protection from external and internal threats, and, at best, to establish policies that will provide the most favorable conditions under which citizens may pursue their lives.

grand jury A judicial body of citizens whose task is to inquire into alleged violations of law and ascertain whether the evidence is sufficient to warrant a trial.

Hamiltonianism The doctrines of Alexander Hamilton or those that are consistent with them, such as belief in a strong central government and strong executive powers, and advocacy of industrialism, urbanism, government aid to business and industry and so forth.

head of government The official who truly exercises the central power of the executive. In the United States, it is the President, in Great Britain, the prime minister.

head of state The official who symbolizes the state and exercises its ceremonial powers. In the United States, it is the President, in Great Britain, the monarch.

higher law Natural or divine law, deemed superior to manmade law.

impeachment The act of indicting a public official and arranging for a trial to consider removal from office. The House of Representatives impeaches by a simple majority vote, the Senate conducts the trial, which requires a two-thirds vote for conviction and removal.

imperialism The attempt to extend the power of a nation to dominate other lands and peoples.

imperial presidency Term recently coined to describe the American presidency as swollen in power and characterized by pomp and ceremony reminiscent of an emperor.

implied powers Powers not spelled out precisely by the Constitution but suggested by its language. They are powers that may be inferred from a study of the specific grants in the Constitution.

impoundment Presidential refusal to spend funds appropriated by Congress.

initiative A device to permit the people in certain states or cities to place proposals on the ballot by petition.

interest groups Organizations, founded for certain purposes, which work to advance their own interests by pressuring the political system ("pressure groups").

item veto The power, denied to the President although possessed by some governors, to veto portions of a bill as well as the entire bill.

Jeffersonianism The doctrines of Thomas Jefferson or those that are consistent with them, such as localism, agrarianism, and an emphasis upon rights, rigid checks upon the exercise of power, and so forth.

judicial review The power of the courts (in the course of a lawsuit) to declare laws or executive actions unconstitutional.

legislative budget A process of budgeting under legislative control, rather than executive agency, found in some states and now in partial form in the United States government.

legislative oversight The power of Congress to oversee or review the manner in which executive agencies administer the laws.

legislature The lawmaking body.

liberal Essentially oriented toward humanism, liberal doctrines emphasize rights and limitations upon governmental power over the individual and welcome change and experimentation. The term is now frequently applied to those favoring maintenance and extension of certain programs such as those pertaining to health care, public welfare, and education.

lobby An organization that brings pressure upon government, especially upon legislators, to favor specific programs.

logrolling The practice among politicians to support one another's favored programs.

loose construction Broad constitutional interpretation.

Manifest Destiny The term applied to justify the United States' imperial sweep across the continent and into territories beyond.

New Deal Franklin D. Roosevelt's programs and policies, characterized by extensive use of old and newly created federal agencies to attack the Great Depression and provide economic security.

nomination The selection of candidates by a political party to run for office in the general election.

Ombudsman An official who functions to protect citizens against arbitrary and unfair actions of government agencies. The position was developed in the Scandinavian countries.

parliamentary government That form of government in which the executive is selected from the legislature and works closely with it. The term of office is irregular in length.

parties (political) Organizations officially formed by citizens to elect candidates to political office.

party responsibility The power of political parties to enforce discipline upon their officeholders. U.S. parties largely lack this power.

Pentagon The building housing the Defense Department; symbolically, the central management of the armed services.

petit jury A group of six to twelve persons who decide the guilt of defendants in all major criminal and some civil cases.

plea bargaining An agreement between the defense and prosecution in a criminal case to plead the defendant guilty to a lesser crime than the one charged in return for a lighter sentence.

pluralism A group theory of politics viewing American democracy as dominated by competition between organized interest groups under the general refereeing of the government; also termed "broker rule."

plural society A society composed of at least two groups that differ in race, religion, nationality, language, or regional subculture.

pocket veto Presidential refusal to sign a bill passed within the last ten days of a congressional session when it cannot become law without his signature.

politics The manner in which human beings collectively organize their affairs.

political science The study of government and politics.

political socialization The means by which a society perpetuates itself and its political ideas by teaching those ideas to the young.

popular sovereignty The doctrine that sovereign power resides in the people and that those chosen to govern as trustees of such power must exercise it in conformity with the people's wishes.

pork barrel A government appropriation that supports local programs, such as river and harbor improvements, generally passed to ingratiate local politicians with their constituents.

President Pro Tempore The senior officer chosen by the U.S. Senate, and empowered to preside in the absence of the Vice President. The position is essentially ceremonial; also found in state senates, where it may have considerable power.

presidential government That form of government in which the executive is selected independently of legislators and serves a fixed term in office.

pressure groups Organized interest groups that operate to obtain favorable policies from the government.

primary A preliminary election held by a party to choose its candidates for office.

primary association A type of interest group built upon characteristics of birth or family background, such as race or sex.

private suit A legal action to settle a point at issue between private persons, such as in marriage or inheritance.

proportional representation The electoral system that attempts to distribute offices according to percentages of party votes. It is often found in multiparty systems but is largely absent from the United States.

public suit A legal action undertaken in disputes over the operation of the state.

referendum A device by which acts passed by a legislature are referred to the people for acceptance or rejection at the polls.

runoff election A second primary election held between the top two or three competitors in the first election to determine which is to secure a party's nomination.

secondary association A type of interest group, such as a club or political party, with which an individual can choose to affiliate.

senatorial courtesy The practice that enables senators to block certain presidential appointments for positions within their states. It applies only to certain positions, and only if the senator and the President are of the same party.

seniority The former rigid practice of Congress to assign committee chairmanships to the member of the majority party with the longest tenure on the committee.

separation of powers The principle that there should be a division of governmental functions and powers among legislative, executive, and judicial branches. Such a division exists in the presidential form of government, which has an independently elected executive serving a fixed term.

single-member district An electoral district common in the United States, in which only one position is to be filled, and a plurality vote is sufficient to capture the position.

Speaker of the House The presiding officer elected by the House of Representatives. The position is a powerful one and is always filled by a member of the party controlling the House.

state A nation; or, in the United States, a political subdivision of the nation.

statutory law Written laws passed by legislatures.

strict construction The assumption that the Constitution grants no authority not specifically spelled out in it.

sunset laws Laws, newly enacted in some states, that require agencies to justify their purposes and functions to continue in existence beyond a certain time.

sunshine laws State statutes requiring open meetings in legislatures and executive agencies. Such laws are intended to make covert lobbying efforts more difficult.

treaty A formal agreement between two nations having the force of law. In the United States it is negotiated by the President and ratified by a two-thirds vote of the Senate.

unicameral legislature A legislature with a single chamber.

unitary government A government with no political subdivisions such as states or provinces, as in France and Great Britain.

veto The power of an executive to reject a legislative enactment. In the United States a two-thirds vote of both houses of Congress may override a veto.

Watergate A collective term for the abuses of governmental authority committed by the Nixon administration (from the Watergate Apartment Building, the scene of a burglary at Democratic headquarters).

writ of assistance A general search warrant, forbidden by the U.S. Constitution, giving unlimited authority for searches and seizures.

zero-based budgeting A budgetary practice that requires a yearly examination of each agency or program to justify continued funding. It replaces the common practice of using the previous year's budget as the basis for requests for further funds.

INDEX

About the Authors

Max J. Skidmore is currently Head of the Department of Political Science at Southwest Missouri State University. He received his Ph.D. from the University of Minnesota, and specializes in American politics and political thought, and political rhetoric and symbolism. From 1965 to 1968 he was Director of American Studies and Associate Professor of Political Science at the University of Alabama. Earlier, he held various positions with the Department of Health, Education, and Welfare in Washington, D.C., including Administrative Assistant in the Office of the Commissioner of Social Security and Program Review Officer in the U.S. Office of Education. Among his publications are *Medicare and the American Rhetoric of Reconciliation*, University of Alabama Press, 1970, and *Word Politics: Essays on Language and Politics*, Freel, 1972.

Marshall Carter Wanke is currently an Assistant Professor and Director of the Criminal Justice Program in the Department of Government at Ohio University. She received her Ph.D. from the University of Wisconsin, where she was a Ford Fellow from 1965 to 1967, a University Fellow from 1967 to 1968, and an Emma Perry Ogg Fellow in 1968. Her specialties are comparative judicial process (especially the Third World), public law, political justice, and political change in Africa. She was an Assistant Professor at Wayne State University from 1969 to 1972 and taught at California State University at Long Beach in 1972 and 1973. From 1973 to 1976 she lectured in Government at Ahmadu Bello   University in Zaria, Nigeria, and from 1976 to 1977 she was Visiting Professor in the Department of Political Science at the University of Texas at El Paso.